Lecture Notes in Artificial Intelligence 6700

Edited by R. Goebel, J. Siekmann, and W. Wahlster

Subseries of Lecture Notes in Computer Science

FoLLI Publications on Logic, Language and Information

Editors-in-Chief

Luigia Carlucci Aiello, *University of Rome "La Sapienza", Italy*
Michael Moortgat, *University of Utrecht, The Netherlands*
Maarten de Rijke, *University of Amsterdam, The Netherlands*

Editorial Board

Sylvain Pogodalla   Myriam Quatrini
Christian Retoré (Eds.)

Logic and Grammar

Essays Dedicated to Alain Lecomte
on the Occasion of His 60th Birthday

 Springer

Series Editors

Randy Goebel, University of Alberta, Edmonton, Canada
Jörg Siekmann, University of Saarland, Saarbrücken, Germany
Wolfgang Wahlster, DFKI and University of Saarland, Saarbrücken, Germany

Volume Editors

Sylvain Pogodalla
INRIA Nancy – Grand Est
615, rue du Jardin Botanique, 54602 Villers-lès-Nancy Cedex, France
E-mail: sylvain.pogodalla@inria.fr

Myriam Quatrini
Université de Marseille
Institut de Mathématiques de Luminy
163, avenue de Luminy, Case 907, 13288 Marseille Cedex 9, France
E-mail: quatrini@iml.univ-mrs.fr

Christian Retoré
Université Bordeaux 1
LaBRI
351, cours de la libération, 33405 Talence cedex, France
E-mail: christian.retore@labri.fr

ISSN 0302-9743   e-ISSN 1611-3349
ISBN 978-3-642-21489-9   e-ISBN 978-3-642-21490-5
DOI 10.1007/978-3-642-21490-5
Springer Heidelberg Dordrecht London New York

Library of Congress Control Number: 2011928314

CR Subject Classification (1998): F.4.2, F.4, I.2.7, I.2.3, I.2.6

LNCS Sublibrary: SL 7 – Artificial Intelligence

Typesetting: Camera-ready by author, data conversion by Scientific Publishing Services, Chennai, India

Printed on acid-free paper

Springer is part of Springer Science+Business Media (www.springer.com)

Preface

"Science longue patience"
Louis Aragon

This volume presents contributed papers of the Colloquium in Honor of Alain Lecomte, held in Pauillac, France, November 2–3, 2007[1]. This event was part of the ANR project *Prélude*[2]. The selected papers belong to the numerous scientific areas in which Alain has worked and to which he has contributed—formal linguistics, computational linguistics, logic and cognition. Being able to work in and across such diverse and active areas requires a bird's eye view from high above. So it might have been predestination that Alain was born in Le Bourget, the former north airport of Paris, in 1947. His father was in fact a mechanic for the Aéropostale and for Air France thereafter, possibly also explaining why Alain is so keen on plane noise, the smell of kerosene and travelling.

After studying in the high school of Drancy, he undertook studies in mathematics in what was to become Jussieu. His interest in philosophy also led him to attend Althusser's seminar. After enjoying May 1968 in Paris and spending a few months in Copenhagen, in 1969 he obtained a master's degree in statistics in Grenoble where he became lecturer (assistant) at the IMSS (Institute of Mathematics for Social Sciences). Resisting the call of the mountains surrounding Grenoble, Alain got more and more interested in linguistics: he was preparing for a PhD under the supervision of Jacques Rouault, who was leading a team called "Traitement automatique des langues et applications" (Natural Language Processing and Applications), issued from the former "Centre d'étude pour la traduction automatique" (Center for Research on Automated Translation) led by Bernard Vauquois. Alain passed his PhD in applied mathematics entitled "Essai de formalisation des opérations linguistiques de prédication" in 1974. Thereafter he spent two years teaching statistics in Oran, and returned to Grenoble at the end of the 1970s.

Jacques Rouault knew Michel Pêcheux because they were both following Antoine Culioli's aproach to the formalization of linguistics. That is how Alain joined the research project conducted by Michel Pêcheux: RCP Adela (Recherche Coopérative Programmée, Analyse du Discours Et Lecture d'Archive) in 1980. Within this project, Alain, with Jacqueline Léon and Jean-Marie Marandin, focused on the incremental analysis of discourse. He was already involved in the logical aspects of such issues. The project also needed a parser and Michel Pêcheux got in touch with Pierre Plante from Montreal who was developing one in Lisp, Deredec. A research program with UQÀM (Université du Québec

---

[1] http://www.loria.fr/ pogodall/AL/
[2] http://www.anr-prelude.fr/

à Montréal) was launched, involving Alain, Jacqueline Léon and Jean-Marie Marandin, among others, on the French side.

Corresponding to this interest in formalizing linguistic phenomena, the first contribution of this volume, by Claire Beyssade, provides a linguistic analysis of bare nouns in French. The main claim of this paper is that interpretative differences between bare nouns and indefinite nouns in predicate position in French derive from a difference between two types of judgements: the attributive ones and the identificational ones. Such a claim relies on an analysis of copular sentences for which the logical forms differ on whether they are built with bare nouns or indefinite noun phrases.

The projects on automatic analysis of discourse (AAD) and the Adela team soon stopped after the death of Michel Pêcheux in 1984. By that time, Jean-Marie Marandin had introduced Alain to Gabriel Bès (GRIL, Clermont-Ferrand). The GRIL was involved in a European project: DYANA (Dynamic interpretation of natural language, DYANA and DYANA-2, that lasted from 1988 to 1995) including a large part on categorial grammars, with people from Edinburgh (such as Claire Gardent, formerly member of the GRIL, or Glyn Morrill) and Utrecht (such as Michael Moortgat). The GRIL was looking for someone comfortable with the mathematical aspects of categorial grammars and Alain thus joined it. There, he familiarized himself with these grammars that would occupy him for several years. In 1990, he organized a DYANA workshop at Clermont-Ferrant and in 1992 he edited *Word Order in Categorial Grammar*, a collection of articles on categorial grammar deriving from this workshop.

Because of his interest in formalization and modelling of linguistic phenomena, in particular from the logical point of view, Alain could not miss what is now a well-established and continuously exciting event: the European Summer School of Logic, Language, and Information, ESSLLI. Indeed, Alain attended ESSLLI in 1990 and since then, he attended, lectured, or presented a communication at most ESSLLI venues: 1990, 1991, 1992, 1995, 1997, 1998, 1999, 2000, 2002, 2005, 2006, 2007, 2008, 2009 and 2010.

His interest in logic for natural language led him to meet Christian Retoré (co-editor of this volume) in 1993. Because Alain was looking for non-commutative versions of linear logic, Vincent Danos suggested he get in touch with Christian who had just obtained a PhD degree with Jean-Yves Girard on partially ordered sequents and the "before" connective (pomset logic). Alain showed Christian how useful non-commutative calculi are for linguistics. Although they never worked in the same location, this was the starting point of a fruitful collaboration. At this time, while teaching in Grenoble, Alain was part of the GRIL and in 1994, he defended his habilitation thesis entitled "Modèles logiques en théorie linguistique" in front of a jury consisting of Michele Abrusci, Gabriel Bès, Jean-Pierre Desclés, Michel Eytan and Michael Moortgat. When Christian moved to Nancy, in October 1994, Alain played an important role in the creation of the INRIA Project team *Calligramme*, led by Philippe de Groote, soon joined by François Lamarche and Guy Perrier. The theoretical center of the team was linear logic, especially proof-nets, and the application areas were concurrency but also—and soon mainly—computational linguistics.

One of the key ideas Alain and Christian had was to map words not to formulas as in categorial grammar, but to partial proof-nets (of Lambek calculus or of pomset logic), and to view parsing as assembling partial proof-nets into a complete correct proof. They presented their work to the Roma workshops organized by Michele Abrusci and Claudia Casadio on Lambek calculus, linear logic and linguistic applications, or to Formal Grammar around ESSLLI venues. In 1995, Alain became professor in epistemology, philosophy of sciences and logic in Grenoble and was the dean of his faculty for several years.

Partial proof-nets as lexical entries was rather a broad notion of a grammar, encompassing rich syntactic formalisms, e.g., TAG, but more symmetrical. This approach permitted one to model discontinuous constituents or relatively free word order while sticking to the idea of "proof as analysis." As in categorial grammar, from this proof could be recovered semantic readings in a Montague-like style. Alain and Christian also thought of inverting this process, and wrote a PhD proposal with Marc Dymetman on this topic: their common student Sylvain Pogodalla (co-editor of this volume) made a contribution to this topic in the more standard framework of Lambek grammars: "Réseaux de preuves et générations pour les grammaires de type logique"(defended in 2001 in Nancy).

In the present volume, the second paper also pertains to the logical view of language. It aims at reconstructing the Cooper storage method for quantifiers within a type-theoretic framework: convergent grammar (CVG). In this paper, Carl Pollard motivates the CVG framework by analyzing the evolutions of Chomsky's transformational model through the minimalist program and by comparing it with the categorial grammar approaches. This leads to considering syntactic trees as proof trees. But, contrary to standard categorial grammar, the semantics terms do not directly result from the syntactic terms. They are instead built in *parallel* using a purely derivational calculus for the syntax-semantics interface.

While the CVG framework itself does not consist in a rephrasing of the Minimalist Program, it highlights some of its relations to type theory and logical grammar. It interestingly echoes that at the beginning of the 2000s, because of Alain's knowledge about generative grammar and Noam Chomsky's work, and because of Christian's interest in this formalism, Alain gave a series of seminars on this topic in Nancy issuing in a joint work for a categorial treatment of minimalism, and in particular of Ed Stabler's minimalist grammars (MG) first presented at Logical Aspects of Computational Linguistics (LACL), a conference launched by Alain and Christian in 1996. The point of giving a categorial view of minimalism was to provide it with better semantic representations. First, the proof expresses valency consumption of linguistic resources, but then a process computes from the proof either word order or semantic representation. This topic was an important one in the INRIA group *Signes* that Christian started in Bordeaux in September 2002 and to which Alain actively took part. In addition to joint papers on that subject, they also co-advised two PhD students: Maxime Amblard, "Calculs de représentations sémantiques et syntaxe générative: les grammaires minimalistes catégorielles," and Houda Anoun, "Approche logique des grammaires pour les langues naturelles," both defended in Bordeaux in 2007.

Witnessing the activity in this area, the next three papers elaborate on various aspects of bridging the minimalist program and categorial grammars. In the first one, Richard Moot builds on proof nets for Lambek grammars to give a graphical perspective on two different categorial grammar-based accounts of the *move* operation of the Minimalist Program. This new perspective allows him to unify the two accounts and to overcome some of their drawbacks, lexicalizing subparts of the proof trees corresponding to syntactic trees where a *move* operation has been triggered. This also makes a very interesting link to the syntactic recipes automatically inferred for categorial grammars on large corpora.

Maxime Amblard's contribution deals with a type-theoretic formulation of minimalist grammars: the minimalist categorial grammars (MCG). This paper is a step in a more general program: to provide MG with a theoretically motivated syntax/semantics interface. It focuses on the first step of the proof of mutual inclusion of languages between MG and MCG. This paper gives an original definition of minimalist grammars based on an algebraic description of trees which allows one to check properties of this framework and which provides a description suitable for comparison with generated languages of frameworks.

The next contribution, by Sylvain Salvati, also provides an original view of MG. This perspective, which relies on reinterpretations of MG in light of logic, is innovative and quite ambitious, and could also be applied to other grammatical formalisms. A first interpretation of MG within abstract categorial grammars is given in which MG derivations are represented as terms. The latter can then be interpreted either as syntactic trees or strings, as usual, or interpreted as semantics terms, providing MG with another syntax-semantics interface. It also shows that the membership problem for MG is at least as difficult as multiplicative exponential linear logic provability. Finally, it also presents a monadic second order-based interpretation of MG derivations, providing them with a descriptive rather than rule-based interpretation.

A very important characteristic of natural language lies in its *learnability*. Taking this property into account is a very interesting feature of MP. This property has also been studied in the framework of type-logical grammars, leading to various results. In this volume, Isabelle Tellier and Daniel Dudau-Sofronie present learnability results for some class of Lambek grammars. It builds on adding semantic information, namely types, to the syntactic available ones under some condition of compositionality.

While these kinds of properties are established on formal and logical systems, this work raises interesting questions on the cognitive abilities exhibited by the language faculty. Alain has also contributed to this area. In 2006 when he decided to move from the university of Grenoble to the one of Paris 8 in order to enjoy a more linguistically oriented department, he started to collaborate with Pierre Pica on the Mundurucu numeral system. In addition to this work and while pursuing his research on categorial minimalist grammars, Alain also became seriously interested in semantics and pragmatics and also in ludics.

In Geocal-Marseille 2006, Alain met Marie-Renée Fleury and Myriam Quatrini (co-editor of this volume), who organized a workshop on Computational Linguistics and Linear Logic. All three were convinced that ludics, a theory of logic conceived by Jean-Yves Girard and presented as a "Theory of Interaction," was a relevant framework to formalize pragmatics, and they decided to explore such a possibility. Alain then launched the national research program on this issue, *Prélude*, that has been renewed for the forthcoming years as *Loci*. Within this program, he has specifically worked on dialogue modelling in ludics with Marie-René Fleury, Myriam Quatrini and Samuel Tronçon. Based on their use of ludics to represent dialogue and pragmatics, in collaboration with Myriam Quatrini, Alain has proposed a new framework for semantics, extending in the ludical framework the intuitionistic idea according to which the semantics of a formula (utterance) is the set of its proofs (justifications). Moreover, the ludical model of semantics that they propose has lots of links with the game semantics tradition.

The last contribution of this volume, by Marie-Renée Fleury, Myriam Quatrini and Samuel Tronçon, gives a formal model for dialogs based on ludics. They show how certain notions of dialogue relate to some fundamental concepts of ludics. In particular, players of a dialogue are not confined within the rigid rules of formal logic but instead can explore a space where a partial, incomplete or even "incorrect" proof can occur. This exploration makes use of the notion of interaction which is central both in ludics and in dialogue.

While this (non-exhaustive) chronology of Alain's work makes it sound as though he could legitimately retire and stop contributing to this multidisciplinary area of logic and linguistics, we are quite confident, given how young in spirit and fit he is, that the aforementioned results are just the beginning and that Alain's best scientific contributions are still to come!

We wish to thank Catherine Péquenat, Alain's wife, for providing us with some biographic elements. We are also very grateful to Jacqueline Léon and Jean-Marie Marandin for their help in setting the scientific chronology of Alain's career and to Nicholas Asher for his stylistic advice. And we are of course responsible for any remaining mistakes.

January 2011

Sylvain Pogodalla
Myriam Quatrini
Christian Retoré

Organization

The Colloquium in Honor of Alain Lecomte was organized by the Laboratoire Bordelais de Recherche en Informatique thanks to the support of l'ANR Prélude.

Program Committee

Maxime Amblard	LORIA/Université de Nancy 2 & NPL
Claire Beyssade	CNRS, Institut Jean Nicod
Marie-Renée Fleury	Institut de Mathématiques de Luminy, Aix-Marseille Université
Richard Moot	CNRS, LaBRI
Sylvain Pogodalla	LORIA/INRIA Lorraine
Carl Pollard	The Ohio State University
Myriam Quatrini	Institut de Mathématiques de Luminy, Aix-Marseille Université
Christian Retoré	Université de Bordeaux, LaBRI
Sylvain Salvati	INRIA, LABRI
Isabelle Tellier	LIFO, Université d'Orléans
Samuel Tronçon	SFL, Université Paris 8

Additional Reviewers

Philippe de Groote	LORIA/INRIA Lorraine
Jean-Yves Marion	LORIA/Institut Polytechnique de Lorraine
Guy Perrier	LORIA/Université de Nancy 2

Sponsoring Institutions

This workshop was supported by the French National Research Agency (ANR[3]) through the ANR-PRÉLUDE project[4].

---

[3] http://http://www.agence-nationale-recherche.fr/Intl

[4] http://www.anr-prelude.fr/

Table of Contents

Logic and Grammar

Bare Nouns in Predicate Position in French

Claire Beyssade

Institut Jean Nicod, CNRS-ENS-EHESS, 29, rue d'Ulm,
75005 Paris, France
claire.beyssade@ehess.fr

Abstract. In this paper we examine the differences between bare singular nouns and indefinite singular NPs in predicate position in French. Our claim is that the semantic value of the singular indefinite determiner is not empty in French and that various interpretative contrasts between bare singular nouns and indefinite nouns in predicate position can be accounted for if a distinction between two rules of predication supported by copular sentences is introduced. We assume that bare nouns denote properties, which can be attributed to individuals, while indefinite noun phrases denote entities, which can be identified with an individual in context. This distinction between two types of statements, attributive ones and identificational ones, takes its source in Higgin's typology, and will be compared with Roy's and Heller and Wolter's works on predicative and specificational sentences.

Keywords: indefinite, bare noun, copular sentence, property.

1 Introduction

It is frequently assumed that French doesn't allow productive bare nouns, neither in argument positions, nor in predicate positions. Such an assumption is in contradiction with the following data, some of which are well-known and studied in the recent literature. (1a) corresponds to autonymic uses of bare nouns, (1b-c) to bare nouns in coordination (cf Roodenburg, 2004), (1d) to bare nouns in compound verbs, (1e) to bare nouns in prepositional phrases, (1f-h) examplify the uses of bare nouns in negative polarity contexts. Such examples need to be explained, and comparison seems to play a crucial role in (1g-h). (1i-j) illustrate some occurences of bare nouns in phrases of the type *N prep N*, (1k-m) present some cases of bare nouns which are not often mentioned in linguistic studies, and (1n-o) show that bare nouns may appear in copular sentences.

(1)   a. *Cordiste est un métier d'avenir qui demande une double compétence, sportive et technique.*
        [A] harnessed climber is a up-and-coming trade which requires both technical and athletic skills[1]

---

[1] We indicate with square brackets [] words which are required in the English translation, but are missing in the French sentence.

S. Pogodalla, M. Quatrini, and C. Retoré (Eds.): Lecomte Festschrift, LNAI 6700, pp. 1–16, 2011.
© Springer-Verlag Berlin Heidelberg 2011

b. *Livres et journaux jonchaient le sol.*
Books and newpapers lay everywhere on the ground
c. *Il faut disposer d'un compte bancaire pour toucher salaire ou retraite.*
You need to have a bank account in order to receive [your] wages or pension
d. *prendre rendez-vous, faire usage, avoir faim, soif, mal au coeur...*
take [an] appointement, make use of, to be hungry, to feel sick
e. *un pot en fer, un problème de taille, une idée de génie...*
a pot made of metal, a problem with size, a genius'idea
f. *Jamais homme n'entra dans ce couvent.*
No man has ever stepped in that convent
g. *Je n'avais jamais vu femme si belle.*
I've never seen such [a] beautiful woman
h. *Vous ne trouverez pas hôtel plus agréable dans la région.*
You won't find [a] more pleasant hotel in the area
i. *Il a bu bière sur bière.*
He drank beer after beer
j. *Elle s'embellit jour après jour.*
She gets prettier day afer day
k. *Ce nouveau téléphone fait appareil photo.*
This new phone can be used as [a] camera
l. Cette explication fait sens.
This explanation makes sense
m. *Si problème il y a, n'hésite pas à me rappeler.*
In case of problem, don't hesitate to call me
n. Jean est ami avec le directeur.
Jean is [a] friend with the director
o. *Jean est professeur.*
Jean is [a] professor

In this paper, we won't analyze all of these configurations. We will only focus on bare nouns in copular sentences, and more specifically on the contrast between bare singular nouns and indefinite singular nouns in copular sentences. Our aim is to show that copular sentences built with indefinite singulars (IS) differ in crucial ways from sentences built with bare singulars (BS): we can explain the interpretative and distributional differences between IS and BS by analyzing copular sentences built with IS as relying on an identity relation rather than on predication.

(2)   a. *Jean est un clown.*   Jean is a clown
        b. *Jean est clown.*   Jean is [a] clown

After a presentation in §2 of various interpretative and distributional contrasts between IS and BS in copular sentences, we propose in §3 to revisit Higgin's typology of copular sentences and to distinguish between predication and equation, grouping copular sentences built with IS together with identificational, specificational and equative sentences. Such an analysis allows to explain both the alternation between *il* and *ce* pronouns in copular sentences (§ 4) and the restrictions on modified bare nouns (§ 5).

2 Contrasts between Bare Nouns and Indefinite Nouns in Copular Sentences

In *Semantics in Generative Grammar,* Heim and Kratzer (1998:61) assume that "the indefinite article *a* is vacuous when it occurs in predicate nominals such as *a cat* in *Kaline is a cat*". This assumption, even if it was true for English, can't be applied to French, since, as (2) illustrates, copular sentences with and without indefinites may convey different meanings. (2b) means that John is a clown by profession, while (2a) just has a metaphoric meaning, and is adequate if John behaves as a clown, i.e. if the speaker judges that John is a funny person. This observation is due to Laca and Tasmovski (1994) and can be added to other contrasts which distinguish between BS and IS in copular sentences.

First of all, ISs, contrary to BSs, are incompatible with small clauses (3). Secondly, ISs, contrary to BSs, cannot appear in sentences with interruptive or intermittent readings (4). Lastly, the difference between ISs and BSs correlates with different pronouns in left dislocation (5).

(3)   *a. Marie imagine Paul ministre.*
        *b. *Marie imagine Paul un ministre.*
            Mary imagines Paul a minister
(4)   *a. Paul est médecin le jour, chanteur la nuit.*
        *a'. * Paul est un médecin le jour, un chanteur la nuit.*
            Paul is a doctor during the day, a singer during the night
        b. Paul est traducteur à ses heures libres.
        *b'. * Paul est un traducteur à ses heures libres.*
            Paul is a translator after hours
        c. Paul a été professeur à trois occasions dans sa vie.
        *c'. * Paul a été un professeur à trois occasions dans sa vie.*
            Paul has been a teacher three times in his life
(5)   *a. Paul, (il / * c') est traducteur.*
        b. Paul, (?il / c') est un traducteur.
            Paul, (he / CE) is a translator

All of these constrasts suggest a possible parallelism between bare nouns and adjectives: like adjectives, bare nouns denote properties, that can be attributed to a stage of individual and that can give rise to temporary interpretation. On the contrary, sentences built with indefinite singulars seem to convey a different meaning, where the indefinite nouns denote a stable property or more precisely denote an individual characterized by a permanent property. A comparison can be made between BS *vs* IS on the one hand, and adjective vs nominalization on the other hand, as in examples (6).

(6)   *a. Jean est bossu*   (temporary property)
        b. Jean est un bossu   (permanent property)
        Jean is a hunchbacked

There are some other differences between IS and BS uses. BSs, contrary to ISs, can be followed by *as qua* expressions (7) and can be modified by a prepositional phrase including a superordinate of the noun (8). Furthermore, BSs and ISs don't trigger the same type of inferences concerning the existence of the subject of the copular sentence. It is usual to consider that (9a) triggers the implicature that Pierre is dead, contrary to (9b), which doesn't trigger any implicature of this kind. Conversely, when one considers sentences built with present tense, the sentence with IS is not associated with any lifetime implicature, while the sentence with BS seems inappropriate when the subject denotes an individual who is dead, like in (10b) (cf Matushansky and Spector 2003, 2005).

(7)   *a. En tant que médecin, Pierre n'a pas voulu prendre position sur ce sujet.*
        *b. * En tant qu'un médecin, Pierre n'a pas voulu prendre position sur ce sujet.*
        As a doctor, Pierre didn't want to take a stand on this subject
(8)   *a. Pierre est avocat de profession. / * Pierre est un avocat de profession.*
        *b. Pierre est chrétien de religion. / * Pierre est un chrétien de religion.*
        *c. Pierre est français de nationalité. / * Pierre est un français de nationalité.*
        Pierre is a (lawyer / christian / French) by (profession / religion / nationality)
(9)   *a. Pierre était un médecin.*
        Pierre was a doctor
        b. Pierre était médecin. Maintenant il est retraité.
        Pierre was [a] doctor. Now he is retired
(10)   *a. Balzac est un écrivain.*
        Balzac is a writer
        b. ? Balzac est écrivain.

The last well-known contrasts between IS and BS concern the modification of the noun, which is much more restricted with BS than with IS.

(11)   *a. Jean est un médecin (généraliste / honnête / qui a plus de 50 ans).*
        *b. Jean est médecin (généraliste / *honnête / * qui a plus de 50 ans).*
        Jean is a general practitioner doctor / an honest doctor / a doctor who is more than 50-year-old

These contrasts are not new, they are presented in different papers, and in particular in Roy (2006) or in de Swart et al. (2006, 2007). Here our aim is just to present them again in order to propose an analysis of copular sentences which can explain some of them.

3 Two Types of Judgments: Predication *vs.* Equation

To account for these interpretative and distributional differences, we propose to introduce a distinction between different types of copular sentences. We focus on two classes of copular sentences, (i) copular sentences built with a bare noun and (ii) copular sentences built with an indefinite noun. We associate these copular sentences to two distinct logical forms.

(12)   *a. Jean est clown*
        b. [[DP is BS]] = 1   iff [[DP]] has P_{BS}
                                      or in other words
                                      iff $P_{BS} \in$ [[DP]]

DP means 'determiner phrase', BS means 'bare singular noun' and P_{BS} refers to the property denoted by the bare noun. Thus the subject DP in (12a) is analyzed as a generalized quantifier.

(13)   *a. Jean est un clown*
        b. [[DP is IS]] = 1   iff [[DP]] = [[IS]]

IS means 'indefinite singular noun'. (13) conveys an identity statement, in which it is claimed that the DP in subject position and the postverbal IS have the same denotation.

Another way to express the difference between these two types of copular sentences is to show that the copula in each of these sentences doesn't play the same role. In (12), the copula corresponds to λPP, while in (13) it corresponds to $\lambda y \lambda x$ (x=y). In (12), the bare noun is comparable to an adjective and denotes a property, which is attributed to a subject. The copula is just used to bind or compose the subject and the post-copular noun.

(14)   is : $\lambda P\ P$
        clown : $\lambda x C(x)$
        is clown : $\underline{\lambda P}\ \underline{(P)}\ \lambda x C(x)$ which reduces to $\lambda x C(x)$

If we analyze any indefinite NP as a generalized quantifier, we obtain the following composition for a VP built with a copula and an IS such as *'est un clown'*. The copular is viewed as expressing relative identity (cf Gupta 1980): $\lambda P\ \lambda x\ (P)\ \lambda y$ (x=y).

(15)   is : $\lambda P\ \lambda x\ (P)\ \lambda y\ (x=y)$
        a : $\lambda Q\ \lambda R\ \exists z\ (Q(z) \wedge R(z))$
        clown : $\lambda x C(x)$
        a clown : $\lambda R\ \exists z\ (R(z) \wedge C(z))$
        is a clown : $\underline{\lambda P}\ \lambda x\ \underline{(P)}\ \lambda y\ (x=y)\ (\underline{\lambda R\ \exists z\ (R(z) \wedge C(z))})$
                        which reduces to

$$\lambda x \ (\lambda \underline{R} \ \exists z \ (R(z) \wedge C(z))) \ \underline{\lambda y \ (x=y)}$$
and finally to
$$\lambda x \ (\ \exists z \ (x=z) \wedge C(z))$$

The present proposal is distinct from what can be found in the literature, and in particular distinct from Higgins', Roy's, and Heller and Wolter's analyses, summarized in table 1.

Table 1. Typology of copular sentences

Higgins	Roy	Heller and Wolter's	Beyssade & Sorin
Predicational	i) characterizing ii) defining iii) situation-descriptive	i) ordinary prediction ii) quiddity prediction (including identificationals)	Predicational
Equative	Equative	Equative	Identity : equatives,
Identificational	Identificational		identificationals,
Specificational	Specificational	Specificational	specificationals

The important point is that here we draw a demarcation line between predicational and non predicational copular sentences, and that we analyze copular sentences built with bare nouns as predicational sentences, while copular sentences built with indefinites nouns are viewed as instances of non predicational sentences. Let's note that in all the other proposals found in the literature no clear distinction is established between copular sentences built with IS *vs* with BS.

In Higgins typology, IS copular sentences may be predicational or non predicational sentences, according to the context.

In Roy's thesis, copular sentences, either built with IS or with BS, are viewed as cases of predication: defining predicates are expressed by ISs, characterizing predicates are expressed by BSs, and situation-descriptive predicates are expressed by adjectives. It should follow from such an analysis that small clauses would be compatible, both with IS and with BS, which is not the case.

(16)   *Marie imagine Paul (ø / *un) ministre.*
         Mary imagine Paul (ø / a) minister

And finally, Heller and Wolter propose to introduce a distinction between two types of predicates: (i) predicates which express ordinary predication, and (ii) what they called quiddity predicates, which provide an answer to the question 'What is that?'. In addition to expressing a property of the entity, quiddity predicates tell us something about the essence or nature of the entity. They don't give any strong argument to justify why they analyze quiddity predicates as instances of predication and not as instances of equatives or specificationals. We have observed that in French, ordinary properties, which express secondary properties, are typically expressed via BS and the verb *faire* (cf (17a)) while quiddity predicates are expressed via IS (cf (17b)). Consequently, we will analyze quiddity sentences as cases of non predicational sentences. The sentence (17a) is not about a camera, but rather about an object that has a secondary function as a camera.

(17)   a. *Ce téléphone fait appareil photo.*   *(ordinary property)*
           This cell phone is a camera.
       b. *C'est un appareil photo.*   *(quiddity)*
           This is a camera.

4 Alternation between *il* and *ce* in French Copular Sentences

It is well-known (cf a.o. Kupferman 1979, Tamba 1983, Boone 1987, Beyssade & Sorin 2005) that there is an alternation between pronouns *ce* / *il* in French left dislocation constructions, which depends on the post-copular element: the pronoun *ce* 'that' appears when the post-copular phrase is an IS, while *il* / *elle* 'he / she' is used with a BS.

(18)   a. *Jean, c'est (un chanteur / *chanteur).*
           John, CE is (a singer / singer)
       b. *Jean, il est (? un chanteur / chanteur).*
           John, IL is (a singer / singer)

We observe that BSs behave as adjectives in this type of configuration, while copular sentences built with IS can be grouped with equative, identificational and specificational sentences since the pronoun which appears in left dislocation constructions is *ce* and not *il /elle*.

(19)   *Jean, (il / * c') est beau.*
        John, (he / CE) is beautiful
(20)   a. *Clark Kent, (c'/?il) est Superman.*   *equative*
        b. *Ça, (c'/ *il) est John.*   *identificational*
        c. *Le problème, (c'/ *il) est John.*   *specificational*

This observation provides a new argument to analyze copular sentences with BS as predicational sentences and to group copular sentences built with IS with equative, identificational and specificational sentences in the class of identity statements.

What does the use of *ce vs il/elle* indicate? Let us recall that pronouns may be used to give some information about the denotation of their antecedents. According to Blanche-Benveniste (1990, 41-42), "pronouns give a grammatical description which may be more fine-grained than lexical words". For instance, the difference between *ils* and *ça* in (21) has to do with the type of denotation of the noun phrase *les chiens*. In (21a), the pronoun refers to a particular set of dogs, while in (21b), it refers to the kind 'dog', and the sentence is a generic one.

(21)   *a. Les chiens, ils aboient.*
        The-dogs-they-are-barking   *The dogs are barking*
        b. Les chiens, ça aboie.
        The-dogs-ÇA-barks   Dogs bark

Furthermore, certain pronouns are sensitive to the difference between singular and plural, some other ones (like for instance the French generic one *ça*) are not. Same thing with the pronoun *le*, when it is anaphoric to a proposition as in (22b). It doesn't vary, whether it refers to one or several propositions.

(22)   *a. (Le chien / Les chiens), ça aboie.*
        (The-dog / The dogs)-ÇA-barks   Dogs bark
        *b. Jean est poète. Marie est danseuse. Tout le monde (le / *les) sait.*
        John is a poet. Mary is a dancer. Everybody (LE-sg / LES–pl) knows.

We can observe that the opposition [+Human] / [-Human] is not relevant here for distinguishing *ce* vs *il/elle*, since in the sentences which we are interested in, every subject NP refers to humans. Moreover, *il / elle* can be used to refer to non human noun phrases, like in (23):

(23)   *La soupe, elle est trop chaude.*
        The-soup–ELLE-is-too-hot

According to us, the relevant difference between *ce* and *il/elle* has to do with the type of denotation. Contrary to *il/elle* which refers to an entity which is identified and can be type-shifted as a set of properties, *ce* refers to an entity without identity. In other terms, the reference of *ce* is not strong, but weak (Dummett 1973, 1981), exactly as indefinite noun phrases can be weak, when they are incorporated (cf van Geenhoven 1996, McNally and van Geenhoven 1998) or when they appear in presentational sentences (Mc Nally 1997, Moltmann 2007). Dummett suggests that *this* and *that* in English refer to pre-individuated portions of reality, and thus involve reference without identity. They involve indeterminate reference that leaves open what entity exactly is being referred to. Our proposal is that *ce*, contrary to *il/elle*, has weak reference, and then can not be type-shifted from type e to type $((e,t),t)$. It is why *ce* can appear in identity sentences, but not in predicational sentences. *Il / Elle* may refer to individual of type e, which can be type-shifted in set of properties (i.e. type $((e,t),t)$).

(24)   Ce can only denote entities (type e). It cannot be type-lifted to denote sets of properties.

Ce is grammatical in identity copular sentences such as *Jean, c'est un chanteur*, because such a sentence doesn't rely on predication, but rather on identity. Inversely, *ce* is ungrammatical in predicational copular sentences such as *Jean, c'est chanteur*, because *ce* doesn't refer to a generalized quantifier, *ce* has weak reference, and can't be type-shifted from type e to type $((e,t),t)$.

5 Modified Bare Nouns in Predicate Positions

We will focus here on the class of expressions that can occupy the post copular position without determiner. It has been observed that in Romance languages only a restricted class of common nouns can be used without any determiner (a.o., Kupferman 1979, Pollock 1983, Boone 1987, Laca and Tasmowski 1994, Roy 2006, Matushansky and Spector 2003, de Swart and al. 2007). This class includes professions, titles and functions:

(25)   Professions (*médecin* 'doctor', *avocat* 'lawyer'...), titles (*prince* 'prince', *baron* 'baron', *roi* 'king'...), hobbies (*chasseur* 'hunter', *alpiniste* 'climber',....), functions (*président* 'president', *ministre* 'minister', *sénateur* 'senator'...), status (*étudiant* 'student', *SDF* 'homeless'...)

This thesis has been recently infirmed by Mari and Martin (2008), which claim that basically every common noun can be used bare in copular sentences, and propose to give an unified analysis for sentences such as (26a) and (26b).

(26)   a. *Marie est docteur.*
           Mary is [a] doctor
         b. *Marie est voiture / salade / mini-jupe.*
            Mary-is (-car / -salad / -mini-skirt)
            Mary is the (car / salad / mini-skirt) type

Even if it is interesting to put examples like (26b) in the picture, it seems to us that it isn't justified to associate the same type of logical form with (26) a and b. Such an analysis blurs important contrasts between (26a) and (26b), as illustrated by (27). If (26b) may be paraphrased by (27d), there is no equivalence between (26a) and (27c).

(27)   a. *Marie est très (*docteur / voiture / salade/ mini-jupe).*
           Mary-is-very (doctor / car / salad / mini-skirt)
         b. *Marie est (un docteur / * une voiture / * une salade/ * une mini-jupe).*
           Mary-is- (a-doctor / a-car / a-salad / a-mini-skirt)
         c. *Marie aime les docteurs.*
           Mary likes doctors
         d. *Marie aime la voiture / la salade / les mini-jupes.*
           Mary-likes- the(sg)-car / the(sg)-salad / the(pl)-mini-skirts

And finally, while (26a) is absolutely non marked, (26b) are marked and need some context to be interpreted as well-formed. It's the reason why we won't consider examples of the type of (26b) in this paper. They deserve a separated study.

Our aim in this part of the paper isn't to propose a new characterization of the class of the nouns which can be bare in copular sentences. We consider that the description proposed in Beyssade and Sorin (2005) is on the good track. They claim that these nouns refer to non sortal properties i.e. to properties that are associated with a principle of application but no principle of identity (cf Gupta 1980). According to

Gupta, the principle of identity is just supplied by the common noun connected with a determiner or a quantifier. When a common noun is used bare, it refers to a role, a guise, which doesn't directly refer to an individual, but to a secondary property of the object. Consequently, bare common nouns are comparable to adjectives, they refer to secondary properties, that are not associated with principles of identity.

What we want to study here is the variety of expressions that can appear in post-copular position, without determiner. It seems that, besides names of role, there are a bunch of more complex expressions that can be used without determination, as illustrated in (28):

(28)   a. *Jean est (professeur de mathématiques / père de trois enfants).*
         John is [a] (professor of Mathematics / [the] father of three children)
         b. *Jean est fils d'avocat.*
         John is [the] son of a lawyer
         c. *Jean est bon danseur.*
         John is [a] good dancer

In each case, a property is attributed to an individual, but in each case, the way to build a complex property from a simple one is different. We describe here three different possibilities, the list may not be exhaustive.

A first type of complex property is shown in (28a), where the noun of guise is modified by another noun preceded by a functional preposition. *Professeur de mathématiques* defines a subtype of professor, and *père de trois enfants* is a subtype of father. It is important to note that (28a) implies that John is a professor, or that John is a father.

Another way to build a complex noun of guise is to use a noun of guise as argument of a relational noun, and more specifically a kinship noun such as *son, wife... Fils d'avocat* or *femme de ministre* denotes a complex property.

(29)   a. *Jean est fils d'avocat.*
         Jean is [a] son of lawyer
         a'. *Jean est (*ø / le) fils (de Marie / d'un avocat).*
         Jean is (ø / the) son (of Mary / of a lawyer)
         b. *Marie est femme de ministre.*
         Marie is [a] minister's wife
         b'. * *Marie est (*ø / la) femme du ministre.*
         Marie is (ø / the) wife of the minister

We assume that kinship nouns such as *fils, femme* may denote a relation not only between two individuals but also between an individual and a property (role/guise). Correspondingly, *fils d'avocat* in (29) denotes a complex property, obtained by applying a function (the word *fils* is represented in (30a) by $\lambda P \lambda x$ fils (x, P)) to a property (*avocat*). (30a) can be reduced in (30b), which shows that *fils d'avocat* denotes a property. It is interesting to note that if the argument of the relational noun does not denote a guise, but an individual (cf (29a') and (29b')), then the complex expression can not be used bare, but need to be preceeded by a determiner.

(30)   a. λP λx fils (x, P) (avocat)
         b. λx fils (x, avocat)

The third way of building a complex property consists in modifying an adjective by a noun of guise. We claim that bare nouns can be taken to denote both a property and a property modifier. This idea is borrowed from Fox (2000), who has proposed to formalize property modifiers in the framework of Property Theory. In example (28c), which illustrates the type of cases, the noun of guise is analyzed as a property modifier rather than as a property: the property attributed to Jean is not the property of being a dancer, but the property of being good, as a dancer.

This analysis presents several advantages compared to some other recent proposals (Larson 1998, de Swart et al. 2007).

First, our analysis predicts that there is no entailment from (31a) to (31b): *danseur* in (31a) does not have the restricted meaning of professional dancer, contrary to what happens with bare nouns. Indeed, the property attributed to the subject in (31a) is not the property to be a dancer, but the property to be good.

(31)   a. *Jean est bon danseur.*
             John is [a] good dancer
         b. *Jean est danseur de profession.*
             John is [a] dancer by profession

It is only when they denote a property that BNs have the restricted meaning of capacity. In all other contexts, they have an underspecified meaning: (31a) can be understood as meaning 'Jean is beautiful when he dances', and not necessarily as 'Jean is a professional dancer who dances beautifully'. According to our proposal, a noun like *danseur* is semantically ambiguous in French, it can denote a property, or a property modifier.

(32)   a. *danseur* as property   D or λx D(x)
         b. *danseur* as a property modifier   λP λx ∀s (D(x,s) → P(x,s))

(32b) translates the fact that *danseur* can modify a property P and yields another property. This new property can be attributed to an individual x if and only if, in a situation s where x has the property D (i.e. when x dances, as a professional dancer or not), x also has the property P. Thus (28c) can be analyzed as a predicative sentence in which *bon danseur* denotes a complex property that is attributed to Jean.

The second advantage of our proposal is that it can be extended to account for examples of the type shown in (33), which are usually analyzed as lexicalizations or idioms. Within our account, they can be instead analyzed in terms of property modification:

(33)   a. *Jean est (beau / gentil) garçon.*
             Jean is [a] (beautiful / nice) guy
         b. *Marie est (vieille fille / jeune grand-mère)*
             Mary is [a] (old maid / young grandmother)

And finally, we can understand why there are restrictions on the adjectives which can be used in examples like (34a). The more usual are *good* and *bad*, and all their variants like *beautiful, awful*... One can find examples with *young* but they are less frequent, and it often seems difficult to use *old* instead of *young*. *Young* in (35a-b) means *young in this function* and can be paraphrased by *depuis peu, recently*.

(34)   a. *Paul est bon élève.*
          Paul is [a] good student
        b. *Jean est piètre avocat.*
          John is [a] very mediocre lawyer
(35)   a. *Quand je serai jeune retraité,....*
          When I am a young retired person, ...
        b. *Marie est jeune députée et ne connaît pas encore les usages.*
          Mary is a young member of Parliament and doesn't know yet the manners

All other adjectives are excluded of these constructions, and in particular I-level adjectives, which denote permament properties, like *rich, parisian*...

(36)   a. **Paul est (beau / riche) professeur.*
          Paul-is(-nice/-rich)-professor
        b. **Paul est professeur parisien.*
          Paul-is-parisian-professor

In fact, the only adjectives that can appear in this type of construction belong to the class of what Siegel (1976) named non intersective but subsective adjectives. According to him, intersective adjectives are of type (e,t) while subsective adjectives are of type ((e,t), (e,t)) and modify the noun with which they are phrased: a sentence like *John is a good dancer* is ambiguous because the adjective *good* is ambiguous, and may be intersective or subsective. Larson (1995) has proposed another analysis for the same type of examples. According to him, the ambiguity doesn't come from the adjectives but from the nouns like *dancer,* which introduce two variables, one event variable and one individual variable. The lexical content associated with the noun *dancer* corresponds to $\lambda x \lambda e.$ dancer (x,e). Larson (1995) proposed to import Davidson's analysis of adverbial modification to adjectival modification. To do that, he relativizes the semantics of common nouns like *dancer* to events, he analyzes adjectives as predicates and he allows adjective phrases to be predicated either of x or e. Consequently, *a beautiful dancer* may be associated with both logical forms given in (37):

(37)   a. $\lambda e \lambda x$ [dancing (x, e) & beautiful(x)]   ' beautiful dancer$_1$'
        b. $\lambda e \lambda x$ [dancing (x, e) & beautiful(e)]   ' beautiful dancer$_2$ '

Larson's analysis accounts for the ambiguity of (38), which can be associated with the two following Logical Forms (38b-c), presented as tripartite structures Quantifier [Restriction] [Nuclear scope].

(38)   *a.   John is a beautiful dancer*
        b. $\forall e$ [dancing(e, j)] [beautiful (j)]
        c. $\forall e$ [dancing(e, j)] [beautiful(e)]

The general situation is the following: some adjectives apply strictly to non-events (for instance *aged*), others apply strictly to events (for instance *former*) and still others apply naturally to both, yielding ambiguity (for instance *beautiful*). Larson's analysis is very interesting and is perhaps adequate for English, but it can't be used to account for French data, because there is a contrast in French between copular sentences with IS and copular sentences with BS, which has no equivalent in English. English doesn't have bare nouns in predicate positions[2].

Our proposal is distinct from Siegel's one and from Larson's one. According to us, *bon danseur* is viewed not as a bare noun modified with an adjective, but as an adjective modified by a noun of property. *Bon danseur* means "bon en tant que danseur", "bon, quand il danse". When one combines a bare noun with an adjective, one obtains a complex property, built from the adjective and modified by the bare noun. We consider that the core of the phrase *bon danseur* is the adjective *bon,* not the noun *danseur*. It is why our analysis is very different from Larson's one: what is relevant in this type of construction is the adjective, which support various constraints, not the noun. We don't analyze the noun in (39) as a noun of event . It is the adjective which supports the major predication in (39), the noun only modifies it, and is used to impose a restriction on the denotation of the subject. The subject is interpreted as a *qua-objet*, as defined by Fine (1982). More generally, we can say that when an adjective is modified by a noun of property, the sentence can be paraphrased by (40). This explains why the noun has to be in a relation with a verb, and the adjective has to be related with an adverb.

(39)   a. *Jean est bon danseur.*
            John is [a] good dancer
(40)   a. DP, as N, is Adj.
        b. DP, when he $V_{\text{derived from N}}$, $V_{\text{derived from N}}$ $Adv_{\text{derived from Adj}}$

Our proposal presents two empirical advantages over others: it can be extended to comparable constructions, including an adjective modified by a noun or a *participe*, which can't be used bare without the adjective, like in (41). In fact, besides nouns of profession which can be used as property modifiers, most of deverbal nouns can also appear in this position.

(41)   a. *Jean est bon/ mauvais perdant*
            John-is-(good / bad)-looser
        a'. * *Jean est perdant*   (with the meaning of a status)
            John-is-looser
        b. *Jean est-il beau parleur, désespéré ou crétin ?*
            Is John [a] smooth talker, [a] desesperate man or [a] moron?
        b'. * *Jean est parleur.*
            John-is-talker

---

[2] Let us note two exceptions: *Chairman* and *President* may be used bare in predicate position.

Furthermore, we can add to the list of adjectives which can appear in these constructions, *grand,* which is in relation with the adverb *grandement,* or *gros,* which may be contextually recategorized as an adverb, as in (42c-d). *Grand* and *gros* are qualified by Szabo (2001) as evaluative adjectives: this means that they present a *as qua* position which may remains unsaturated (cf (43)).

(42)   a. *Jean est grand amateur d'art.*
             John-is-big-lover-of-art
         b. *Jean est gros buveur de bière.*
             John-is-big-drinker-of-beer
         c. *Jean joue gros*
             John-plays-GROS   'John plays a lot of money'
         d. *Ça peut te coûter gros.*
             ÇA-may-dative-cost-GROS   'It may cost you a lot'

(43)   a. *John is tall*   *John is tall as a person.*
         b. *Everest is tall*   *Everest is tall as a mountain.*

6 Conclusion

The main claim of this paper is that interpretative differences between bare nouns and indefinite nouns in predicate position in French derive from a difference between two types of judgments. We have proposed to analyze copular sentences built with bare nouns as predicational sentences, and copular sentences built with indefinite noun phrases as identity sentences. Consequently, bare nouns present some similarities with adjectives, which denote properties, whereas indefinite noun phrases are viewed as individual denoting phrases, just like proper names or definite noun phrases.

We have also shown how to account for modified bare nouns in this framework. Very frequently, when a bare noun co-occurs with an adjective in a copular sentence, the head of the postcopular phrase is not the bare noun, but the adjective. Nevertheless, in certain cases such as (44), both analyses may be possible : either the head of the postcopular phrase is the adjective (and the bare noun is an adjective modifier), or the head of the phrase is the bare noun (and the adjective modifies the noun). Thus, *simple soldat, petit commerçant* and *danseur professionel* are ambiguous and may be analyzed either as an adjective phrase or as a noun phrase.

(44)   a. *Jean est (simple soldat / petit commerçant).*
             John is [a] (regular soldier / little storekeeper)
         b. *Paul est danseur professionel.*
             John is [a] professional dancer

Finally, some issues concerning bare nouns in French have been leave aside. In particular, nothing was said about restrictions on the class of nouns which can appear without determiner in predicate position. However, we hope that the line of thought proposed here may provide some pointers for further studies of bare nominals and their special status at the syntax-semantics interface.

References

Beyssade, C., Dobrovie-Sorin, C.: A syntax-based analyis of predication. In: Georgala, E., Howell, J. (eds.) Proceedings of Semantics and Linguistic Theory 15, pp. 44–61. CLC Publications, Ithaca (2005)

Blanche-Benveniste, C.: le français parlé. CNRS Editions (1990)

Boone, A.: Les Constructions Il est linguiste/C'est un linguiste. Langue Française 75, 94–106 (1987)

Chierchia, G.: Formal Semantics and the Grammar of Predication. Linguistics Inquiry 16, 417–443 (1985)

Comorovski, I.: Constituent questions and the copula of specification. In: Comorovski, I., von Heusinger, K. (eds.) Existence: Semantics and Syntax, pp. 49–77. Springer, Dordrecht (2007)

Dummett, M.: Frege. Philosophy of Language. Duckworth (1973)

Dummett, M.: The interpretation of Frege's Philosophy. Duckworth (1981)

Fine, K.: Acts, Events, and Things. In: Leinfellner, W., et al. (eds.) Language and Ontology, pp. 97–105 (1982)

Fox, C.: The Ontology of Language. Properties, Individuals and Discourse. CSLI Publications, Stanford (2000)

Geach, P.T.: Reference and Generality, 3rd edn. Cornell University Press, Ithaca (1980)

Gupta, A.: The Logic of Common Nouns. Yale Univ. Press, New Haven (1980)

Heim, I., Kratzer, A.: Semantics in Generative Grammar. Blackwell, Malden (1998)

Heller, D., Wolter, L.: That is Rosa: Identificational sentences as intensional predication. In: Grønn, A. (ed.) Proceedings of Sinn & Bedeutung 12, Oslo, pp. 226–240 (2008)

Heycock, C., Kroch, A.: Pseudocleft Connectedness: Implications for the LF Interface Level. Linguistic Inquiry 30(3), 365–397 (1999)

Higgins, R.F.: The Pseudocleft Construction in English. Garland, New York (1979)

Kratzer, A.: Stage-Level and Individual-Level Predicates. In: Bach, E., Kratzer, A., Partee, B. (eds.) Papers on Quantification, University of Massachusetts, Amherst (1989); Also published in Carlson G.N., Pelletier, F.J. (eds.) The Generic Book, pp. 125–175. University of Chicago Press, Chicago (1995)

Kupferman, L.: Les Constructions Il est un médecin/C'est un médecin: Essai de solution. Cahiers linguistiques 9 (1979)

Laca, B., Tasmovski, L.: Le pluriel indéfini de l'attribut métaphorique. Linguisticae Investigatione XVIII(1), 27–48 (1994)

Larson, R.: Olga is a Beautiful Dancer. Presented at the Winter Meetings of the Linguistic Society of American, New Orleans (1995)

Larson, R.: Events and Modification in Nominals. In: Strolovitch, D., Lawson, A. (eds.) Proceedings from Semantics and Linguistic Theory VIII, pp. 145–168. Cornell University Press, Ithaca (1998)

Mari, A., Martin, F.: Bare and Indefinites NPs in Predicative Position in French. In: Schäfer, F. (ed.) SinSpec, Working Papers of the SFB 732, vol. 1. University of Stuttgart, Stuttgart (2008)

Matushansky, O., Spector, B.: To be (a) human. Talk given at JSM 2003 (2003)

Matushansky, O., Spector, B.: Tinker, tailor, soldier, spy. In: Maier, E., Bary, C., Huitink, J. (eds.) Proceedings of Sinn & Bedeutung 9, pp. 241–255. NCS, Nijmegen (2005)

Mc Nally, L., Van Geenhoven, V.: Redefining the weak/strong distinction. Expanded Version of a Paper Presented at the CSSP 1997 (1998)

Mc Nally, L.: A Semantics for the English Existential Construction. Garland Press, New York (1997)

Mikkelsen, L.: Specifying Who: On the Structure, Meaning, and Use of Specificational Copular Clauses. PH. D. Diss., University of California, Santa Cruz (2004)

Mikkelsen, L.: Copular clauses. In: von Heusinger, K., Maienborn, C., Portner, P. (eds.) Semantics: An International Handbook of Natural Language Meaning. Mouton de Gruyter, Berlin (to appear)

Moltmann, F.: Weak Reference or the True Semantics of of Relative Identity Statements, ms (2007)

Moro, A.: There-raising: principles across levels. Presentation at the 1990 Glow colloquium, Cambridge (1990)

Moro, A.: The Raising of Predicates: Predicative Noun Phrases and the Theory of Clause Structure. Cambridge University Press, Cambridge (1997)

Munn, A., Schmitt, C.: Number and indefinites. Lingua 115, 821–855 (2005)

Musan, R.: On the Temporal Interpretation of Noun Phrases. MIT dissertation (1995)

Musan, R.: Tense, Predicates, and Lifetime Effects. Natural Language Semantics 5(3), 271–301 (1997)

Partee, B.: Noun phrase interpretation and type-shifting principles. In: Groenendijk, J., de Jongh, D., Stokhof, M. (eds.) Studies in Discourse Representation Theory and the Theory of Generalized Quantifiers, pp. 115–143. Foris, Dordrecht (1987)

Pollock, J.-Y.: Sur quelques propriétés des phrases copulatives en français. Langue Française 58, 89–125 (1983)

Roodenburg, J.: Pour une approche scalaire de la déficience nominale: la position du français dans une théorie des 'noms nus'. Ph.D. Diss., Utrecht Lot (2004)

Roy, I.: Non verbal predications: a syntactic analysis of copular sentences. Ph.D Diss., USC (2006)

Siegel, E.: Capturing the Adjective. Ph.D. Diss., University of Massachusetts, Amherst, MA (1976)

de Swart, H.: Adverbs of quantification. A Generalized Quantifier Approach, Garland (1993)

de Swart, H., Winter, Y., Zwarts, J.: Bare nominals and reference to capacities. Natural Language and Linguistic Theory 25, 195–222 (2007)

de Swart, H., Zwarts, J.: Less form, more meaning: why bare nominals are special. Ms Nias/Utrecht/Nijmegen (2006)

Szabo, Z.: Adjectives in context. In: Kenesei, I., Harnish, R.M. (eds.) Perspectives on Semantics, Pragmatics, and Discourse, pp. 119–146 (2001)

Tamba, I.: Pourquoi dit-on "Ton neveu, il est orgueilleux" et "Ton neveu, c'est un orgueilleux". L'information Grammaticale 19, 3–10 (1983)

van Geenhoven, V.: Semantic Incorporation and Indefinite Descriptions: Semantic and Syntactic Aspects of West Greenlandic Noun Incorporation. Ph.D. Diss., Universität Tübingen (1996)

Williams, E.: Pseudoclefts and the order of the logic of English. Linguistic Inquiry 21, 485–489 (1990)

Williams, E.: The asymmetry of predication. Texas Linguistic Forum 38, 323–333 (1997)

Wolter, L.K.: That's that : the semantics and pragmatics of demonstrative noun phrases. Ph.D Diss., University of California, Santa Cruz (2006)

Covert Movement in Logical Grammar

Carl Pollard*

INRIA-Lorraine and Ohio State University
pollard@ling.ohio-state.edu

Abstract. We propose a formal reconstruction of the well-known storage-and-retrieval technique for scoping quantifiers and other 'covertly moved' semantic operators due to Cooper (1975). In the proposed reconstruction, grammar rules are presented in the familiar term-labelled Gentzen-sequent style of natural deduction. What is new is that, in addition to the usual contexts to the left of the turnstile (recording undischarged pairs of hypotheses, with each pair consisting of a syntactic variable ('trace') and a corresponding semantic variable), our typing judgments also include a **co-context** to the right of the **co-turnstile** (⊣). A co-context consists of a list of semantic variables, each paired with a quantifier that corresponds to the meaning expressed by a quantified noun phrase whose scope has not yet been specified. Besides the usual logical rules, the grammar also contains rules called **Commitment** and **Responsibility** that implement, respectively, storage and retrieval of semantic operators.

1 Introduction

From the mid-1970s until the emergence of Chomsky's Minimalist Program (MP, 1995) in the 1990s, the mainstream of research on natural-language syntax in

* For helpful discussion and comments on earlier stages of this work, I am grateful to Chris Barker, Patrick Blackburn, Wojciech Buszkowski, Robin Cooper, David Dowty, Jonathan Ginzburg, Philippe de Groote, Jirka Hana, Martin Jansche, Ruth Kempson, Brad Kolb, Yusuke Kubota, Alain Lecomte, Tim Leffel, Jim Lambek, Scott Martin, Vedrana Mihalicek, Glyn Morrill, Michael Moortgat, Reinhard Muskens, Guy Perrier, Andy Plummer, Ken Shan, Elizabeth Smith, Chris Worth, workshop participants at ESSLLI Workshop on New Directions in Type-Theoretic Grammar (Dublin 2007), the Fourth Workshop on Lambda Calculus and Formal Grammar (Nancy, 2007), the Colloque en l'honneur d'Alain Lecomte (Pauillac 2007), the Second Workshop on Types, Logic, and Grammar (Barcelona, 2007), the NaTAL Workshop on Semantics and Inference (Nancy 2008), the ESSLLI Workshop on Continuationd and Symmetric Calculi (Hamburg 2008), and audiences at the Séminaire de l'UMR 7023, CNRS/ Université de Paris 8 (2008), the Séminaire Calligramme, INRIA-Lorraine (2008), and the Centre de Lingüística Teòrica, Universitat Autònoma de Barcelona (2008). In addition, I benefited greatly from the comments of two anonymous referees. For their help in providing the conditions that made this research possible, I am grateful to Carlos Martin Vide, Philippe de Groote, and to the Department of Linguistics and College of Humanities of Ohio State University. The research reported here was supported by grant no. 2006PIV10036 from the Agència de Gestió d'Ajuts Universitaris i de Recerca of the Generalitat de Catalunya.

S. Pogodalla, M. Quatrini, and C. Retoré (Eds.): Lecomte Festschrift, LNAI 6700, pp. 17–40, 2011.
© Springer-Verlag Berlin Heidelberg 2011

much of the world embraced a theoretical architecture for syntactic derivations
that came to be known as the **T-model**. According to this model, which underlay
Chomsky's (1976, 1977) Extended Standard Theory (EST) of the 1970s and its
successor, the Government-Binding (GB) Theory (Chomsky 1981) of the 1980s
and early 1990s, a tree called a **deep structure** (DS) is generated from lexical
entries by essentially context-free **base rules**. The DS is then converted into a
surface structure (SS) by **transformations**, destructive structural operations
that can delete, copy, or (most significantly for us) move subtrees. From SS, the
derivation branches (the two arms of the T): in one direction the SS is further
transformed into a **phonetic form** (PF), which determines what the expression
being analyzed sounds like, and in the other direction the SS is transformed into
a **logical form** (LF), which determines what the expression means.

In the T-model, the tranformations that convert DS to SS are called **overt**,
because their effects are (at least potentially) audible (since the branch of the
derivation that leads to PF is yet to come). The prototypical case of overt movement is **overt wh-movement** in languages like English, where constituent questions are formed (so the theory goes) by moving a wh-expression (or, in so-called
pied-piping constructions, an expression properly containing a wh-expression)
to the left periphery of a clause. Since both PF and LF are derived from SS, this
movement is subsequently reflected in both how the sentence sounds, and what
it means:

(1) **Overt Wh-Movement in the T-Model**

    a. I wonder who Chris thinks Kim likes.

    b. DS: (I wonder (Chris thinks (Kim likes who)))

    c. SS: (I wonder (who$_t$ (Chris thinks (Kim likes t))))

    d. LF: (I wonder (who$_x$ (Chris thinks (Kim likes x))))

Here, the **wh-operator** *who* occupies an **argument (A)** position at DS.
After overt movement, it occupies a **nonargument (Ā)** position in SS on the
left periphery of one of the clauses that contained it; in this sentence, the only
clause it can move to is the middle one (with subject *Chris*), because the verb
wonder is the kind of verb that requires an interrogative complement clause.
When *who* moves, it leaves behind a **trace** or **syntactic variable** (here, t),
which it **binds** at SS; this is essentially the same position it will occupy at LF.
Now since derivations branch to PF (and LF) *after* SS, the movement of *who* has
an audible reflex (you hear it in the position it moved to). And finally, during
the SS-to-LF derivation, a **rule of construal** replaces t with a **logical variable**
(here, x), which is bound by *who* at LF.

Now nobody with even a rudimentary knowledge of lambda calculus or predicate logic could fail to notice that the SS in (1c) and the LF in (1d) look a
lot like formal terms containing operators that bind variables. But, at least as
far as I know, no logician has ever suggested that λ's, or $\exists$'s, or $\forall$'s, actually
start out in the position of the variables they bind, and then move to the left.
So one might well ask why transformational grammarians, right down to the

present day, believe that binding operators in NL do. At least 30 years ago, practicioners of **categorial grammar (CG)** (e.g. David Dowty, Emmon Bach) and **phrase structure grammar (PSG)**(e.g. Gerald Gazdar, Geoff Pullum) started asking this very question, and in the intervening decades researchers in these frameworks have proposed a wealth of carefully thought out theories in which NL binding operators do **not** move. We will come back to this.

By contrast with overt movement (within the T-model), transformations that convert SS to LF are called **covert** because they take place too late in the derivation—after the SS branch point—to have a reflex at PF. One standardly assumed covert movement is **quantifier raising** (QR, May 1977, 1985), which moves a quantificational NP (QNP) to a position in LF (reflective of its semantic scope) higher than the one it occupied at SS.

(2) **Covert Wh-Movement in the T-Model: QR**

    a. I know Chris thinks Kim likes everyone.

    b. DS: (I know (Chris thinks (Kim likes everyone)))

    c. SS: (I know (Chris thinks (Kim likes everyone))) [no change]

    d. LF (narrow scope reading): (I know (Chris thinks (everyone$_x$ (Kim likes x))))

    e. LF (medium scope reading): (I know (everyone$_x$ (Chris thinks (Kim likes x))))

    f. LF (wide scope reading): (everyone$_x$ (I know (Chris thinks (Kim likes x))))

Here, the QNP *everyone* occupies an **argument (A)** position at DS, and nothing happens to it between DS and SS (no overt movement). But after covert movement, it occupies a **nonargument (Ā)** position in LF on the left periphery of one of the clauses that contained it. Now when *everyone* moves, it leaves behind a **logical variable** (here, x), which it **binds** at LF. But since derivations branch after SS to PF and LF, and the movement of *everyone* is on the the the SS-to-LF branch, it has no audible reflex (you hear it in its pre-movement position).

Another standardly assumed covert movement is **covert wh-movement** in languages like Chinese (Huang et al. 1992), (Pesetsky 1987)[1]. Covert wh-movement is supposed to be essentially the same as overt wh-movement, except that, since—like QR— it takes place *after* the SS branch point, it is *heard* just as if it had never moved (or, to use the syntactician's term of art, it remains **in situ**).

(3) **Covert Wh-Movement in the T-Model: *Wh*-in-Situ**

    a. Zhangsan xiang-zhidao shei mai-le shenme. [Chinese]

    b. Zhangsan wonder who bought what [English word-for-word gloss]

---

[1] But see Aoun and Li (1993) for a dissenting view (that Chinese *wh*-movement is overt movement of an inaudible operator, with the *wh*-expressions as bindees, not binders.)

    c. DS: (Zhangsan xiang-zhidao (shei mai-le shenme))

    d. SS: (Zhangsan xiang-zhidao (shei mai-le shenme)) [no change]

    e. LF (*shei* and *shenme* both narrow):
    (Zhangsan xiang-zhidao (shei$_x$ shenme$_y$ (x mai-le y)))
    'Zhangsan wonders who bought what'

    f. LF (*shenme* narrow, *shei* wide):
    (shei$_x$(Zhangsan xiang-zhidao (shenme$_y$ (x mai-le y))))
    'Who does Zhangsan wonder what (s/he) bought?'

    g. LF (*shenme* wide, *shei* narrow):
    (shenme$_y$(Zhangsan xiang-zhidao (shei$_x$ (x mai-le y))))
    'What does Zhangsan wonder who bought?'

Here, as with QR, there is no change between DS and SS. Each of the *wh-* (or, in Chinese, *sh-*)operators can scope to any of the clauses containing it. However, in this example, at least one of them must scope to the lower clause, since the clausal complement of the verb *xiang-xhidao* 'wonder' has to be a question.

In fact, even languages like English with overt wh-movement also have in situ wh, in two different respects. First, in **multiple constituent questions**, all but the leftmost wh-expression remain in situ. And second, in cases of pied piping, the wh-expression that is properly contained within the moved constituent remains in situ, relative to the displaced constituent that contains it. In this paper, however, we will limit our attention henceforth to phenomena that transformational grammar (TG) has analyzed purely in terms of covert movements.

In the rest of the paper, we sketch an approach to so-called covert phenomena in which (as in logic) binding operators never move. (For the extension of this approach to so-called overt movement phenomena, see Pollard 2008b.)

2   Toward a New, Nontransformational Synthesis

The T-model has long since been abandoned. Within the Chomskyan syntactic tradition, the Minimalist Programm (MP, Chomsky 1995) provides much more flexibility than EST or GB did, by discarding the notions of DS and SS. Instead, merges (corresponding to EST/GB base rules) need not all take place before any moves do. And the possibility of multiple branch points in a single derivation ('Spell-outs') means that not all overt moves must occur 'lower' in the derivation than any of the covert ones. These are not exactly negative developments; but it is well worth noting that, had transformational grammarians followed the lead of CG and PSG practicioners from the 1970s on in informing their theory by ideas from logic (as opposed to logic metaphors), the architectural problems of EST/GB that the MP has sought to repair could have been addressed much early, or even avoided altogether. Here are a few examples.

First, in EST/GB, as noted above, LF is derived from SS. But an LF looks a lot like a semantic lambda-term, and so, in light of the Curry-Howard (types as formulas, terms as proofs) conception (Curry et al. 1958, Howard 1980), we should be able to think of it as an (intuitionistic) proof in its own right. So there is no reason why it has to be derived from SS (or anything else).

Second, also as noted above, an EST/GB labelled bracketing, which typically contains traces (syntactic variables) and inaudible operators which bind them, also looks a lot like a lambda term. But by then (1970s to early 1980s), Lambek (1958) had already long since proposed that NL syntax be formulated in terms of a substructural proof theory. Moroever the idea of extending the Curry-Howard conception to substructural logics was continually being redis-covered[2]; so, in hindsight at least, it is easy perceive these labelled bracketings as Curry-Howard terms for some resource-sensitive logic or other. But in that case, linguists should think of NL syntactic trees as *proof trees*, as Moortgat (1991) and other categorial grammarians had already realized in the mid-to-late 1980s, not as *structures* whose subtrees can be deleted, copied, or moved by transformations (and whose internal structural configurations could be relevant in the formulation of linguistically significant generalizations).

Third (given the preceding), there is no need to stipulate a Strict Cycle Con-dition (Chomsky 1976) on rule application (roughly, that once a rule has applied to a given tree, it is already too late for any rule to apply solely to one of that tree's proper subtrees), for the simple reason that a proof cannot go back and change earlier parts of itself!

And fourth, also in hindsight, it is clear that the notion of SS is not only unnecessary but pernicious. That is because SS is the stage of the derivation at which all base rule applications (merges) have taken place but none of the transformational rule applications (moves). In proof theoretic terms, what SS amounts to is a point in a proof subsequent to which only instances of Hypo-thetical Proof (but not Modus Ponens) are admitted! But there is no requirement on proofs that all instances of Modus Ponens appear lower in the proof tree than all instances of Hypothetical Proof, just as there is no well-formedness condition on lambda terms that all the abstractions occur on the left periphery of the term.

If these observations are on the right track, then the syntax and semantics of NL expressions are both proofs in their own right. But then, a grammar should not be in the business of tranforming syntax into semantics; rather, it should be specifying which syntax-semantics *pairs of proofs*[3] go together. To put it another way, the syntax-semantics interface should be at once **purely derivational** and **parallel**. Here, by *purely* derivational, we mean simply that derivations are *proofs*, as opposed to nondeterministic algorithms that build arboreal structures via successive destructive modification. And by *parallel*, we mean that there are separate proofs theories that provide, respectively, candidate syntactic and semantic proofs; whereas it is the job of the syntax-semantics interface to recursively define the set of proof pairs that belong to the language in question.

---

[2] E.g. (Mints 1981; van Benthem 1983; Buszkowski 1987; Jay 1989; Benton et al. 1992; Wansing 1992; Gabbay and de Queiroz 1992; Mackie et al. 1993).

[3] Or triples, if phonology is also taken into account.

The pure derivationality of the proposed approach comes straight out of CG, and the syntactic proof theory we will adopt below will be readily taken for what it is, a variant of (multimodal) applicative categorial grammar. However, the mainstream of CG[4] has eschewed parallelism, in favor of the **functional** approach to semantic interpretation bequeathed by Montague, which mandates that there can never be a purely semantic ambiguity. Rather, on the functional approach, there must be a *function* from syntactic proofs/terms[5] to semantic proofs/terms; or, to put it another way, all meaning differences must be disambiguated in the syntax.[6]

But I am not aware of any scientific basis for requiring that the relation between syntactic derivations and semantic ones be a function. Indeed, there is a long tradition[7] which rejects the premise that the syntax-semantics relation is a function from the former to the latter. I will refer to this tradition as the **parallel** approach to the syntax-semantics interface. The framework I will be using below, called **Convergent Grammar (CVG)**, while purely derivational, also lies squarely within this parallel tradition.[8]

In fact, the idea of a purely derivational parallel grammar architecture has already been proposed independently and considerably earlier in this decade by Lecomte and Retoré (Lecomte and Retoré 2002, Lecomte 2005), and there are numerous points of similarity between their approach and CVG. However, unlike their approach, which is part of a larger intellectual enterprise (**categorial minimalism**) which seeks to bring about a marriage of CG and MP, the intellectual tradition to which CVG belongs is one that parted company with (to use Culicover and Jackendoff's term) mainstream generative grammar (MGG) more than three decades ago. As will be made clear shortly, CVG is really a proof-theoretic embodiment not of minimalism but rather of the storage and retrieval technology proposed by Cooper (1975, 1983) as an alternative to the then-current EST/GB.

---

[4] E.g. (van Benthem 1983; Lambek 1988; Morrill 1994; Steedman 1996; Moortgat 1996; Carpenter 1997; Jacobson 1999; de Groote 2001b; Ranta 2004; Muskens 2003; Pollard 2004; Anoun and Lecomte 2007; Bernardi and Moortgat 2007).

[5] Or, in the case of Montague, analysis trees.

[6] There is a trivial respect in which any relational syntax-semantics interface can be rendered functional by allowing *sets* of usual meanings to serve as 'meanings', since there is a canonical correspondence between binary relations and functions from the domain of the relation to the powerset of the codomain (the category of relations is the Kleisli category of the powerset monad on sets). But linguists generally require of meanings, however they are modelled, that they provide a deterministic interpretation for contextualized utterances. Thus, we rule out as meanings nondetermistic (or underspecified) representations (as in the MRS (minimal recursion semantics) employed in some versions of head-driven phrase structure grammar (HPSG)) that have to be postprocessed to resolve scopal ambiguities.

[7] See, e.g. (Cooper 1975, 1983; Bach and Partee 1980; Hendriks 1993; Pollard and Sag 1994; Lecomte and Retoré 2002; Lecomte 2005; Culicover and Jackendoff 2005).

[8] This is scarcely surprising, since it originated as an effort to reformulate HPSG along type-theoretic lines (Pollard 2004).

The kinds of ambiguities associated with the so-called covert-movement phenomena, illustrated above in (2) and (3), bear directly on the functional vs. parallel issue. Indeed, on parallel approaches, they readily lend themselves to analyses that locate the ambiguities wholly in the semantics, rather than complicating the syntax for the mere sake of preserving the (putative) functionality of the syntax-semantics interface at any cost. To put it simply, it is entirely permissible, at a certain point in a pair of simultaneous derivations (one syntactic; one semantic), to do something on the semantic side while doing nothing at all on the syntactic side. And as we will see shortly, the Cooper-inspired storage and retrieval rules in terms of which we analyze covert movement are of this precise character.

3   Syntax, Semantics, and Their Interface

For present purposes, we take a CVG to consist of three things: (1) a **syntax**, (2) a **semantics**, and (3) a **syntax-semantics interface** (hereafter, **interface** *simpliciter*).[9] For the fragment developed here, we can take the syntax to be a proof theory for a simple multi-applicative categorial grammar.[10] The semantics will be another proof theory closely related to the familiar typed lambda calculus (TLC). And the interface will recursively define a set of pairs of proofs. The two proof theories are both presented in the Gentzen-sequent style of natural deduction with Curry-Howard proof terms (see e.g. Mitchell and Scott (1989)), because this style of proof theory is visually easy to relate to EST/GB-style or HPSG-style linguistic analyses.

3.1   Semantics

Rather than the familiar TLC, we employ a new semantic calculus RC (the calculus of **Responsibility and Commitment**[11] which, we argue, is better adapted to expressing the semantic compositionality of natural language. (But we will also provide a simple algorithm for transforming RC semantic terms into TLC, more specifically, into Ty2.) Here we present only the fragment of RC needed to analyze covert movement; the full calculus, with the two additional schemata needed to analyze overt movement, is presented in (Pollard 2008b).

Like TLC, RC has types, terms, and typing judgments. One important difference is that in TLC, the **variable context** of a typing judgment is just a

---

[9] For the simple fragment developed here, it is easy to read the word order off of the syntactic analyses (proof terms). But to do serious linguistics, we also will require a **phonology** and a **syntax-phonology interface**. Thus CVG is **syntactocentric**, in the sense that syntax has interfaces to phonology and semantics, but only **weakly** so, in the sense that the relations defined by the two interfaces need not be functions.

[10] But in order to extend the theory to cover so-called overt movement phenomena, we will need to add some form of hypothetical reasoning to the syntactic proof theory (Pollard 2008b).

[11] See (Pollard 2008a) and references cited there for background and discussion.

set of variable/type pairs, written to the left of the turnstile. But an RC typing judgment has a **Cooper store**, written to the right and demarcated by a **co-turnstile** $\dashv$:

(4) **Format for RC Typing Judgments**

$\vdash a : A \dashv \Delta$

The Cooper store is also called the **variable co-context**[12]; the 'co-' here is mnemonic not only for 'Cooper'; but also for 'Commitment' (for reasons to be explained presently), for 'Covert Movement', and for 'Continuation' (since the operators stored in them will scope over their own continuations). Thus a judgment like (4) is read 'the (semantic) term a is assigned the (semantic) type A in the co-context Δ.'

(5) **RC Semantic Types**

    a. There are some **basic** semantic types.

    b. If A and B are types, then $A \to B$ is a **functional** semantic type with **argument** type A and **result** type B.

    c. If A, B, and C are types, then $O[A, B, C]$, usually abbreviated (following Shan 2004) to A_B^C, is an **operator** semantic type with **binding** type A, **scope** type B, and **result** type C.[13]

(6) **Basic Semantic Types**

For present purposes, we use three basic semantic types:
ι (individual concepts), π (propositions), and κ (polar questions).[14]

(7) **Functional Semantic Types**

We employ the following abbreviations for (necessarily curried) functional types:

    a. Where σ ranges over strings of types and ϵ is the null string:

       i. $A_\epsilon =_{\text{def}} A$

      ii. $A_{B\sigma} =_{\text{def}} B \to A_\sigma$ (e.g. $\pi_{\iota\iota} = \iota \to \iota \to \pi$)

    b. For $n \in \omega$, $\kappa_n =_{\text{def}} \kappa_\sigma$ where σ is the string of ι's of length n.

    For n-ary constituent questions where the constituents questioned all have type ι. E.g. *who likes what* will get type κ_2.

(8) **Operator Types**

    a. These will be the semantic types for expressions which would be analyzed in TG as undergoing $\bar{\text{A}}$-movement (either overt or covert).

---

[12] The full RC calculus, including the schemata for analyzing overt movement, also employs ordinary variable contexts to the left of the turnstile.

[13] That is, a term a of type $O[A, B, C]$ binds a variable x of type A in a term of type B, resulting in a term $a_x b$ of type C.

[14] Here κ is mnemonic for 'Karttunen' because its transform (see below) into Ty2 will be the Karttunen type for questions.

b. The O-constructor is like Moortgat's (1996) q-constructor, but it belongs to the *semantic* logic, *not* the syntactic one.

c. Thus, for example, while for Moortgat (1996) a QNP would have category q[NP, S, S] and semantic type $(\iota \rightarrow \pi) \rightarrow \pi$, for us it has category (simply) NP and semantic type ι_π^π.[15]

(9) **RC Semantic Terms**

a. There is a denumerable infinity of **semantic variables** of each type.

b. There are finitely many **basic semantic constants** of each type.

c. There are **functional** semantic terms of the form $(f\ a)$, where f and a are semantic terms.

d. There are **binding** semantic terms of the form $(a_x b)$ where a and b are semantic terms and x is a semantic variable.

e. But there is no λ!

(10) **Cooper Stores**

a. The Cooper stores (co-contexts) will contain semantic operators to be scoped, each paired with the variable that it will eventually bind.

b. We call such stored pairs **commitments**, and write them in the form a_x, where the type of x is the binding type of a.

c. Then we call x a **committed** variable, and say that a is **committed** to bind x.

Then the rule schemata of RC are the following:

(11) **Semantic Schema A (Nonlogical Axioms)**

$\vdash c : A \dashv$ (c a basic semantic constant of type A)

The basic constants notate meanings of syntactic words (see (26)).

(12) **Semantic Schema M (Modus Ponens)**

If $\vdash f : A \rightarrow B \dashv \Delta$ and $\vdash a : A \dashv \Delta'$, then $\vdash (f\ a) : B \dashv \Delta; \Delta'$

a. This is the usual natural-deduction (ND) Modus Ponens, except that co-contexts have to be propagated from premises to conclusions.

b. Semicolons in co-contexts represent set union (necessarily disjoint, since variables are always posited fresh).

(13) **Semantic Schema C (Commitment)**

If $\vdash a : A_B^C \dashv \Delta$ then $\vdash x : A \dashv a_x : A_B^C; \Delta$ (x fresh)

a. This is a straightforward ND formulation of Cooper storage.

---

[15] Actually QNPs have to be polymorphically typed. See (Pollard 2008a, fn. 4).

b. It generalizes Carpenter's (1997) Introduction rule for Moortgat's (1991) ⇑ (essentially the special case of q where the scope type and the result type are the same), but **in the semantics, not in the syntax**.

(14) **Semantic Schema R (Responsibility)**

If $\vdash b : B \dashv a_x : A_B^C; \Delta$ then $\vdash (a_x b) : C \dashv \Delta$ (x free in b but not in Δ)

a. This is a straightforward ND formulation of Cooper retrieval.

b. It generalizes Carpenter's (1997) Elimination rule for Moortgat's ⇑, but, again, **in the semantics, not in the syntax**.

c. It is called Responsibility because it is about fulfilling commitments.

To give the reader a familiar point of reference, we provide a transform of RC into the standard higher-order semantic representation language Ty2 (Gallin 1975).[16] We follow Carpenter (1997, Sect. 11.2) in using individual concepts as the basic type for NPs. But we use use the Gallin/Montague names for the basic types e (entities, Carpenter's individuals), t (truth values, Carpenter's booleans), and s (worlds), rather than Carpenter's Ind, Bool, and World respectively. Hence our (and Montague's) type s → e for individual concepts corresponds to Carpenter's type World → Ind.[17]

We also follow Carpenter's convention that functional meaning types take their world argument last rather than first, e.g. the type for an intransitive verb is (s → e) → s → t (the transform of RC type $\iota \to \pi$) rather than s → (s → e) → t, so that the verb meaning combines with the subject meaning by ordinary function application.

The price, well worth paying, is that, except for individual concepts and propositions, our Ty2 meanings are technically not intensions (functions from worlds). Consequently the extension at a world w of a Ty2 meaning is defined by recursion on types as follows:

(15) **Ty2 Meaning Types**

a. s → e (individual concepts) is a Ty2 meaning type.

b. s → t (propositions) is a Ty2 meaning type.

c. If A and B are Ty2 meaning types, then so is $A \to B$.

(16) **Extensional Types Corresponding to Ty2 Meaning Types**

These are defined as follows:

---

[16] This transform is not a proper part of our framework, but is provided in order to show that familiar meaning representations can be algorithmically recovered from the ones we employ. Readers who are not concerned with this issue can just ignore this transform.

[17] Types for Ty2 variables are as follows: $x, y, z : $ s → e (individual concepts); $p, q : $ s → t (propositions); $w : $ s (worlds); and $P, Q : $ (s → e) → s → t (properties of individual concepts).

a. $E(s \rightarrow e) = e$

b. $E(s \rightarrow t) = t$

c. $E(A \rightarrow B) = A \rightarrow E(B)$

(17) Extensions of Ty2 Meanings

The relationship between Ty2 meanings and their extensions is axiomatized as follows, where the family of constants $\text{ext}_A : s \rightarrow A \rightarrow E(A)$ is parametrized by the Ty2 meaning types:[18]

a. $\vdash \forall_x \forall_w (\text{ext}_w(x) = x(w)$ (for $x : s \rightarrow e)$

b. $\vdash \forall_p \forall_w (\text{ext}_w(p) = p(w)$ (for $p : s \rightarrow t)$

c. $\vdash \forall_f \forall_w (\text{ext}_w(f) = \lambda_x \text{ext}_w(f(x))$ (for $f : A \rightarrow B$, A and B Ty2 meaning types.

(18) The Transform τ from RC Types to Ty2 Meaning Types

a. $\tau(\iota) = s \rightarrow e$

b. $\tau(\pi) = s \rightarrow t$

c. $\tau(\kappa) = \tau(\pi) \rightarrow \tau(\pi)$

d. $\tau(A \rightarrow B) = \tau(A) \rightarrow \tau(B)$

e. $\tau(A_B^C) = (\tau(A) \rightarrow \tau(B)) \rightarrow \tau(C)$

(19) The Transform τ on Terms

a. Variables and basic constants are unchanged except for their types. (We make abundant use of meaning postulates, e.g. (20) rather than giving basic constants nonbasic transforms.)

b. $\tau((f\ a)) = \tau(f)(\tau(a))$

   The change in the parenthesization has no theoretical significance. It just enables one to tell at a glance whether the term belongs to RC or to Ty2, e.g. (walk' Kim') vs. walk'(Kim').

c. $\tau((a_x b)) = \tau(a)(\lambda_x \tau(b))$

(20) Ty2 Meaning Postulates for Generalized Quantifiers

$\vdash$ every' $= \lambda_Q \lambda_P \lambda_w \forall_x (Q(x)(w) \rightarrow P(x)(w))$

$\vdash$ some' $= \lambda_Q \lambda_P \lambda_w \exists_x (Q(x)(w) \wedge P(x)(w))$

$\vdash$ everyone' $=$ every'(person')

$\vdash$ someone' $=$ some'(person')

---

[18] We omit the type subscript A on ext_A when it is inferrable from context. Moreover we abbreviate $\text{ext}(w)$ as ext_w.

3.2   Syntax

For the fragment developed here, our syntactic calculus is just a simple multi-modal applicative CG.[19] Again, there are types, now called **(syntactic) categories**, terms, and typing judgments, which have the form

(21) **Format for CVG Syntactic Typing Judgments**
$\vdash a : A$
read 'the (syntactic) term a is assigned the category A.'

(22) **CVG Categories**
  a. There are some **basic** categories.
  b. If A and B are categories, so are $A \multimap_F B$, where F belongs to a set F of **grammatical function names**[20]; these are called **functional** categories with **argument** category A and **result** category B.

(23) **Basic Categories**
For now, just S and NP.

(24) **Functional Categories**
We start off with the grammatical function names s (subject) and c (complement).[21] Others will be added as needed.

(25) **CVG Syntactic Terms**
  a. There are finitely many **(syntactic) words** of each category.
  b. There are **syntactic functional terms** of the forms $(f\, a^{\,F})$ and $(^{F} f\, a)$

(26) **(Syntactic) Words**
  a. These correspond not just to Bloomfield's "minimal free forms", but also to minimal syntactic units realized phonologically as phrasal affixes, sentence particles, argument clitics, etc.
  b. Some of these might be realized nonconcatenatively, e.g. by pitch accents, (partial) reduplication, phonological zero (inaudibility), etc.

---

[19] But to analyze overt movement, it will have to be extended with schemata for traces and syntactic binding by 'overtly moved' syntactic operators (Pollard (2008b)).

[20] Thus grammatical functions are abstract tectogrammatical primitives, and not defined in terms of word order, phonology, or the positions in which they occur in proof trees. And so the role grammatical functions play in CVG is strongly analogous to the role that they play in such frameworks as HPSG, lexical-functional grammar (LFG), and relational grammar (RG). Multiple modes of implication can be replaced by a single linear implication (see (de Groote et al. 2009) for details), at the expense of considerably elaborating the set of basic types.

[21] Here CVG betrays its HPSG pedigree.

(27) **Syntactic Functional Terms**

    a. In principle these could always be written $(f\ a\ ^{\mathrm{F}})$, but we write $(f\ a\ ^{\mathrm{C}})$ and $(^{\mathrm{S}}\ a\ f)$ as a mnemonic that in English subjects are to the left and complements to the right.

    b. This enables us to read the word order off the syntactic terms, as in EST/GB labelled bracketings.

The CVG syntactic rule schemata are as follows:

(28) **Syntactic Schema W (Words)**

    $\vdash w : A$ (w a syntactic word of category A)

(29) **Syntactic Schema M_S (Subject Modus Ponens)**

    If $\vdash a : A$ and $\vdash f : A \multimap_S B$, then $\vdash (^{\mathrm{S}}\ a\ f) : B$

(30) **Syntactic Schema M_C (Complement Modus Ponens)**

    If $\vdash f : A \multimap_C B$ and $\vdash a : A$, then $\vdash (f\ a\ ^{\mathrm{C}}) : B$

3.3 The CVG Syntax-Semantics Interface

The interface recursively specifies which syntactic proofs are paired with which semantics ones. Unsurprisingly, the recursion is grounded in the lexicon:

(31) **Interface Schema L (Lexicon)**

    $\vdash w, c : A, B \dashv$ (for certain pairs $\langle w, c \rangle$ where w is a word of category A and c is a basic constant of type B)

The following two schemata are essentially ND reformulations of HPSG's Subject-Head and Head-Complement schemata:

(32) **Interface Schema M_S (Subject Modus Ponens)**

    If $\vdash a, c : A, C \dashv \Delta$ and $\vdash f, v : A \multimap_S B, C \to D \dashv \Delta'$
    then $\vdash (^{\mathrm{S}}\ a\ f), (v\ c) : B, D \dashv \Delta; \Delta'$

(33) **Interface Schema M_C (Complement Modus Ponens)**

    If $\vdash f, v : A \multimap_C B, C \to D \dashv \Delta$ and $\vdash a, c : A, C \dashv \Delta'$
    then $\vdash (f\ a\ ^{\mathrm{C}}), (v\ c) : B, D \dashv \Delta; \Delta'$

And finally, the following two rules, both of which leave the syntax unchanged, are ND reformulations of Cooper storage and retrieval, respectively.

(34) **Interface Schema C (Commitment)**

    If $\vdash a, b : A, B_C^D \dashv \Delta$, then $\vdash a, x : A, B \dashv b_x : B_C^D; \Delta$ (x fresh)

(35) **Interface Schema R (Responsibility)**

    If $\vdash e, c : E, C \dashv b_x : B_C^D; \Delta$ then $\vdash e, (b_x c) : E, D \dashv \Delta$
    (x free in c but not in Δ)

It should be noted that, since co-contexts are sets, not lists, retrieval is nondeterministic not only with respect to which node in the proof tree it takes place at, but also with respect to which of the stored operators is retrieved.

4   Analysis of Quantifier Raising in English

Our English fragment will employ the following lexicon. By convention, for any lexical entry, the words and the semantic constants are presupposed to have already been licensed, respectively, by the syntactic and semantic logics.

(36) **Lexicon for English Fragment**

$\vdash$ Chris, Chris' : NP, ι $\dashv$ (likewise other names)

$\vdash$ everyone, everyone' : NP, ι_π^π $\dashv$

$\vdash$ someone, someone' : NP, ι_π^π $\dashv$

$\vdash$ likes, like' : NP $\multimap_C$ NP $\multimap_S$ S, $\iota \to \iota \to \pi$ $\dashv$

$\vdash$ thinks, think' : S $\multimap_C$ NP $\multimap_S$ S, $\pi \to \iota \to \pi$ $\dashv$

(37) **A Simple Sentence**

a. Chris thinks Kim likes Dana.

b. $\vdash$ (^{S} Chris (thinks (^{S} Kim (likes Dana ^{C}) ^{C}))) : ((think' ((like' Dana') Kim')) Chris') : S, π $\dashv$

c. Ty2: think'(like'(Dana')(Kim'))(Chris')

(38) **Quantifier Scope Ambiguity**

a. Chris thinks Kim likes everyone.

b. Syntax (both):
(^{S} Chris (thinks (^{S} Kim (likes everyone ^{C}) ^{C}))) : S

c. Semantics (scoped to lower clause):
RC: ((think' (everyone'$_x$((like' x) Kim'))) Chris') : π
Ty2: think'($\lambda_w(\forall_x$(person'$(x)(w) \to$ like'(x)(Kim')(w)))))(Chris') : s $\to$ t

d. Semantics (scoped to upper clause):
RC: (everyone'$_x$((think' ((like' x) Kim')) Chris')) : π
Ty2: $\lambda_w(\forall_x$(person'$(x)(w) \to$ think'(like'(x)(Kim'))(Chris')(w)))) : s $\to$ t

(39) **Raising of Two Quantifiers to Same Clause**

a. Everyone likes someone.

b. Syntax (both): (^{S} everyone (likes someone ^{C}) ^{C}) : S

c. $\forall\exists$-reading (RC): (everyone'$_x$(someone'$_y$((like' y) x))) : π

d. $\exists\forall$-reading (RC): (someone'$_y$(everyone'$_x$((like' y) x))) : π

e. These are possible because for generalized quantifiers, the result type is the same as the scope type.

f. Things are not so straightforward in the case of multiple in-situ wh-operators, as we will see in the next section.

5   Background for the Analysis of *Wh*-in-Situ

In dealing with the semantics of (possibly multiple) in-situ constituent questions, we take as our target (Ty2) semantics a variant (Pollard 2008c) of Karttunen's (1977) semantics of interrogatives, which analyzes interrogative denotations as sets of propositions. We follow Karttunen in the case of polar questions; but for n-place constituent questions, we take the denotation to be (the curried form of) a function from n-tuples to propositions:[22]

(40) **Types for Polar Questions**

    a. RC meaning type: κ

    b. Meaning type of Ty2 transform: $(s \rightarrow t) \rightarrow s \rightarrow t$ (property of propositions)

    c. Type of Ty2 extension: $(s \rightarrow t) \rightarrow t$ (characteristic function of) a (singleton) set of propositions)

    d. Example: at w, *Does Chris walk* (or *whether Chris walks*) denotes the singleton set whose member is whichever is true at w, the proposition that Chris walks or the proposition that s/he doesn't.

(41) **Types for Unary Constituent Questions**

    a. RC meaning type: κ_1

    b. Meaning type of Ty2 transform: $(s \rightarrow e) \rightarrow (s \rightarrow t) \rightarrow (s \rightarrow t)$ (function from individual concepts to properties of propositions).

    c. Type of Ty2 extension: $(s \rightarrow e) \rightarrow (s \rightarrow t) \rightarrow t$ (function from individual concepts to sets of propositions). Technically, the curried version of the characteristic function of a certain binary relation between individual concepts and propositions.

    d. Example: at w, *who walks* denotes the (functional) binary relation between individual concepts x and propositions p that obtains just in case x is a w-person and and p is whichever proposition is a w-fact, that x walks or that x does not walk.

(42) **Types for Binary Constituent Questions**

    a. RC meaning type: κ_2

    b. Meaning type of Ty2 transform: $(s \rightarrow e) \rightarrow (s \rightarrow e) \rightarrow (s \rightarrow t) \rightarrow (s \rightarrow t)$ (curried function from pairs of individual concepts to properties of propositions).

---

[22] A set of propositions can then be recovered as the *range* of this function. This set differs from the Karttunen semantics in having both positive and negative 'atomic answers' as members. Additionally, our interrogative meanings yield a refinement of the Groenendijk-Stokhof partition semantics by taking the induced equivalence relation on worlds. See (Pollard 2008c) for detailed discussion.

c. Type of Ty2 extension: $(s \rightarrow t) \rightarrow (s \rightarrow e) \rightarrow (s \rightarrow t) \rightarrow t$ (curried function from pairs of individual concepts to sets of propositions). Technically, the curried version of the characteristic function of a certain ternary relation between individual concepts, individual concepts, and propositions.

d. Example: at w, *who likes what* denotes the (functional) ternary relation between individual concepts x and y and propositions p that obtains just in case x is a w-person, y is a w-thing, and p is whichever proposition is a w-fact, that x likes y or that x does not like y.

The fact that not all questions have the same type complicates the analysis of in-situ multiple constituent questions as compared with the analysis of multiple quantifier retrieval (39). For example, scoping one in-situ *wh*-operator at a proposition produces a unary constituent question, so its type must be $\iota_\pi^{\kappa_1}$. Thus, if we want to scope a second in-situ *wh*-operator over that unary constituent question to form a binary constituent question, then *its* type must be $\iota_{\kappa_1}^{\kappa_2}$, and so forth. So unlike QNPs, *wh*-operators must be (in principal infinitely) polymorphic. Note that this polymorphism has nothing to do with the depth of embedding of the *sentences* at which the operator is retrieved, but only with the operator's scoping order (in the sequence of all the wh-operators scoped within a given sentence).

Our analysis will make use of a number of Ty2 logical constants, defined by the following meaning postulates:

(43) **Ty2 Meaning Postulates for Some Useful Logical Constants**

a. $\vdash \mathsf{id}_n = \lambda_Z Z$ (for $Z : \tau(\kappa_n)$)

b. $\vdash \mathsf{and}' = \lambda_p \lambda_q \lambda_w (p(w) \wedge q(w))$

c. $\vdash \mathsf{or}' = \lambda_p \lambda_q \lambda_w (p(w) \vee q(w))$

d. $\vdash \mathsf{not}' = \lambda_p \lambda_w \neg p(w)$

e. $\vdash \mathsf{equals}'_A = \lambda_x \lambda_y \lambda_w (x = y)$

f. $\vdash \mathsf{whether}' = \lambda_q \lambda_p (p \wedge ((p \ \mathsf{equals}' \ q) \vee (p \ \mathsf{equals}' \ \mathsf{not}'(q))))$

g. $\vdash \mathsf{which}^0 = \lambda_Q \lambda_P \lambda_x \lambda_p (Q(x) \ \mathsf{and}' \ \mathsf{whether}'(P(x))(p))$

h. $\vdash \mathsf{which}^n = \lambda_Q \lambda_Z \lambda_{x_0} \ldots \lambda_{x_n} \lambda_p (Q(x) \ \mathsf{and}' \ Z(x_0) \ldots (x_n)(p)) \ (n > 0)$

The last two are the Ty2 meanings of the interrogative determiner *which*. We do not include determiners in this fragment, but these meanings are used to define the following nonlogical constants:

(44) **Ty2 Meaning Postulates for some Nonlogical Constants**
For $n \in \omega$:

a. $\vdash \mathsf{who}^n = \mathsf{which}^n(\mathsf{person}')$

b. $\vdash \mathsf{what}^n = \mathsf{which}^n(\mathsf{thing}')$

6   Chinese Interrogatives

We turn now to the analysis of so-called covert *wh*-movement in Chinese.[23]

Our Chinese fragment uses the same types, categories, and (semantic, syntactic, and interface) rule schemata as the English, but a different lexicon:

(45) **Lexicon for Chinese Fragment**

$\vdash$ Zhangsan, Zhangsan' : NP, ι $\dashv$

$\vdash$ xihuan, like' : NP $\multimap_C$ NP $\multimap_S$ S, $\iota \to \iota \to \pi$ $\dashv$

$\vdash$ xi-bu-xihuan, like?' : NP $\multimap_C$ NP $\multimap_S$ S, $\iota \to \iota \to \kappa$ $\dashv$

$\vdash$ xiang-zhidao, wonder'$_n$: S $\multimap_C$ NP $\multimap_S$ S, $\kappa_n \to \iota \to \pi$ $\dashv$

$\vdash$ shei, who^0 : NP, $\iota_\pi^{\kappa_1}$ $\dashv$

$\vdash$ shei, who^n : NP, $\iota_{\kappa_n}^{\kappa_{n+1}}$ $\dashv$ (for $n > 0$)

$\vdash$ shenme, what^0 : NP, $\iota_\pi^{\kappa_1}$ $\dashv$

$\vdash$ shenme, what^n : NP, $\iota_{\kappa_n}^{\kappa_{n+1}}$ $\dashv$ (for $n > 0$)

(46) **Meaning Postulate for an Interrogative Verb Meaning**

$\vdash$ like?' $= \lambda_y \lambda_x$ whether'(like'$(y)(x)$)

Note that *xibuxihuan* 'like?' is a partial-reduplicative interrogative verb form, used for forming (both root and embedded) polar questions. The verb *xiang-zhidao* 'wonder' has to be type-schematized according to the type of question expressed by the sentential complement. And the *sh*-interrogative words have to be type-schematized according by their scope type (and corresponding result type). This fragment produces analyses such as the following:

(47) **A Simple Chinese Sentence**

    a. Zhangsan xihuan Lisi.

    b. Zhangsan like Lisi

    c. Zhangsan likes Lisi.'

    d. $\vdash$ (^{S} Zhangsan (xihuan Lisi ^{C})) : S

    e. Ty2: $\vdash$ like'(Lisi')(Zhangsan') : $\tau(\pi)$

(48) **A Chinese Polar Question**

    a. Zhangsan xi-bu-xihuan Lisi?

    b. Zhangsan like? Lisi

    c. 'Does Zhangsan like Lisi?'

    d. $\vdash$ (^{S} Zhangsan (xi-bu-xihuan Lisi ^{C})) : S

    e. Ty2: $\vdash$ whether'(like'(Lisi')(Zhangsan')) : $\tau(\kappa_0)$

---

[23] The analysis we will propose here improves on an earlier version (Pollard 2007a, 2007b) which required construction-specific rules for different in-situ operators.

(49) **A Chinese Unary Constituent Question**

    a. Zhangsan xihuan shenme?

    b. Zhangsan like who

    c. 'What does Zhangsan like?'

    d. $\vdash (^S$ Zhangsan (xihuan shenme $^C)) : S$

    e. RC: $\vdash ($what$^0_y(($like' $y)$ (Zhangsan'$)) : \kappa_1 \dashv$

(50) **A Chinese Binary Constituent Question**

    a. Shei xihuan shenme?

    b. who like what

    c. Who likes what?

    d. $\vdash (^S$ Shei (xihuan shenme $^C)) : S$

    e. RC: $\vdash ($who$^1_x($what$^0_y(($like' $y)$ $(x))) : \kappa_2 \dashv$

    f. RC: $\vdash ($what$^1_y($who$^0_x(($like' $y)$ $(x))) : \kappa_2 \dashv$

The ambiguity is inessential: the two functions are the same modulo permutation of their arguments.

Finally, we consider so-called Baker-type ambiguities. Baker (1970) noticed that English sentences like the following are ambiguous:

(51) **Baker-Type Ambiguity in English**

    a. A: Who knows where we bought what?

    b. B: Chris does. (Appropriate when *what* scopes to the embeded question.)

    c. B: Chris knows where we bought the books, and Kim knows where we bought the records. (Appropriate when *what* scopes to the root question.)

    d. The 'overtly moved' *wh*-expressions must scope at their 'surface' positions: *who* can only scope to the root question, and *where* can only scope to the embedded question.

    e. But the in-situ *wh*-expression *what* can scope high or low.

A full account of thus phenomenon in English depends on an analysis of *overt* movement, which is beyond the scope of this paper (but see (Pollard 2008a)). Instead, we analyze the corresponding facts of Chinese, which involve only covert movement.

(52) **A Chinese Baker-Type Wh-Scope Ambiguity**

    a. Zhangsan xiang-zhidao shei xihuan shenme./?

    b. Zhangsan wonder who like what

    c. $\vdash (^S$ Zhangsan (xiang-zhidao $(^S$ shei (xihuan shenme $^C)$ $^C))) : S$

    d. $\vdash (($wonder'$_2$ (who$^1_x($what$^0_y(($like' $y)$ $x)))) Zhangsan') : \pi \dashv$
       'Zhangsan wonders who likes what.'

e. $\vdash$ (who$_x^0$((wonder'$_1$ (what$_y^0$((like' y) x)))) Zhangsan') : κ_1 $\dashv$
'Who does Zhangsan wonder what (that person) likes?'

f. $\vdash$ (what$_y^0$((wonder'$_1$ (who$_x^0$((like' y) x)))) Zhangsan') : κ_1 $\dashv$
'What does Zhangsan wonder who likes?'

(53) **The Gist of the Preceding**

a. Both *sh*-expressions are in situ, so they can each scope high or low.

b. If both scope low (52d), then the root sentence expresses a proposition and the embedded sentence expresses a binary question.

c. If one scopes high and the other low (52e,52f), then the root sentence and the embedded sentence both express unary questions.

d. But they cannot *both* scope high, since then the complement sentence would express a proposition, while the first argument of wonder' must be a question.

7   Conclusion

We have presented a new, simple, and formally precise account of so-called covert movement phenomena. The key ideas of the account are these:

(54) **The Key Ideas Summarized**

– As in CG, both the syntax and the semantics of a linguistic expression are proofs.

– But unlike mainstream CG, the syntax-semantics interface is not a function, so operator-scope ambiguities need not have syntactic reflections.

– Thus the syntax is simple.

– And unlike TG, the interface is not a nondeterministic process made up of sequences of structural operations on trees.

– Instead, it is just a recursive specification of which proof pairs go together (parallel derivational architecture).

– The key insights embodied in the the semantic logic RC go back to the 1970s: Cooper's storage and retrieval.

– The RC formulation generalizes Carpenter's ND rules for Moortgat's $\Uparrow$, but only in the semantic logic (not the syntactic one).

– The transform from RC to TLC is simple.[24]

---

[24] It would be instructive to understand the the connection between this transform and ones employed in many recent CG approaches (e.g. (de Groote 2001a; Barker 2002; Shan 2002, 2004; Moortgat 2007; Bernardi and Moortgat 2007)) based on CPS transforms (Plotkin 1975; Felleisen 1988; Danvy and Filinski 1990; Parigot 1992, 2000; Curien and Herbelin 2000).

A number of issues remain to be addressed. For one thing, the relationship between covert and overt movement needs to be clarified. Some preliminary steps in this direction are taken in (Pollard 2008b, 2008d). In essence, the approach taken there is to reconstruct the analysis of overt movement in Gazdar (1981) , using (abstract) syntactic operators paired with operator meanings of the the same general character as those that occur in the co-context. Such syntactic operators bind a syntactic variable ('trace of overt movement') in a sentence in much the same way that a quantifier retrieved from the co-store binds a semantic variable in a proposition, except that rather then being retrieved, it is just an ordinary logical premiss.

Second, it remains unclear how ultimately to make sense of the co-store, and the storage and retrieval mechanisms, in logical (or categorical) terms. In this connection, de Groote et al. (2009) show that the analysis of covert movement set forth above can be assimilated to the CVG analysis of overt movement just mentioned, provided we analyze an *in situ* operator as an ordinary premiss with an operator type, which, when applied to its 'gappy' sentential argument, in effect lowers itself into the trace position via β-reduction.[25] In other words, a CVG with co-store can be algorithmically converted into an ordinary multimodal categorial grammar without co-store, with CVG derivations being globally transformed into ordinary proofs that make no use of storage or retrieval.

This state of affairs is vaguely analogous to CPS transforms that map programs with control operators into pure functional programs. But what is missing is a convincing logical or categorical characterization of the CVG-to-CG transform. In the absence of such a characterization, perhaps the best face we can put onto the the storage-and-retrieval machinery is that it provides a kind of syntactic sugar for linguists with a taste for surface-oriented syntax. To put a more positive spin on it, the de Groote et al. transform can be taken as establishing that Cooper-style storage-and-retrieval machinery actually has a precise meaning (which is given by the transform).

A third, and potentially more serious challenge for the framework presented above is the existence of the linguistic phenomenon of *parasitic scope* discussed by Barker (2007) . This has to do with seemingly quantificational expressions whose scope, as Barker puts it, 'depends on the scope of some other scope-taking element in the sentence'. For example, in the following sentences

(55)

    a. Anna and Bill read the same book.

    b. John hit and killed the same man.

the interpretations of the NPs introduced by *the same* depend on the interpretations of the coordinate expressions *Anna and Bill* and *hit and killed*. Barker argues persuasively that such phenomena resist coherent analysis under familiar approaches to quantifer scope, and offers a type-logical analysis that makes

---

[25] This analysis is broadly similar to Oehrle's (1994) simulation of Montagovian 'quantifying in', except that on Oehrle's approach, the β-reduction that effects the 'lowering' is in the concrete (rather than the abstract) syntax.

use of both continuations and choice functions. Ongoing investigation of parasitic scope (broadly construed to include similar phenomena such as remnant comparatives and internal readings of superlatives) suggest that, although neither continuations nor choice functions are required for the analysis of parasitic scope, a convincing characterization of such constructions in terms of storage-and-retrieval is simply not available.[26] If so, then it may well be that, after 35 years of yeoman service, storage-and-retrieval technology is overdue for retirement.

References

1. Anoun, H., Lecomte, A.: Linear grammars with labels. In: Satta, G., Monachesi, P., Penn, G., Wintner, S. (eds.) Proceedings of Formal Grammar 2006. CSLI, Stanford (2007)
2. Aoun, J., Li, A.: Wh-elements in situ: syntax or lf? Linguistic Inquiry 24(2), 199–238 (1993)
3. Bach, E., Partee, B.: Anaphora and semantic structure. In: Krieman, J., Ojeda, A. (eds.) Proceedings the Chicago Linguistic Society, Papers from the Parasession on Pronouns and Anaphora, pp. 1–28 (1980)
4. Baker, C.: Note on the description of english questions: the role of an abstract question morpheme. Foundations of Language 6, 197–219 (1970)
5. Barker, C.: Continuations and the nature of quantification. Natural Language Semantics 10 (2002)
6. Barker, C.: Parasitic scope. Linguistics and Philosophy 30(4), 407–444 (2007)
7. Benton, N., Bierman, G., de Paiva, V., Hyland, M.: Term assignment for intuitionistic linear logic. Technical Report 262, University of Cambridge (August 1992)
8. Bernardi, R., Moortgat, M.: Continuation semantics for symmetric categorial grammar. In: Leivant, D., de Queiroz, R. (eds.) WoLLIC 2007. LNCS, vol. 4576, pp. 53–71. Springer, Heidelberg (2007)
9. Buszkowski, W.: The logic of types. In: Srzednicki, J. (ed.) Initiatives in Logic, pp. 180–206. M. Nijhoff, Dordrecht (1987)
10. Carpenter, B.: Type-Logical Semantics. The MIT Press, Cambridge (1997)
11. Chomsky, N.: Conditions on rules of grammar. Linguistic Analysis 2, 303–351 (1976)
12. Chomsky, N.: On wh-movement. In: Culicover, P., Wasow, T., Akmajian, A. (eds.) Formal Syntax, pp. 71–132. Academic Press, New York (1977)
13. Chomsky, N.: The Minimalist Program. MIT Press, Cambridge (1995)
14. Chomsky, N.: Lectures on government and binding. Foris, Dordrecht (1981)
15. Cooper, R.: Montague's Semantic Theory and Transformational Syntax. PhD thesis, University of Massachusetts at Amherst (1975)
16. Cooper, R.: Quantification and Syntactic Theory. Reidel, Dordrecht (1983)
17. Copestake, A., Flickinger, D., Sag, I., Pollard, C.: Minimal recursion semantics: An introduction. Journal of Research on Language and Computation 3, 281–332 (2005)
18. Culicover, P.W., Jackendoff, R.: Simpler Syntax. Oxford University Press, Oxford (2005)

---

[26] Unless one is willing to countenance new rule schemas which allow elements within co-stores to interact with other (rather than merely being stored and retrieved).

19. Curien, P.L., Herbelin, H.: The duality of computation. In: ICFP 2000, pp. 233–243 (2000)
20. Curry, H., Feys, R.: Combinatory Logic, vol. 1. North-Holland, Amsterdam (1958)
21. Gallin, D.: Intensional and Higher Order Modal Logic. North-Holland, Amsterdam (1975)
22. Danvy, O., Filinski, A.: Abstracting control. In: 1990 ACM Conference on Lisp and Functional Programming, pp. 151–160. ACM Press, New York (1990)
23. de Groote, P.: Type raising, continuations, and classical logic. In: van Rooy, R., Stokhof, M. (eds.) Proceedings of the Thirteenth Amsterdam Colloquium, Amsterdam, Institute for Logic, Language, and Computation, Universiteit van Amsterdam, pp. 97–101 (2001)
24. de Groote, P.: Towards abstract categorial grammars. In: Proceedings of ACL, pp. 148–155 (2001)
25. de Groote, P., Pogodalla, S., Pollard, C.: About parallel and syntactocentric formalisms: what the encoding of convergent grammer into abstract categorial grammer tells us. Fundamenta Informaticae (2009) (submitted)
26. Felleisen, M.: The theory and practice of first-class prompts. In: POPL 1988, pp. 180–190. ACM Press, New York (1988)
27. Gabbay, D., de Queiroz, R.: Extending the curry-howard interpretation to linear, relevant, and other resource logics. Journal of Symbolic Logic 57(4), 1319–1365 (1992)
28. Gazdar, G.: Unbounded dependencies and coordinate structure. Linguistic Inquiry 12, 155–184 (1981)
29. Groenendijk, J., Stokhof, M.: Studies on the Semantics of Questions and the Pragmatics of Answers. PhD thesis, University of Amsterdam (1984)
30. Hendriks, H.: Studied Flexibility: Categories and Types in Syntax and Semantics. PhD thesis, Universiteit van Amsterdam (1993)
31. Howard, W.A.: The formulæ-as-types notion of construction. In: Hindley, J., Seldin, J. (eds.) To H. B. Curry: Essays on Combinatory Logic, Lambda Calculus and Formalism., Academic Press, New York (1980)
32. Huang, C.T.J.: Logical Relations in Chinese and the Theory of Grammar. PhD thesis, MIT (1992)
33. Jacobson, P.: Towards a variable-free semantics. Linguistics and Philosophy (1999)
34. Jay, B.: Languages for monoidal categories. Journal of Pure and Applied Algebra 59, 61–85 (1989)
35. Karttunen, L.: Syntax and semantics of questions. Linguistics and Philosophy 1, 3–44 (1977)
36. Lambek, J.: Categorial and categorical grammars. In: Oehrle, R., Bach, E., Wheeler, D. (eds.) Categorial Grammars and Natural Language Structures, pp. 297–317. Reidel, Dordrecht (1988)
37. Lambek, J.: The mathematics of sentence structure. American Mathematical Monthly 65(3), 154–170 (1958)
38. Lecomte, A., Retoré, C.: Bi-grammars: a logical system for syntax, semantics, and their correspondence. Presented at Formal Grammar 2002, Trento (2002) (unpublished)
39. Lecomte, A.: Categorial grammar for minimalism. In: Casdio, C., Scott, P., Seely, R. (eds.) Language and Grammar: Studies in Mathematical Linguistics and Natural Language, pp. 163–188. CSLI, Stanford (2005)
40. Leivant, D., de Queiroz, R. (eds.): WoLLIC 2007. LNCS, vol. 4576. Springer, Heidelberg (2007)

41. Mackie, I., Román, L., Abramsky, S.: An internal language for autonomous categories. In: Proceedings of the First Imperial College Department of Computing Workshop on Theory and Formal Methods, pp. 235–246. Springer, London (1993)
42. May, R.C.: Logical Form: Its Structure and Derivation. MIT Press, Cambridge (1985)
43. May, R.C.: The Grammar of Quantification. PhD thesis, Massachusetts Institute of Technology. Dept. of Linguistics and Philosophy (1977)
44. Mints, G.: Closed categories and the theory of proofs. Journal of Soviet Mathematics 15(1), 45–62 (1981); Translated From Zapiski Nauchnykh Seminarov Leningradskogo Otdeleniya Matematicheskogo Insititutaim. V.A. Steklova AN SSSR, vol. 68, pp. 83–114 (1977)
45. Mitchell, J., Scott, P.: Typed lambda models and cartesian closed categories. Contemporary Mathematics 92, 301–316 (1989)
46. Montague, R.: The proper treatment of quantification in ordinary english. In: Thomason, R. (ed.) Formal Philosophy: Selected Papers of Richard Montague, pp. 247–270. Yale University Press, New Haven (1974); Originally published in Hintikka, J., Moravcsik, J., Suppes, P. (eds.) Approaches to Natural Language: Proceedings of the 1970 Stanford Workshop on Grammar and Semantics. Reidel, Dordrecht
47. Moortgat, M.: Symmetries in natural language syntax and semantics. In: Leivant, D., de Queiroz, R. (eds.) WoLLIC 2007. LNCS, vol. 4576, pp. 53–71. Springer, Heidelberg (2007)
48. Moortgat, M.: Categorial Investigations: Logical and Linguistic Aspects of the Lambek Calculus. Mouton de Gruyter/Foris Publications, Berlin (1991)
49. Moortgat, M.: Generalized quantifiers and discontinuous type constructors. In: Bunt, H., van Horck, A. (eds.) Discontinuous Constituency, pp. 181–207. De Gruyter, Berlin (1996)
50. Moortgat, M.: Categorial type logics. In: van Benthem, J., ter Meulen, A. (eds.) Handbook of Logic and Language, pp. 93–177. Elsevier Science Publishers, Amsterdam (1996)
51. Morrill, G.V.: Type Logical Grammar Categorial Logic of Signs. Kluwer Academic Publishers, Dordrecht (1994)
52. Muskens, R.: Lambdas, Language, and Logic. In: Kruijff, G.J., Oehrle, R. (eds.) Resource Sensitivity in Binding and Anaphora. Studies in Linguistics and Philosophy, pp. 23–54. Kluwer, Dordrecht (2003)
53. Oehrle, R.T.: Term-labeled categorial type systems. Linguistic and Philosophy 17(6), 633–678 (1994)
54. Parigot, M.: On the computational interpretation of negation. In: Clote, P.G., Schwichtenberg, H. (eds.) CSL 2000. LNCS, vol. 1862, pp. 472–484. Springer, Heidelberg (2000)
55. Parigot, M.: $\lambda\mu$-calculus: an algorithmic interpretation of classical natural deduction. In: Voronkov, A. (ed.) LPAR 1992. LNCS, vol. 624. Springer, Heidelberg (1992)
56. Pesetsky, D.: Wh-in-situ: movement and unselective binding. In: Reuland, E., Meulen, A. (eds.) The Representation of (In-) Definiteness, pp. 98–129. MIT Press, Cambridge (1987)
57. Plotkin, G.: Call-by-name, call-by-value, and the λ-calculus. Theoretical Computer Science 1(2), 125–159 (1975)
58. Pollard, C.: Type-logical hpsg. In: Proceedings of Formal Grammar (2004), http://www.ling.ohio-state.edu/~hana/hog/pollard2004-FG.pdf

59. Pollard, C.: The logics of overt and covert movement in a relational type-theoretic grammar. Presented at the Fourth Workshop on Lambda Calculus and Formal Grammar, LORIA, Nancy (September 2007),
http://www.ling.ohio-state.edu/~hana/hog/pollard2007-lcfg.pdf

60. Pollard, C.: The logic of pied piping. Presented at Colloque en l'honneur d'Alain Lecomte, Pauillac (November 2007),
http://www.ling.ohio-state.edu/~hana/hog/pollard2007-pied.pdf

61. Pollard, C.: The calculus of responsibility and commitment. Unpublished paper accepted for presentation at the Workshop on Ludics, Dialog, and Interaction, Autrans (May 2008)

62. Pollard, C.: A parallel derivational architecture for the syntax-semantics interface. Presented at the ESSLLI 2008 Workshop on What Syntax Feeds Semantics, Hamburg (August 2008),
http://www.ling.ohio-state.edu/~pollard/cvg/para-slides.pdf

63. Pollard, C.: What do interrogative sentences refer to? Unpublished paper, Ohio State University, Universitat Rovira i Virgili, and INRIA-Lorraine. Presented at the Workshop on Reference to Abstract Objects, Universitat Pompeu Fabra, Barcelona (March 2008), http://www.ling.ohio-state.edu/~pollard/cvg/absobj.pdf

64. Pollard, C.: Convergent grammar. In: Slides for ESSLLI 2008, Course, Hamburg (August 2008), http://www.ling.ohio-state.edu/~pollard/cvg/day2.pdf

65. Pollard, C.: Hyperintensions. Journal of Logic and Computation 18(2), 257–282 (2008)

66. Pollard, C.: Hyperintensional questions. In: Hodges, W., de Queiroz, R. (eds.) WoLLIC 2008. LNCS (LNAI), vol. 5110, pp. 261–274. Springer, Heidelberg (2008),
http://www.ling.ohio-state.edu/~pollard/cvg/wollic08.pdf

67. Pollard, C., Sag, I.A.: Head-Driven Phrase Structure Grammar. CSLI Publications, Stanford (1994); Distributed by University of Chicago Press

68. Ranta, A.: Grammatical Framework: A type-theoretical grammar formalism. Journal of Functional Programming 14(2), 145–189 (2004)

69. Shan, C.: A continuation semantics of interrogatives that accounts for baker's ambiguity. In: Jackson, B. (ed.) Proceedings of Semantics and Linguistic Theory 12, pp. 246–265. Cornell University Press, Ithaca (2002)

70. Shan, C.: Delimited continuations in natural language: quantification and polar sensitivity. In: Continuation Workshop 2004, Venice (2004)

71. Steedman, M.: Surface Structure and Interpretation. MIT Press, Cambridge (1996)

72. van Benthem, J.: The semantics of variety in categorial grammar. Technical Report 83-29, Department of Mathematics, Simon Fraser University, Vancouver (1983); Reprinted in Buszkowski, W., van Benthem, J., Marciszewski, W. (eds.) Categorial Grammar, pp. 37–55. John Benjamins, Amsterdam

73. Wansing, H.: 'formulas-as-types' for a hierarchy of sublogics of intuitionistic proposiitonal logic. In: Pearce, D.J., Wansing, H. (eds.) All-Berlin 1990. LNCS (LNAI), vol. 619, pp. 125–145. Springer, Heidelberg (1992)

Categorial Grammars and Minimalist Grammars

Richard Moot*

LaBRI CNRS, INRIA Bordeaux SW & Bordeaux University
Domaine Universitaire
351, Cours de la Libération
33405 Talence Cedex
France
Richard.Moot@labri.fr

Abstract. This paper explores some of the connections between minimalist grammars and categorial grammars in the tradition of the Lambek calculus and its various extensions. It provides a new graphical perspective on the lexical items of both minimalist and categorial grammars and uses this perspective to suggest a reconciliation between two different ways of embedding minimalist grammars into categorial grammars, while keeping the good properties of both.

1 Introduction

Since their introduction, it was clear that the minimalist program [1] used ideas close to resource-sensitive grammar formalisms such as (extensions of) the Lambek calculus [2]. This is especially clear in Stabler's formalization of the minimalist program [3]. The links between categorial and minimalist grammars have been widely investigated [4, 5, 6, 7, 8], with the goal to 'rebuild the minimalist program on a logical ground' [6].

Minimalist grammars are a lexicalized formalism with two operations: a tree building operation *merge* and a tree reconfiguration operation *move*. While there is little divergence between different authors on how to model the *merge* operation, there are (at least) two different ways of modeling *move*, exemplified by [4] and [8].

The goal of this paper is twofold. Firstly, I will introduce a graph-based presentation of proofs for (extensions of) the non-associative Lambek calculus NL. These *proof nets* — besides being useful as a computational device [9,10] — also make the correspondence between minimalist and categorial grammars visually clear. Secondly, proof nets will provide a simple path to a unified treatment of the *move* operation. As a surprising set of supporting data for this unified treatment, I will show how this unified approach is in fact very close to the one used for large-coverage categorial grammars.

2 Merge and AB Grammars

This section introduces the basics: AB grammars, minimalist grammars and the *substitution* and *merge* operations in addition to several useful theoretical notions.

---

* This research has been supported by the ANR Project 'Prélude'.

S. Pogodalla, M. Quatrini, and C. Retoré (Eds.): Lecomte Festschrift, LNAI 6700, pp. 41–60, 2011.

2.1   AB Grammars

AB grammars, named after the pioneering work of Ajdukiewicz and Bar-Hillel [11, 12], can be seen as a restriction on the formulas of the Lambek calculus in the sense made clear by the following definition.

Definition 1. *Given a set of atomic formulas $\mathcal{A}$ the* formulas *of AB grammars are defined as follows.*

$$\mathcal{N} ::= \mathcal{A} \mid \mathcal{N} / \mathcal{P} \mid \mathcal{P} \backslash \mathcal{N}$$
$$\mathcal{P} ::= \mathcal{A} \mid \mathcal{P} \bullet \mathcal{P}$$

The definition distinguishes between *negative* formulas $\mathcal{N}$ and *positive* formulas $\mathcal{P}$. The left and right implication '$\backslash$' and '$/$' can only be used on negative (sub)formulas whereas the conjunction or product '$\bullet$' can only be used on positive (sub)formulas.

Definition 2. *For the set of negative formulas $\mathcal{N}$ the set of* antecedent trees $\mathcal{T}$ *is defined as follows.*

$$\mathcal{T} ::= \mathcal{N} \mid (\mathcal{T}, \mathcal{T})$$

That is to say, an antecedent tree is a (non-empty) binary branching tree with negative formulas as its leaves.

Definition 3. *A* sequent *is a pair $\langle \mathcal{T}, \mathcal{P} \rangle$ — written $\mathcal{T} \vdash \mathcal{P}$ — where $\mathcal{T}$ is an antecedent tree and $\mathcal{P}$ is a positive formula.*

Table 1 lists the rules for AB: the axiom rule $[Ax]$ states that the antecedent tree containing just a single formula A as its leaf is a tree of type A. The rule $[\bullet I]$ allows us to combine two arbitrary trees of type A and B into a tree of type $A \bullet B$.

The rule $[\backslash E]$ states that whenever we have shown an antecedent tree Δ to be of type $A \backslash B$ and an antecedent tree Γ to be of type A then we can construct a complex tree (Γ, Δ) of type B. In other words an antecedent tree of type $A \backslash B$ combines with an antecedent tree of type A to its left to form an antecedent treeof type B. Symmetrically, the rule $[/E]$ allows an antecedent tree of type B / A to combine with and antecedent tree of type A to its right to form an antecedent tree of type B.

Table 1. Natural deduction rules for AB grammars

$$\frac{\quad}{A \vdash A} \, [Ax] \qquad \frac{\Delta \vdash A \quad \Gamma \vdash B}{(\Delta, \Gamma) \vdash A \bullet B} \, [\bullet I]$$

$$\frac{\Gamma \vdash A \quad \Delta \vdash A \backslash B}{(\Gamma, \Delta) \vdash B} \, [\backslash E] \qquad \frac{\Delta \vdash B / A \quad \Gamma \vdash A}{(\Delta, \Gamma) \vdash B} \, [/E]$$

2.2 Trees and Substitution

The rules for the connectives are perhaps best seen as tree construction rules. Figure 1 shows the rules for the connectives of Table 1 in tree form.

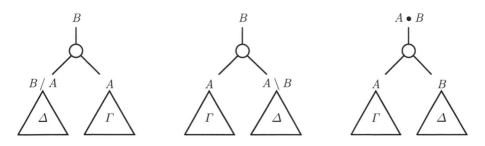

Fig. 1. The rules of AB as tree construction rules

Given a list of formulas, we can determine by looking at just the form of the formulas which rules we need to apply in order to form a correct derivation. This is especially clear in the tree form: we recursively decompose each of the formulas until we reach the atoms.

Figure 2 shows this pre-compilation of the rules for the sequence of formulas.

$$d, (d \setminus v) / d, d / n, n$$

An example of lexical assignments which would correspond to this sequence is shown inside of the square boxes. All trees have a negative atomic formula as their root and all leaves are positive atomic formulas — with the exception of the lexical formula which is negative and can be complex.

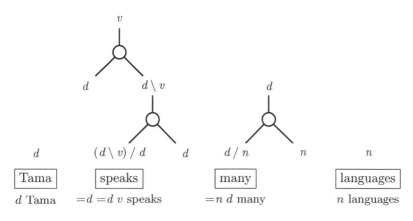

Fig. 2. Lexical Unfolding

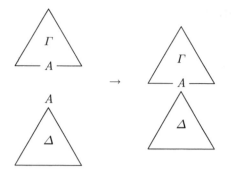

Fig. 3. Axiom/Cut as Substitution

In order to use these trees as a system for deriving sentences, we only need to add a single rule: the substitution rule — shown in Fig. 3 — which allows us to substitute a tree Δ with root A for a leaf A in a tree Γ. In other words, it identifies a positive and a negative occurrence of the same atomic formula.

This is exactly the substitution rule from tree adjoining grammars [13] and from the view of natural deduction, it corresponds to the possibility of substituting a proof $\Delta \vdash A$ for a proof of $\Gamma[A] \vdash C$ with axiom $A \vdash A$ to obtain a proof of $\Gamma[\Delta] \vdash C$.

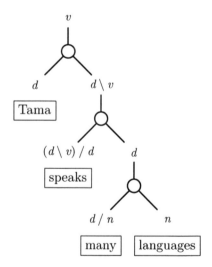

Fig. 4. Result after two d substitutions and one n substitution

Figure 4 shows how one application of the substitution rule for the n atomic formula and two applications of the substitution rule for the np formula produce a tree of type s with 'Tama speaks many languages' as its yield.

2.3   Merge

In Stabler's formalization of Chomsky's minimalist grammars [1, 3], grammars have a set of features: syntactic features, which play an active role in the derivations of the formalism and non-syntactic features, which are the phonetic symbols (and semantic symbols, but in the current paper these will not be treated at the same level as the phonetic features) in the lexicon — the words and morphemes of the language.

Given a set of base syntactic categories $\mathcal{B}$, typically containing categories like n for nouns, d for determiner phrases, v for verb phrases and c for complementizers, the *selectors* for these base categories, written $=A$ for a base category A, select a base category of type A to form a complex tree.

The lexicon assigns lists of features to words and morphemes — possibly including the empty string. The grammatical functions *merge* and *move* construct and rearrange trees by eliminating matched pairs of features from the first positions of their respective lists. Throughout this paper, I will use A to denote the first feature on the feature list — the *head* or *car*, depending on your favorite progamming language — the and Bs to denote the rest of the features — the *tail* or *crd*. In addition, I will often differentiate among the different possibilities for A, using $= A$ for the first element of a feature list which has the additional requirement that it has a selector feature.

The function *merge* allows a lexical list of features with first feature $=A$ to combine with a tree with principal feature A. We distinguish two cases: in case $=A$ is a lexical feature, it combines with a (possibly complex) tree Γ of category A to its right. In case $=A$ is derived, it combines with tree Γ of category A to its left. Figure 5 shows the two cases in tree form[1]. The similarity with Fig. 1 should be clear, but let's remark the differences explicitly. First of all, there is no equivalent of the $[\bullet I]$ rule in minimalist grammars. More importantly, merge imposes a clear order on the selection of the arguments: the first argument needs to selected to the right whereas any additional arguments need to be selected to the left.

As a consequence, minimalist grammars which use merge only are — from the point of view of AB grammars — a restriction on the allowed formulas. The lexical categories of Fig. 2 satisfy the required restrictions, as shown by the corresponding lists of minimalist features beneath each lexical tree.

Minimalist grammars allow the same type of lexical unfolding as we used to AB grammars. Figure 6 shows this explicitly: the unfolding of the list of features for 'speaks' produces the tree on the left, whereas the unfolding of the corresponding AB formula produces the tree on the right. Discounting the labels on the internal nodes and the lexical leaves, the two trees are identical.

Since the substitution rule operates only on the positive atomic leaves and the negative roots of the trees, we can simplify our tree representations by

---

[1] I will not consider Stabler's head movement categories here. In addition, I will follow [8] in not distinguishing between left-headed and right-headed structures, though it is easy to add this information in case of need [14, 7, show how this can be done in the general and in the minimalist case].

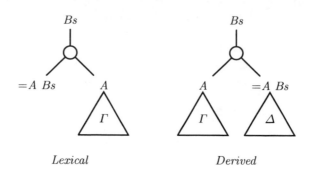

Lexical   *Derived*

Fig. 5. The minimalist merge operation

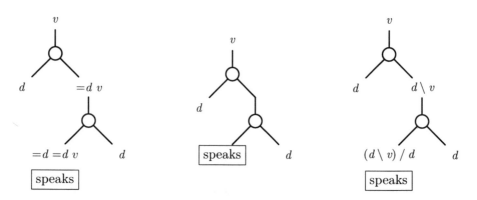

Fig. 6. A transitive verb in MG and in AB grammars, with a simplified representation for both in the middle

erasing all complex formulas and non-singleton feature lists, obtaining a simplified representation which is functionally equivalent to the fully annotated trees and from which we can — when needed — extract all information which has been erased.

3   Move and Extensions of Lambek Grammars

The correspondence between merge and AB grammars of the previous section is very simple and direct. In order to model the minimalist move operation as well, we will need some more machinery. First, I will follow Lambek [2, 15] by adding the 'missing' rules for the connectives to AB. That is to say, we add the logical rules for negative occurrences of the conjunction and for positive occurrences of the implications.

Secondly, since *move* rearranges a tree by moving a marked subtree to the front, essentially changing the word order of the tree yield, I will follow [16, 17] by adding modally controlled versions of the associativity and commutativity rules to the calculus.

3.1   The Non-associative Lambek Calculus

Lambek's seminal paper [2] extends the rules of AB (Table 1) by adding the introduction rules for the implications — which show how to use positive B / A and $A \backslash B$ formulas — and the elimination rule for the product — which shows how to use negative $A \bullet B$ formulas — to the calculus. In addition to giving numerous linguistic uses of the calculus, Lambek proves basic results like cut elimination and decidability.

The non-associative Lambek Calculus NL [15] is a restriction of the associative Lambek Calculus L. It requires all antecedents to be trees of formulas, where antecedents for L were simply lists of formulas.

Table 2. Natural deduction rules for NL grammars

$$\frac{}{A \vdash A} \, [Ax]$$

$$\frac{\Delta \vdash A \bullet B \quad \Gamma[(A, B)] \vdash C}{\Gamma[\Delta] \vdash C} \, [\bullet E] \qquad \frac{\Delta \vdash A \quad \Gamma \vdash B}{(\Delta, \Gamma) \vdash A \bullet B} \, [\bullet I]$$

$$\frac{\Gamma \vdash A \quad \Delta \vdash A \backslash B}{(\Gamma, \Delta) \vdash B} \, [\backslash E] \qquad \frac{(A, \Gamma) \vdash B}{\Gamma \vdash A \backslash B} \, [\backslash I]$$

$$\frac{\Delta \vdash B / A \quad \Gamma \vdash A}{(\Delta, \Gamma) \vdash B} \, [/ E] \qquad \frac{(\Gamma, A) \vdash B}{\Gamma \vdash B / A} \, [/ I]$$

Definition 2 in Sect. 2.1 already uses trees of formulas as antecedents, so our basic sequents are suitable objects for NL. Table 2 shows the natural deduction rules for NL.

The $[\bullet E]$ rule is the most complicated of the new rules. Figure 7 shows the rule in a graphical representation. On the left hand side of the figure, we have the two premises of the rule, a structure Δ with a negative root formula $A \bullet B$ and a structure Γ with a negative root formula of type C. This structure Γ has the additional property that it has a subtree occurrence (A, B) — that is to say a binary branch with positive leaves A and B, in that order — which is displayed explicitly. For the conclusion of the rule, shown on the right hand side, the subtree (A, B) has been replaced by Δ.

The structure in the middle of Fig. 7 shows an intermediate structure we will use for computational purposes. It splits up the conversion of the structure on the left into the structure on the right into two steps. The first step, indicated by the first arrow, 'unfolds' the $A \bullet B$ formula into its A and B sub-formulas, while keeping track of the position of the main formula by means of an arrow. The new constructor, which is portrayed with a filled center and which we will call an *auxiliary* constructor, connects the two structures shown on the left hand side,

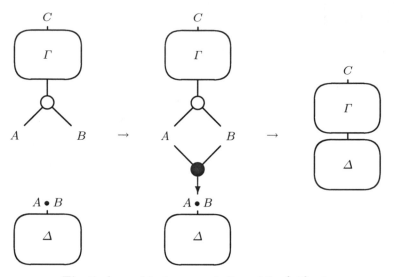

Fig. 7. A graphical representation of the [•E] rule

but in such a way that the result is no longer a tree.[2] The use of ovals instead of triangles instead of triangles in the figure is to remind us of the fact that the structures Γ and Δ are no longer necessarily trees. The second step contracts an auxiliary and a tree constructor which are connected at both ports which do not have the arrow, eliminating the two constructors and the intermediate A and B nodes while keeping Γ and Δ connected. The intuition behind the auxiliary constructor and the corresponding contraction should be clear: it verifies that A and B occur as sister leaves of a tree constructor then erases both of them.

Figure 8 shows the [/I] rule in graphical form — the [\I] rule is left-right symmetric. Here, the premiss of the rule is a graph (Γ, A) of type B, as shown on the left of the figure. The conclusion of the rule is the graph Γ of type B / A. Again, we divide the calculation into two steps: the first step consists of decomposing the goal formula B / A into its B and A subformulas and connecting these subformulas to the B root and A leaf of the graph on the left to produce the structure in the middle of the figure. Then, as before we contract the two links which are shown in the middle of the figure to arrive at the final structure on the right hand side. The intuition behind the [/I] contraction is then: verify that a formula A occurs as the right daughter of a B tree, then delete both to obtain an B / A graph.

Remark that this contraction is similar to the contraction shown in Fig. 7: in both cases an auxiliary and a tree constructor are connected at the two points of the auxiliary constructor which do not have the arrow pointing towards them, the two constructors and shared vertices are erased and the graph is reconnected.

---

[2] In fact, the graphs we obtain are still quite close to trees: they are *term graphs*, a data structure used, for example, to share common sub-terms in arithmetic expressions. In this case $A \bullet B$ is shared by two paths from C.

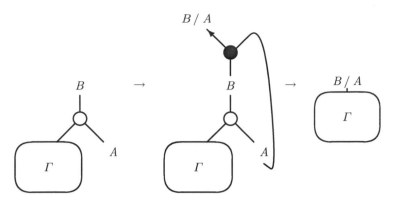

Fig. 8. A graphical representation of the [/I] rule

Similar to the way we have seen in Sect. 2.2, we can recursively unfold a lexical formula until we reach its atoms. This time, there will be a possibility for each pair of main connective and polarity, though it requires us to slightly generalize our structures. In addition to the constructor with an empty circle in the center there are now three auxiliary constructors with a filled circle. Each of these auxiliary constructors has a single arrow which points to the main formula of the link, whereas the two active formulas are not explicitly marked.

As shown in Fig. 9 there is an auxiliary constructor for each of the connectives and the rules for the connectives of positive polarity on the top row are the up-down symmetric duals of the connectives of negative polarity on the bottom row, with one of the pair being a tree constructor and the other an auxiliary constructor.

In each of the six figures the oval Γ corresponds to the graph which has been constructed so far, with the main formula either on top of it (for the negative occurrences) or at its bottom (for the positive occurrences). For reference, the inductive definition of formulas (which adds the missing cases to those of Definition 1 is shown above the unfolding rule for the positive cases and below it for the negative cases.

Remark that after an unfolding step, the positive subformulas are always drawn below the constructor while the negative sub-formula are drawn above it. The substitution or axiom/cut rule connects positive and negative atomic formulas as before. The only difference is that — unlike what is suggested by Fig. 3 — the two connected structures need not be disjoint.

A graph is *correct* if we can contract all auxiliary constructors to form a tree. Valid structures correspond exactly to natural deduction proofs [9].

As an example, Fig. 10 shows the sentence 'Someone speaks Yoruba' unfolded on the left hand side of the picture. To save space, the simple d tree 'Yoruba' has already been substituted for the object determiner phrase of 'speaks'. As before, the information on the internal nodes is superfluous and can be deduced from the combination of the graph structure and the formulas at the external nodes.

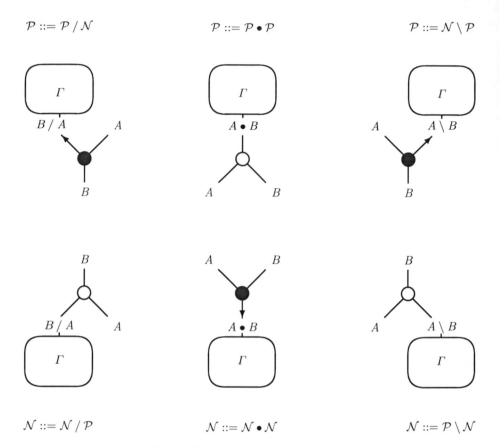

$$\mathcal{P} ::= \mathcal{P} / \mathcal{N} \qquad\qquad \mathcal{P} ::= \mathcal{P} \bullet \mathcal{P} \qquad\qquad \mathcal{P} ::= \mathcal{N} \setminus \mathcal{P}$$

$$\mathcal{N} ::= \mathcal{N} / \mathcal{P} \qquad\qquad \mathcal{N} ::= \mathcal{N} \bullet \mathcal{N} \qquad\qquad \mathcal{N} ::= \mathcal{P} \setminus \mathcal{N}$$

Fig. 9. Formula decomposition rules

Note that since 'someone' has a complex positive subformula $d \setminus v$, its unfolding uses the unfolding for $\mathcal{P} ::= \mathcal{N} \setminus \mathcal{P}$ shown on the top right of Fig. 9. Intuitively, someone searches for a verb phrase $d \setminus v$ to its right to give a v and we will verify this by means of substitutions and contractions.

Performing the d and v substitutions gives the graph shown on the right. The d and v node in the graph are connected respectively to the left and to the top node of a tree constructor, which means we are in the proper configuration to perform a $[\setminus I]$ contraction. Performing this contraction erases the part of the graph shown in the gray box, while identifying the two $d \setminus v$ nodes. After the contraction, the remaining part of the graph is a tree, showing the initial structure to be valid.

3.2 Extensions of NL

Before returning to minimalist grammars, I will quickly discuss the ways to extend NL to allow the controlled use of structural rules. The first of these is the use of unary control operators [16]. Unlike the exponentials of linear logic [18],

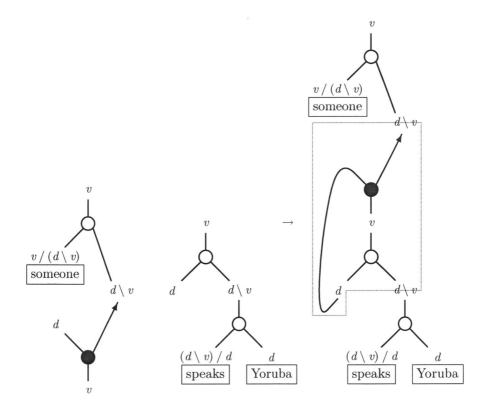

Fig. 10. Lexical Unfolding and Axioms

these unary connectives are a simple generalization of the binary ones. They have their own constructors and contractions which are shown in Fig. 11.

The similarity with the contractions for the binary connectives becomes clear once we see that the right hand side of Fig. 11 — showing the $[\Diamond E]$ contraction — is just the contraction for $[\bullet E]$ shown in Fig. 7, but with the A formula and its link to the two connectors removed. The $[\Box I]$ contraction on the left is just the $[/I]$ contraction shown in Fig. 8, again with the A formula and links to it removed.

The principles illustrated in Fig. 11, and which we will use in what follows, are the following:

$$\Diamond \Box A \vdash A \qquad A \vdash \Box \Diamond A$$

It states that — in a negative context, such as shown in Fig. 11 on the left — we can contract a $\Diamond \Box A$ structure into an A structure. In other words, it is a sort of subtype of A with some special properties.

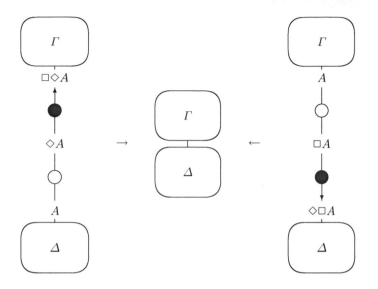

Fig. 11. Constructors and Contractions for Unary Connectives

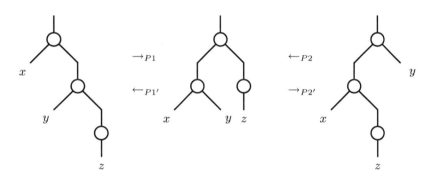

Fig. 12. Structural Rules: Right Branch

The special property we are interested in here is the access to structural rules which are not globally available. This make a formula $\Diamond\Box A$ a formula which can permute throughout the tree and then convert to a normal A formula.[3]

In the graph representation of proofs we have been working with, structural rules correspond to a rewrite of one tree into another. Tree rewriting allows us to restructure a graph in such a way that a contraction becomes possible. A graph

---

[3] Compare this a formula $!A$ in linear logic, which can use the structural rules of contraction and weakening, then convert to a normal A formula using the dereliction rule $!A \vdash A$.

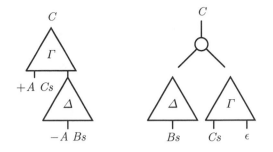

Fig. 13. The minimalist move operation

is *correct* if it converts to a tree using a combination of the structural rules and the contractions [9].

The set of structural rules we use for this purpose is shown in Fig. 12. This figure shows the possibilities for combining a unary connective with a pair of binary connectives, while keeping the unary connective with its daughter z as one of the branches of one of the binary constructors.

The arrows pointing inwards to the center structure, move z up towards the root. Depending on whether we are in a configuration as shown on the left or in a configuration as shown on the right only one of rules [P1] and [P2] applies. The arrows pointing outwards, offer a non-deterministic choice between moving down towards subtree x or towards subtree y.

3.3   Move

With the required machinery in place, it is time to return to minimalist grammars. Besides the *merge* operation, minimalist grammars define a *move* operation. In order to model this move operation, Stabler introduced *licensor* features $+X$ and *licensee* features $-X$. Licensor features 'attract' subtrees with a licensee feature and move them to the licensors specifier position.

Figure 13 shows a graphical representation of the minimalist move operation. In the figure, Δ is the largest tree of which $-X$ is the head.

We have seen in Sect. 2.3 that a minimalist grammar with only the merge rule naturally generates sentences in SVO order. Stabler [3] shows how the move operation can be used to derive SOV order instead.

Suppose 'speaks', which was assigned feature list $=d\ =d\ v\ speaks$ before is now assigned $=d\ +k\ =d\ v\ speaks$ instead. That is to say, it still selects its object to the right, but then 'attracts' the subtree with the case feature k to its left. In case the determiner phrase 'Maori' is assigned the feature list $d-k\ Maori$, we derive 'Maori speaks' as shown in Fig. 14. Remark that combining the structure on the right with a subject determiner phrase will produce the SOV order as required.

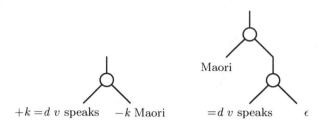

Fig. 14. An example of move to derive SOV word order

3.4 Different Categorial Perspectives on Move

There are two basic approaches to implementing the *move* operation into categorial grammars: the approach of Vermaat [4], who analyses *move* using the introduction rules for the implications and the approach of Lecomte & Retoré [8], who analyse *move* using the elimination rule for product. Both use a form of commutativity to handle the actual movements.

Vermaat's presents two ways of implementing *move*: the first [4, Section 4.2.2,4.2.3] provides a translation of minimalist feature lists into categorial formulas, but it has the disadvantages that it assigns formulas to the empty string and that it doesn't assign the correct semantics to the assigned structures. The second [4, Section 4.2.4] avoids these two problems but doesn't answer the question if this method is sufficiently general to handle arbitrary minimalist grammars. No general translation for this second implementation is offered and no formal equivalence result between either of the two implementations and minimalist grammars is proved.

Lecomte & Retoré's proposal is close — in spirit if not in the actual details — to Vermaat's first implementation. It provides a general mapping from minimalist feature lists into categorial formulas, but requires formula assignments to the empty string to make the translation work. Because the translation stays close to the definition of minimalist grammars, equivalence is relatively easy to establish [19]. On the other hand, this closeness to minimalist grammars also means it requires some work to compute the correct semantics from a derivation [19, 20].

A slightly simplified version of the translation proposed by Amblard [19, Section 6.2.1] is shown below.[4]

Figure 15 shows on the right how this translation produces formulas and graphs for the lexical entries $=n$ d $-wh$ *which* and $=v$ $+wh$ c. These two lexical entries allow us to treat *wh* extraction, for sentences such as 'which languages does Tama speak?'.

---

[4] It is simplified in the sense that only one licensee feature $-f$ can be present in a lexical entry and that a licensee feature necessarily occurs in a type with at least one selector feature. This suffices for the example later and is just to simplify the presentation.

$$\|{=}f\ Bs\|^{\alpha} = \|Bs\|^{\beta} \,/\, f$$
$$\|f\|^{\alpha} = f$$
$$\|{=}f\ Bs\|^{\beta} = f \setminus \|Bs\|^{\beta}$$
$$\|{+}f\ Bs\|^{\beta} = f \setminus \|Bs\|^{\beta}$$
$$\|f\ {-}g\|^{\beta} = g \bullet \Diamond\Box f$$
$$\|f\|^{\beta} = f$$

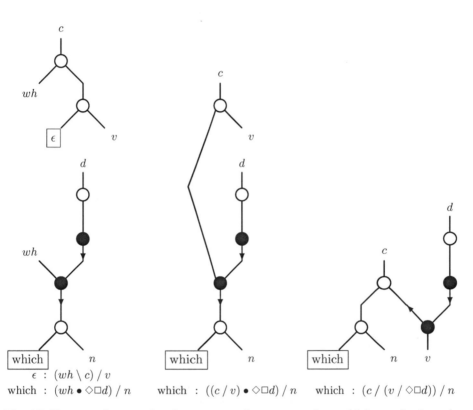

$$\epsilon \ :\ (wh \setminus c) \,/\, v$$
$$which \ :\ (wh \bullet \Diamond\Box d) \,/\, n \qquad which \ :\ ((c \,/\, v) \bullet \Diamond\Box d) \,/\, n \qquad which \ :\ (c \,/\, (v \,/\, \Diamond\Box d)) \,/\, n$$

Fig. 15. From products and assignments to the empty string to higher order formulas

The analysis is divided into two parts. The first part is performed by the lexical entry 'which', shown on the bottom left: it selects an n to its right to become a d which is marked for movement to a wh licensor. The second part, performed by the empty lexical element shown on the top left, closes of a verb domain to produce a clause c while adding a movement trigger to the left of this empty element.

In this case, we can simplify the two lexical graphs a bit. Given that the positive and negative wh elements can only occur together, we can combine the two lexical graphs into a single graph. In addition this allows us to remove the

ϵ element from the graph. The result, with the corresponding formula, is shown in the middle of Fig. 15.

Using a second translation step, we can specialize the sub-formula of the form $(A/\Diamond\Box C) \bullet B$ into $A/(C/\Diamond\Box B)$. The resulting formula and the corresponding graph on the right of the figure correspond quite well to our intuitions of lexical formula assignments for categorial grammars and has the desired *semantic* form as well.

These two operations: elimination of assignments to the empty string by joining the licensor and licensee into a single lexical entry and the formula specialization rule seem to form the 'missing link' between Vermaat's and Lecomte & Retoré's implementation of minimalist grammars. It can be used as a stepping stone both for a proof of equivalence for Vermaat's proposal and for an easy way of obtaining a sort of 'higher order' minimalist grammars as well as the correct semantics for Lecomte & Retoré's proposal.

4   Extracting Grammars from Corpora

In the previous section, we have seen that the different ways of implementing minimalist grammars into categorial grammar are actually quite close. In this section, I will provide some surprising support for this claim in the form of large-coverage categorial grammars which are automatically extracted from corpora.

4.1   The Spoken Dutch Corpus

The Spoken Dutch Corpus (Corpus Gesproken Nederlands, or CGN) is an annotated corpus of around nine million words of contemporary spoken Dutch [21]. A core corpus of slightly over one million words has been assigned syntactic annotations in the forms of directed acyclic graphs, where the vertices are labeled with constituent information and the edges are labeled with dependency relations between these constituents.

Figure 16 shows an example of such an annotated graph. Vertices are drawn as ovals, with the syntactic category inside and edges connect vertices by lines, with the vertex label inside a rectangle. The arrows are not explicitly indicated but are assumed to move down, with the mother nodes portrayed above their respective daughters.

The graph of Fig. 16 is a *wh* question, as indicated by the category WHQ, which has two daughters: a noun phrase (NP) which is the head of the *wh* question (whd) and its body (body), which is a verb-initial sentence (SV1).

The CGN annotation has no assignments to the empty string. Instead, when a Chomskyan analysis would require an empty 'trace' element, the annotation gives a constituent multiple dependencies. In our example, the NP 'welke idioot' is the head of the *wh* question (whd) as well as the subject (su) of the verb-initial sentence. In the graph the NP node has therefore both the WHQ and the SV1 vertices as its parents.

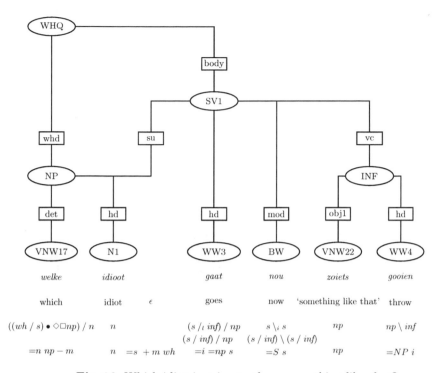

Fig. 16. Which idiot is going to throw something like that?

4.2   Grammar Extraction

Moortgat & Moot [22, 23] propose a parametric algorithm for extracting categorial lexicons from these annotation graphs. I will only briefly sketch the way this algorithm transforms the annotation graphs into a categorial lexicon, using the preceding graph as an example.

The SV1 node has four daughters: a subject (su), which is the extracted noun phrase, a head (hd), which is the main verb of the sentence, a sentence modifier (mod), which is the adverb 'nou' and finally a verbal complement (vc) which is an infinitival group (INF).

The categorial formulas corresponding to the vertex label are a parameter to the algorithm. Here we assume SV1 is translated into s, NP is translated into np and INF is translated into inf. Other choices are possible: for example, we could use a complex $np \backslash s$ category for the infinitive.

Another parameter of the extraction algorithm is the set of dependency relations which correspond to modifiers. Typically, this includes (mod) but some syntactic categories have additional dependency roles which are, from a categorial point of view, best analyzed as modifiers. As usual in categorial grammars, modifiers are assigned formulas of the form X / X or $X \backslash X$. There is a single modifier daughter, which is assigned the category $s \backslash_i s$, indicating it modifies the sentence but does so using a special 'infixation mode' i. We can avoid using different modes here by assigning the category $(s \, / \, inf) \setminus (s \, / \, inf)$ to 'nou' instead, but this would result in a considerable increase in the number of lexical possibilities for adverbs. There is a trade-off to be made between lexical ambiguity and additional structural rules here which is beyond the scope of the current article.

A final parameter identifies the functor of each constituent by its dependency relation. This is typically the head of the constituent, as in the current case. All daughters of a syntactic category which are neither functor nor modifier, the subject and verbal complement in this case, are arguments. A functor F selects its argument A and marks whether it occurs on its left or on its right by the direction of the implication used: $F \, / \, A$ if the argument occurs to the right and $A \setminus F$ if the argument occurs to the left.

Though the position of the NP in the annotation graph is to the left of the verb, the subject is considered to be directly on its right instead: the canonical position of a subject in a verb initial phrase is directly after the verb eg. 'gaat Piet nou zoiets gooien?'. This is an explicit use of linguistic information in order to obtain structures which are as close as possible to manually assigned categories.

To obtain the category for the verb, we integrate the argument daughters from right to left. Obtaining first $s \, / \, inf$ after the infinitive daughter and then $(s \, / \, inf) \, / \, np$ as the result category for the verb.

All of this produces a (possibly multimodal) AB grammar. However, we haven't dealt with multiple dependencies yet. If a constituent play several roles in a phrase, we need to assign it a formula for each of these roles. The simplest and most general way of encoding this is to use the product of the different categories. However, since typically only one of these roles is a local one we must allow for the additional roles to be played in other constituents. This means the appropriate formula for a constituent which is locally of category A and which is of category B elsewhere would be $A \bullet \Diamond \Box B$, where $\Diamond \Box B$ is a B formula with a permute modality.

This gives the NP constituent the type $(wh \, / \, s) \bullet \Diamond \Box np$. This is a slightly unusual formula for a wh element in a categorial grammar. However, it is exactly the type of formula we saw for the translation of the minimalist grammar in Sect. 3.4 and Fig. 15 and we translate it in the same way to $wh \, / \, (s \, / \, \Diamond \Box np)$.

Continuing the formula assignment to the remaining vertices, we get the lexical results shown in the penultimate line of Fig. 16. The unimodal possibilities for 'gaat' and 'nou', the only types requiring a multimodal annotation in order to reduce the number of lexical entries for the adverb, are shown below the other types.

The closeness of the extracted types in this section to the translated minimalist types of Sect. 3.4 suggests the possibility of extracting a minimalist lexicon using more or less the same strategy. The last line in Fig. 16 shows a minimalist lexicon inspired by the categorial lexicon. In the cases where the first argument is selected to the left, I used a head movement with adjunction solution, indicated by a selector with an upper case feature. Note that — when we abstract from the category names — it is quite similar the minimalist grammars we have seen before, including the assignment of the licensor $=s \, +m \, wh$ to the empty string.

All this suggests that the results from [22, 23] can adapt to the minimalist case and produce a lexicon which would not be far from one assigned by hand. However, verifying the size and quality of a lexicon thus extracted would be an interesting subject requiring a considerable amount of additional research.

5 Conclusion

We have seen how looking at categorial grammars and minimalist grammars in a graph theoretic way makes the correspondence between the two systems quite clear. In addition, it it make the effect of different choices of the translation function visible in a way which has permitted us to move towards an unification of different translation. Finally, grammars extracted from corpora turn out to have a similar shape to translated minimalist grammars, which suggests the possibility to automatically extract minimalist grammars from treebanks.

References

1. Chomsky, N.: The Minimalist Program. MIT Press, Cambridge (1995)
2. Lambek, J.: The mathematics of sentence structure. American Mathematical Monthly 65, 154–170 (1958)
3. Stabler, E.: Derivational minimalism. In: Lecomte, A., Perrier, G., Lamarche, F. (eds.) LACL 1997. LNCS (LNAI), vol. 1582. Springer, Heidelberg (1997)
4. Vermaat, W.: Controlling movement. Minimalism in a deductive perspective. Master's thesis, Utrecht University, Utrecht (1999)
5. Retoré, C., Stabler, E.: Generative grammars in resource logics. Research on Language and Computation 2(1), 3–25 (2004)
6. Lecomte, A.: Rebuilding MP on a logical ground. Research on Language and Computation 2(1), 27–55 (2004); Special Issue on Resource Logics and Minimalist Grammars
7. Vermaat, W.: The minimalist move operation in a deductive perspective. Journal of Language and Computation 2(1), 69–85 (2004); Special Issue on Resource Logics and Minimalist Grammars
8. Lecomte, A., Retoré, C.: Extending Lambek grammars: A logical account of mininalist grammars. In: Proceedings of the 39th Meeting of the Association for Computational Linguistics, Toulouse, France, pp. 354–361 (2001)
9. Moot, R., Puite, Q.: Proof nets for the multimodal Lambek calculus. Studia Logica 71(3), 415–442 (2002)
10. Moot, R.: Filtering axiom links for proof nets. In: Kallmeyer, L., Monachesi, P., Penn, G., Satta, G. (eds.) Proccedings of Formal Grammar 2007 (2007) (to appear with CSLI)
11. Ajdukiewicz, K.: Die syntaktische Konnexität. Studies in Philosophy 1, 1–27 (1935)
12. Bar-Hillel, Y.: Language and Information. In: Selected Essays on their Theory and Application. Addison-Wesley, New York (1964)
13. Joshi, A., Schabes, Y.: Tree-adjoining grammars. In: Rosenberg, G., Salomaa, A. (eds.) Handbook of Formal Languages 3: Beyond Words, pp. 69–123. Springer, New York (1997)

14. Moortgat, M., Morrill, G.: Heads and phrases: Type calculus for dependency and constituent structure. Technical report, Research Institute for Language and Speech (OTS), Utrecht (1991)
15. Lambek, J.: On the calculus of syntactic types. In: Jacobson, R. (ed.) Structure of Language and its Mathematical Aspects, Proceedings of the Symposia in Applied Mathematics, vol. XII, pp. 166–178. American Mathematical Society, Providence (1961)
16. Kurtonina, N., Moortgat, M.: Structural control. In: Blackburn, P., de Rijke, M. (eds.) Specifying Syntactic Structures, pp. 75–113. CSLI, Stanford (1997)
17. Moortgat, M.: Categorial type logics. In: van Benthem, J., ter Meulen, A. (eds.) Handbook of Logic and Language, pp. 93–177. Elsevier/MIT Press (1997)
18. Girard, J.Y.: Linear logic. Theoretical Computer Science 50, 1–102 (1987)
19. Amblard, M.: Calculs de représentations sémantique et syntaxe générative: les grammaires minimalistes catégorielles. PhD thesis, University of Bordeaux (2007)
20. Lecomte, A.: Semantics in minimalist-categorial grammars. In: Kallmeyer, L., Monachesi, P., Penn, G., Satta, G. (eds.) Proceedings of Formal Grammar 2008 (2008)
21. Schuurman, I., Schouppe, M., Hoekstra, H., van der Wouden, T.: CGN, an annotated corpus of spoken dutch. In: Proceedings of the 4th International Workshop on Linguistically Interpreted Corpora, Budapest, Hungary (2003)
22. Moortgat, M., Moot, R.: Using the Spoken Dutch Corpus for type-logical grammar induction. In: Proceedings of the Third International Language Resources and Evaluation Conference, Las Palmas (2002)
23. Moot, R.: Automated extraction of type-logical supertags from the spoken dutch corpus. In: Bangalore, S., Joshi, A. (eds.) Complexity of Lexical Descriptions and its Relevance to Natural Language Processing: A Supertagging Approach. MIT Press, Cambridge (2010) (to appear)

Minimalist Grammars and Minimalist Categorial Grammars: Toward Inclusion of Generated Languages

Maxime Amblard

Nancy Université – INRIA Nancy-Grand Est
amblard@loria.fr

Abstract. Stabler proposes an implementation of the Chomskyan Minimalist Program [1] with Minimalist Grammars (MG) [2]. This framework inherits a long linguistic tradition. But the semantic calculus is more easily added if one uses the Curry-Howard isomorphism. Minimalist Categorial Grammars (MCG), based on an extension of the Lambek calculus, the mixed logic, were introduced to provide a theoretically-motivated syntax-semantics interface [3]. In this article, we give full definitions of MG with algebraic tree descriptions and of MCG, and take the first steps towards giving a proof of inclusion of their generated languages.

The Minimalist Program (MP), introduced by Chomsky [1], unified more than fifty years of linguistic research in a theoretical way. MP postulates that a *logical form* and a *sound* could be derived from *syntactic relations*. Stabler [2], proposes a framework for this program in a computational perspective with Minimalist Grammars (MG). These grammars inherit a long tradition of generative linguistics. The most interesting contribution of these grammars is certainly that the derivation system is defined with only two rules: *merge* and *move*. The word *Minimalist* is introduced in this perspective of simplicity of the definitions of the framework. If the *merge* rule seems to be classic for this kind of treatment, the second rule, *move*, accounts for the main concepts of this theory and makes it possible to modify relations between elements in the derived structure.

Even if the phonological calculus is already defined, the logical one is more complex to express. Recently, solutions were explored that exploited Curry's distinction between tectogrammatical and phenogrammatical levels; for example, Lambda Grammars [4], Abstract Categorial Grammars [5], and Convergent Grammars [6]. First steps for a convergence between the Generative Theory and Categorial Grammars are due to S. Epstein [7]. A full volume of *Language and Computation* proposes several articles in this perspective [8], in particular [9], and Cornell's works on links between Lambek calculus and Transformational Grammars [10]. Formulations of Minimalist Grammars in a Type-Theoretic way have also been proposed in [11,12,13]. These frameworks were evolved in [14,3,15] for the syntax-semantics interface.

Defining a syntax-semantics interface is complex. In his works, Stabler proposes to include this treatment directly in MG. But interactions between syntax

S. Pogodalla, M. Quatrini, and C. Retoré (Eds.): Lecomte Festschrift, LNAI 6700, pp. 61–80, 2011.

and semantic properties occur at different levels of representation. One solution is to suppose that these two levels should be synchronized. Then, the Curry-Howard isomorphism could be invoked to build a logical representation of utterances. The Minimalist Categorial Grammars have been defined from this perspective: capture the same properties as MG and propose a synchronized semantic calculus. We will propose definitions of these grammars in this article. But do MG and MCG generate the same language? In this article we take the first steps towards showing that they do.

The first section proposes new definitions of Minimalist Grammars based on an algebraic description of trees which allows to check properties of this framework [3]. In the second section, we will focus on full definitions of Minimalist Categorial Grammars (especially the phonological calculus). We will give a short motivation for the syntax-semantics interface, but the complete presentation is delayed to a specific article with a complete example. These two parts should be viewed as a first step of the proof of mutual inclusion of languages between MG and MCG. This property is important because it enables us to reduce MG's to MCG, and we have a well-defined syntax-semantics interface for MCG.

1   Minimalist Grammars

Minimalist Grammars were introduced by Stabler [2] to encode the Minimalist Program of Chomsky [1]. They capture linguistic relations between constituents and build trees close to classical Generative Analyses.

These grammars are fully lexicalized, that is to say they are specified by their lexicon. They are quite different from the traditional definition of lexicalized because they allow the use of specific items which do not carry any phonological form. The use of theses items implies that MG represent more than syntactic relations and must be seen as a meta-calculus lead by the syntax.

These grammars build trees with two rules: *merge* and *move* which are trigged by features. This section presents all the definitions of MG in a formal way, using algebraic descriptions of trees.

1.1   Minimalist Tree Structures

To provide formal descriptions of Minimalist Grammars, we differ from traditional definitions by using an algebraic description of trees: a sub-tree is defined by its context, as in [16] and [17]. For example, the figure on the left of Fig. 1 shows two subtrees in a tree (t_1 and t_2) and their context (C_1 and C_2). Before we explain the relations in minimalist trees, we give the formal material used to define a tree by its context.

Graded Alphabets and Trees. Trees are defined from a *graded set*. A graded set is made up of a support set, noted Σ, the alphabet of the tree, and a *rank* function, noted σ, which defines node arity (the *graded* terminology results from the rank function). In the following, we will use Σ to denote a graded (Σ, σ).

The set of trees built on Σ, written T_Σ, is the smallest set of strings ($\Sigma \cup \{(;);,\}$)*. A leaf of a tree is a node of arity 0, denoted by α instead of $\alpha()$. For a tree t, if $t = \sigma(t_1, \cdots, t_k)$, the root node of t is written σ .

Moreover, a set of variables $X = \{x_1, x_2, \cdots\}$ is added for these trees. X_k is the set of k variables. These variables mark positions in trees. By using variables, we define a substitution rule: given a tree $t \in T_{\Sigma(X_k)}$ (*i.e.* a tree which contains instances of k variables $x_1, \cdots, x_k$) and $t_1, \cdots, t_k$, k trees in T_Σ, the tree obtained by simultaneous substitution of each instance of x_1 by $t_1, \ldots, x_k$ by t_k is denoted by $t[t_1, \cdots, t_k]$. The set of all subtrees of t is noted $\mathcal{S}_t$.

Thus, for a given tree t and a given node n of t, the subtree for which n is the root is denoted by t with this subtree replaced by a variable.

Minimalist trees are produced by Minimalist Grammars and they are built on the graded alphabet $\{<, >, \Sigma\}$, whose ranks of $<$ and $>$ are 2 and 0 for strings of Σ. Minimalist Trees are binary ones whose nodes are labelled with $<$ or $>$, and whose leaves contain strings of Σ.

Relations between Sub-Trees. We formalise relations for different positions of elements in $\mathcal{S}_t$. Intuitively, these define the concept of *be above, be on the right* or *on the left*. A specific relation on minimalist trees is also defined: *projection* that introduces the concept of *be the main element* in a tree.

In the following, we assume a given graded alphabet Σ. Proofs of principal properties and closure properties are all detailed in [3]. The first relation is the dominance which informally is the concept of *be above*.

Definition 1. *Let* $t \in T_\Sigma$, *and* $C_1, C_2 \in \mathcal{S}_t$, C_1 **dominates** C_2 *(written* $C_1 \lhd^* C_2$*) if there exists* $C' \in \mathcal{S}_t$ *such that* $C_1[C'] = C_2$.

Figure 1 shows an example of dominance in a tree. One interesting property of this algebraic description of trees is that properties in sub-trees pass to tree. For example, in a given tree t, if there exists C_1 and C_2 such that $C_1 \lhd^* C_2$, using a 1-context C, we could build a new tree $t' = C[t]$ (substitution in the position marked by a variable). Then, $C[C_1]$ and $C[C_2]$ exist (they are part of t') such that $C[C_1] \lhd C[C_2]$.

Definition 2. *Let* $t \in T_\Sigma$, $C_1, C_2 \in \mathcal{S}_t$, C_1 **immediately precedes** C_2 *(written* $C_1 \prec C_2$*) if there exists* $C \in \mathcal{S}_t$ *such that:*

1. $C_1 = C[\sigma(t_1, \ldots, t_j, x_1, t_{j+2}, \ldots, t_k)]$ *and*
2. $C_2 = C[\sigma(t_1, \ldots, t_j, t_{j+1}, x_1, \ldots, t_k)]$.

Precedence, written $\prec^\sim$, *is the smallest relation defined by the following rules (transitivity rule, closure rule and relation between dominance and precedence relation):*

$$\frac{C_1 \prec^\sim C_2 \quad C_2 \prec^\sim C_3}{C_1 \prec^\sim C_3} [trans] \qquad \frac{C_1 \prec C_2}{C_1 \prec^\sim C_2} [*] \qquad \frac{C_1 \lhd^* C_2}{C_2 \prec^\sim C_1} [dom]$$

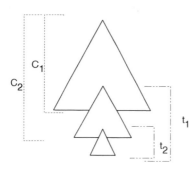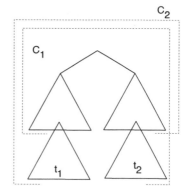

- C_1 is the context of the sub-tree t_1
- C_2 is the context of the sub-tree t_2
- $C_1 \vartriangleleft^* C_2$ means that the root node of t_1 is higher than the root node of t_2 in the full tree

- C_1 is the context of the sub-tree t_1
- C_2 is the context of the sub-tree t_2
- $C_1 <^* C_2$ means that the root node of t_1 is on the left side of the root node of t_2 in the tree

Fig. 1. Dominance and precedence relations in trees

Precedence encodes the relation *be on the left* (and then *be on the right*) or *be above* another element (using the dominance). These two relations stay true for substitution (as mentioned above).

The next relation does not define a tree relation. It realises a linguistic property by leading the concept of *be the main* element in a structure (or a substructure).

Definition 3. *Let $t \in T_{\Sigma_{MG}}(A)$, and $C_1, C_2 \in S_t$, C_1 **immediately projects** on C_2 (written $C_1 < C_2$) if there exists $C \in S_t$ such that one of the two following properties holds:*

1. $C_1 = C[<(x_1, t_2)]$ and $C_2 = C[<(t_1, x_1)]$,
2. $C_1 = C[>(t_2, x_1)]$ and $C_2 = C[>(x_1, t_1)]$,

in this case $C \vartriangleleft C_1$ and $C \vartriangleleft C_2$. If $C_1 < C_2$ or $C_2 < C_1$, then there exists C such that $C \vartriangleleft C_1$ and $C \vartriangleleft C_2$.

$<^\sim$ is the smallest relation defined by the following system of rules:

$$\frac{C \in S_t}{C <^\sim C} \, [0] \qquad \frac{C_1 <^\sim C_2 \quad C_2 <^\sim C_3}{C_1 <^\sim C_3} \, [trans] \qquad \frac{C_1 < C_2}{C_1 <^\sim C_2} \, [\sim]$$

$$\frac{C_1 \vartriangleleft^* C_2 \quad C_3 \vartriangleleft^* C_4 \quad C_2 < C_3}{C_1 <^\sim C_4} \, [A] \qquad \frac{C_1 \vartriangleleft C_2 \quad C_2 < C_3}{C_2 <^\sim C_1} \, [B]$$

Note that the projection relation is transitive. All the properties of these three relations are proven in [3]. Figure 2 presents three minimalist trees where in t the *main* element is the verb *walks* (which is accessible by following the projection relation).

These three relations could seem quite complicated for a reader who is not familiar with these notations or the zipper theory. But their expressiveness allows to prove the structural properties assumed for MG and moreover to give the proof of languages inclusion with MCG. Finally, in this section, we have defined the concept of parent and child relations in trees plus the projection relation which defines constituents in linguistic descriptions.

1.2   Linguistic Structures in Trees

From the linguistic perspective, trees represent relationships between the grammatical elements of an utterance. Linguistic concepts are associated with minimalist tree structures. These relationships have been proposed for the analysis of structural analogies between verbal and nominal groups. Thus, groups of words in a coherent statement (phrases), whatever their nature, have a similar structure. This is supposed to be the same for all languages, regardless of the order of sub-terms. This assumption is one of the basic ideas of the X-bar theory introduced in the seventies [18] and in the MP [1].

The Head. is the element around which a group is composed. An easy way to find the head of a minimalist tree is to follow the projection relation of the nodes.

Definition 4. *Let $t \in T_{MG}$, if for all $C' \in S_t$, $C<^{\sim}C'$ then C is called the **head** of t. For a given tree $t \in T_{MG}$, we write $H_t[x] \in S_t$ a sub-tree of t of which x is the head, and $head(t)$ is a leaf which is the head of t. Then $t = H_t[head(t)]$.*

For a minimalist tree, there always exists a unique minimal element for the projection relation and it is a leaf (which is the head of the tree) [3].

For example, the head of the minimalist tree in Fig. 2 is the leaf *walks* (follow the direction of the projection relation in nodes and stop in a leaf). Subtrees have their own head, for example the leaf a is the head of the subtree t_1 (in Fig. 2) and the preposition *in* is the head ot t_3.

Maximal Projection. is, for a leaf l, the largest subtree for which l is the head. This is the inverse notion of *head*. In the minimalist tree of Fig. 2, the maximal projection of the leaf *walks* is the full tree t. To describe other maximal projections in this example, the maximal projection of a is the subtree which contains a *man* and the maximal projection of the *man* is the leaf *man*. In a more formal way, the maximal projection is defined as follows:

Definition 5. *Let $t \in T_{MG}$, $C \in S_t$. The **maximal projection** of C (denoted by $proj_{max}(C)$) is the subtree defined by:*

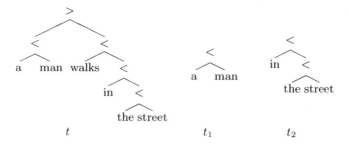

Fig. 2. A minimalist tree t and two of its sub-tree

- $if\ C = x_1,\ proj_{max}(C) = x_1$
- $if\ C = C'[< (x_1, t)]\ or\ C = C'[> (t, x_1)],\ proj_{max}(C) = proj_{max}(C')$
- $if\ C = C'[< (t, x_1)]\ or\ C = C'[> (x_1, t)],\ proj_{max}(C) = C$

Then $proj_{max}(walks) = t$. This logical characterization of minimalist trees and structural relations allows to prove different properties of MG (for example that the projection is anti-symmetric) [3].

Complement and Specifier. are relations on subtrees with respect to the head.

Elements coming after the head provide information and they are in the *complement* relation. Let $t \in S_{MG}$, C_1 is a complement of $head(t) = C$, if $proj_{max}(C) \lhd^* C_1$ and $C \prec^+ C_1$, denoted by $C_1\ comp\ C$.

In the tree t of Fig. 2, the subtree t_2 is in a complement relation with the head *walks*. It *adds* information to the verb.

By contrast, elements placed before the head determine who (or what) is in the relationship. Let $t \in S_{MG}$, C_1 is a specifier of $head(t) = C$, if $proj_{max}(C) \lhd^* C_1$ and $C_1 \prec^+ C$, denoted by $C_1\ spec\ C$.

In the tree t of Fig.2, the subtree t_1 is in a specifier relation with the head *walks*. It *specifies* interpretation of the verb.

1.3   Minimalist Grammars

The computational system of MG is entirely based on features which represent linguistic properties of constituents. Rules are trigged by these features and they build minimalist trees. A *Minimalist Grammar* is defined by a quintuplet $\langle V, Features, Lex, \Phi, c \rangle$ where:

- V is a finite set of non-syntactic features, which contains two sets: P (phonological forms, marked with $/\ /$), and I (logical forms, marked with $()$).
- $Features = \{B \cup S \cup L_a \cup L_e\}$ is a finite set of syntactic features,
- Lex is a set of complex expressions from P and $Features$ (lexical items),
- $\Phi = \{merge, move\}$ is the set of generative rules,
- $c \in Features$ is the feature which allows to accept derivations.

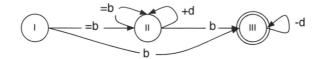

Fig. 3. Automata of acceptable sequences of features where $b \in B$ and $d \in D$

The final tree of a derivation which ends with acceptance is called a *derivational tree*, which corresponds to a classical generative analysis. Phonological forms are used as lexical items (and they could be seen as the grammar's terminal symbols). A left-to-right reading of phonological forms in derived and accepted structures provides the recognized string. But intermediate trees in a derivation do not stand for this. Only the derivational tree allows to recognize a string. This results from the *move* rule which modifies the tree structure. For a MG G , the language L_G recognized by G is the closure of the lexicon by the generation rules.

1.4 Features

A MG is defined by its lexicon which stores its resources. Lexical items consist of a phonological form and a list of syntactic features. The syntactic set of features is divided in two subsets: one for basic categories, denoted B, and one for *move* features, denoted D. Different types of features are:

- $B = \{v,\ dp,\ c, \cdots\}$ the set of **basic features**. Elements of B denote standard linguistic categories. Note that this set contains c, the *accepting feature* (I assume it is unique at least).
- $S = \{=d \mid d \in B\}$ the set of **selectors** which expresses the necessity of another feature of B of the same type (for $d \in B$, $=d$ is the dual selector).
- $L_a = \{+k \mid k \in D\}$ the set of **licensors**. These features assign an expression's property to complement another in a specifier-head relation.
- $L_e = \{-k \mid k \in D\}$ the set of **licensees**. These features state that the expression needs to be complemented by a similar licensor.

Lexical sequences of features follow the syntax: $/FP/ : (S(S \cup L_a)^*)^* B(L_e)^*$

Vermaat [19], proposes an automata which recognises the acceptable sequences, proposed in Fig. 3. This structure could be divided in two parts: the first containing a sequence of selectors and licensors (features which trigger rules, as we shall see), and the second which contains only one basic feature (the grammatical category associated to the expression) and a sequence of licensees. The first part corresponds to stat I and II and the second to stat III and transitions to this state. In the following, e will denote any feature and E a sequence of features (possibly empty).

For example, the sequence associated with an intransitive verb will be:

$$=d\ +case\ v$$

which means that this verb must be jointed with a *determinal phrase* (*determinal* comes from the Generative Theory), a complex expression with feature d. Then it must be combined with a $-case$, we will see how in the next section, an then there is a structure associated with *verb* (feature v).

Transitive verbs will extend the intransitive ones wth the list:

$$=d + case =d + case \ v$$

The two $=d$ correspond to the subject and the object of the verb. The first *case* will be *accusative* and the second *nominative*.

Another example is determiners: they are combined with a noun to build a determiner phrase and need to be unified in the structure (see the next section). Here is an example of lexicon which contains a verb, a noun and a determiner:

$$walks : \ =d + case \ v$$
$$a : \ =n \ d - case$$
$$man : n$$

1.5   MG Rules

Φ, the set of generating rules, contains only: *merge* and *move*. A derivation is a succession of rule applications which build trees. These trees are partial results: the structural order of phonological forms does not need to correspond to the final one. In the MP, a specific point, called *Spell-Out* is the border between the calculus of derivations and the final result. Rules are trigged by the feature occurring as the first element of list of features of the head.

Merge. is the process which connects different parts. It is an operation which joins two trees to build a new one:

$$merge : T_{MG} \times T_{MG} \to T_{MG}$$

It is triggered by a selector $(=x)$ at the top of the list of features of the head and it is realised with a corresponding basic feature (x) at the top of the list of features of the head of a second tree. *Merge* adds a new root which dominates both trees and cancels the two features. The specifier/complement relation is implied by the lexical status of the tree which carried the selector. The new root node points to this tree.

Let $t, t' \in T_{MG}$ be such that $t = H_t[l : =h \ E]$ and $t' = H_{t'}[l' : h \ E']$ with $h \in B$:

$$merge(t, t') = \begin{cases} < (l : \ E, H_{t'}[l' : \ E']) & \text{if } t \in Lex, \\ > (H_{t'}[l' : \ E'], H_t[l : \ E]) & \text{otherwise.} \end{cases}$$

Figure 4 presents the graphical representation of *merge*.

For example, to derive *a man walks*, we first need to combine *a* with *man*, and then to combine the result with the verb:

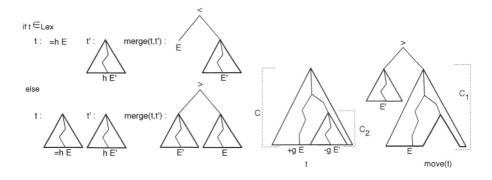

Fig. 4. Tree representation of *merge* and *move*.

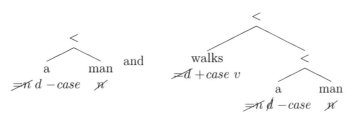

Obtained trees do not verify the word order (only the final tree will check the right word order). In this example, the selectors are carried by lexical items, then projection relations point to the left in both cases.

Move. encodes the main idea of the Minimalist Program. It corresponds to the movement of a constituent to the top position of the derivation. *Move* is trigged by a licensor $(+x)$ at the top of the list of features of the head of a tree. Then, it looks for a corresponding licensee $(-x)$ at the top of the list of features of the head inside the tree. If these conditions are met, the maximal projection of the node which carries the licensee is moved to the left of a new root. This node points to the right (the subtree which carries the former head). Both licensor and licensee are cancelled. The root of the moved maximal projection is substituted by an empty leaf (ϵ). This new leaf is called the *trace* of the move.

Figure 4 shows a graphical representation of the move rule where the head of C carries a $+g$ in its top features list. Then we look for a leaf with $-g$ in its top features list and then find its maximal projection (C_2) which contains all the elements which depend on it. Finally this sub-tree is moved to the left position of a new root node. Intuitively, a linguistic property is checked and the consequence is a move in first position in the tree. And strictly:

$$move : T_{MG} \to T_{MG}$$

For all tree $t = C[l : +g\ E, l' : -g\ E']$, such that $t = H_t[l : +g\ E]$, there exists $C_1, C_2 \in S_t$ such that: C_2 is the maximal projection of the leaf l' and C_1 is t deprived of C_2. Then, $t = C_1[l : +g\ E, C_2[l' : -g\ E']]$ where:

- $C_2[l' : -g\ E'] = proj_{max}(C[l' : -g\ E])$
- $C_1[l : +g\ E, x_1] = proj_{max}(C[l : +g\ E, x_1])$

$$move(t) = >(C_2[l' : E'], C_1[l : E, \epsilon])$$

Figure 4 presents the graphical representation of *move*.

Stabler introduces some refinements to these grammars. Let us mention them. He introduces a second *move*: *weak move*, which does not move the phonological forms. The precedent *move* is then called *strong move*, which is trigged with capital features. The *weak move* is, like *strong move*:

$$move(t) = >(C_2[\epsilon : E'], C_1[l : E, l'])$$

Variations on *strong/weak* values achieve variations on phonological order. This is an instance of the use of *parameters* of the Minimalist Program.

Moreover, restrictions can be introduced on MG derivations. An important one is the Shortest Move Condition (SMC) which blocks *move* in case of ambiguity on licensees. Then, the move operation of MG with SMC is deterministic.

A locality condition could also be introduced: Specifier Island Condition (SPIC). "Islands" define areas which prohibit extractions. With SPIC, a subtree cannot be moved if it is in a specifier relation within a subtree. This condition was introduced by Stabler [20] drawing on [21] and [22], who proposes that moved elements had to be in a complement relation.

In the previous example, the head of the last tree is the leaf *walks* which contains a +*case* feature as first element of its list. Then, a *move* is trigged in the tree with the leaf *a* which carries a (−*case*). The resulting tree is the following:

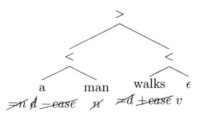

The move operation modifies the position of the maximal projection of the leaf which carries the −*case*. The old position is substituted by an empty leaf (ϵ). Finally, the tree contains only one feature which is v. In this small example, I did not discuss the validity of the final feature, but in a real derivation, we assume that it is not the verb which carries the +*case* licensor which corresponds to the nominal case, but it is a specific item. This item corresponds to the morphological mark of the verb. Then each acceptable derivation assumes that a verb has received its time (and other properties). But exhibiting the use of this item needs other refinements of the two rules (Head-movement and Affix-Hopping).

This section did not propose a new framework for computational linguistics. This is a new definition of Stabler proposal. This way, assumed properties of minimalist trees have been fully proved [3]. Moreover this algebraic definition of MG is a perfect description to compare generated languages with other frameworks. Finally, this modifies the point of view on derivations and shows all steps of the calculus as substitution. One missing point is still the introduction of a semantic calculus. Let us now develop MCG which are defined with a syntax-semantics interface.

2   Minimalist Categorial Grammars (MCG)

In this section, we define a new Type-Theoretic Framework which is provided by the mixed calculus, a formulation of Partially Commutative Linear Logic. It proposes to simulate MG and then keep linguistic properties of the Minimalist Program. MCG are motivated by the syntax-semantics interface [3]. This interface, as for Lambek calculus, is based on an extension of the Curry-Howard isomorphism [23]. Even though this interface is not the aim of this paper, let us discuss some important points.

The idea of encoding MP with Lambek calculus arises from [11] and extended versions of this work. In these propositions, the calculus is always non-commutative, a property needed to model the left-right relation in sentences. But the *move* operation could not be defined in a proper way with non-commutative relation. In particular, in complex utterances, the non-commutativity implies that a constituent (for example the object DP) must be fully treated before another one is introduced (for example the subject DP). Otherwise, features are mixed and non-commutativity blocks resolutions. It is not acceptable to normalize the framework with such a strong property and it makes the system inconsistent in regard to linguistics.

The solution we propose is to define a new framework which allows to deal with commutative and non-commutative connectors: the mixed calculus. The main consequence on the model of this calculus is that variables in logical formulae are introduced at different places and must be unified later. In [3] we show how the unification is used to capture semantic phenomena which are not easily included. In few words, the idea is to consider proofs of mixed calculus as *phases* of a verb. Phases have been introduced by Chomsky to detail different modifications which occur on a verb. Several linguists have showed that phases have implications on semantics, for example the theta-roles must be allocated after a specific phase. This is exactly the result of the syntax-semantics interface of MCG. Full explanations need more space to be presented, but the main contribution of MCG is to propose an efficient syntax-semantics interface in the same perspective as MG.

In this section, we will detail MCG and expose their structural link with MG. First we present the mixed calculus, then we give definitions of MCG and show proofs of the mixed calculus produced by MCG (together with their linguistic properties).

2.1   Mixed Calculus

MCG are provided with mixed calculus [24], a formulation of Partially Commutative Linear Logic. Hypotheses are either in a non-commutative order ($<;>$) or in a commutative one ($(,)$) The plain calculus contains introduction and elimination rules for:

- the non-commutative product $\odot$:

$$\frac{\Delta \vdash A \odot B \quad \Gamma, < A; B >, \Gamma' \vdash C}{\Gamma, \Delta, \Gamma' \vdash C} \, [\odot_e] \qquad\qquad \frac{\Delta \vdash A \quad \Gamma \vdash B}{< \Delta; \Gamma > \vdash A \odot B} \, [\odot_i]$$

- its residuals (/ and \\):

$$\frac{\Gamma \vdash A \quad \Delta \vdash A \backslash C}{< \Gamma; \Delta > \vdash C} \, [\backslash_e] \qquad\qquad \frac{\Delta \vdash A/C \quad \Gamma \vdash A}{< \Delta; \Gamma > \vdash C} \, [/_e]$$

$$\frac{< A; \Gamma > \vdash C}{\Gamma \vdash A \backslash C} \, [\backslash_i] \qquad\qquad \frac{< \Gamma; A > \vdash C}{\Gamma \vdash C/A} \, [/_i]$$

- the commutative product $\otimes$:

$$\frac{\Delta \vdash A \otimes B \quad \Gamma, (A, B), \Gamma' \vdash C}{\Gamma, \Delta, \Gamma' \vdash C} \, [\otimes_e] \qquad\qquad \frac{\Delta \vdash A \quad \Gamma \vdash B}{(\Delta, \Gamma) \vdash A \otimes B} \, [\otimes_i]$$

- its residual $\multimap$:

$$\frac{\Gamma \vdash A \quad \Delta \vdash A \multimap C}{(\Gamma, \Delta) \vdash C} \, [\multimap_e] \qquad\qquad \frac{(A, \Gamma) \vdash C}{\Gamma \vdash A \multimap C} \, [\multimap_i]$$

The product connectors of the mixed calculus use in a first step hypotheses to mark positions in the proof and in a second one substitute the result of an another proof in these positions using a product elimination (the commutative/non-commutative status depends on relations between hypotheses). This is exactly the process we will use to define the *move* rule of MCGs.

Moreover, the calculus contains an axiom rule and an entropy rule. This last one allows to relax the order between hypotheses. We will use this rule to define *merge* in MCG as we will see in the following section.

$$\frac{}{A \vdash A} \, [axiom] \qquad\qquad \frac{\Gamma \vdash C}{\Gamma' \vdash C} \, [\text{entropy—whenever } \Gamma' \sqsubset \Gamma]$$

This calculus has been shown to be normalizable [25] and derivations of MCG will be proofs of the mixed calculus in normal form.

2.2   Minimalist Categorial Grammars

As MG, MCG are lexicalized grammars. Derivations are led by formulae associated with lexical items built with connectors of the mixed logic. They are specific proofs of the mixed logic, labelled to realise the phonological and semantic tiers. Phonological labels on proofs will be presented with definitions of MCG rules.

A MCG is defined by a quintuplet $\langle N, \text{P}, Lex, \varPhi, C \rangle$ where :

- N is the union of two finite disjoint sets Ph and I which are respectively the *set of phonological forms* and the one of *logical forms*.

- P is the union of two finite disjoint sets P_1 and P_2 which are respectively the *set of constituent features* (the set B of MG) and the one of *move features* (the set D of MG).
- *Lex* is a finite subset of $E \times F \times I$, the set of lexical items [1].
- $\Phi = \{merge, move\}$ is the set of generative rules,
- $C \in P$ is the accepting formulae.

As mentioned in the previous section, *move* is defined using a product elimination. In MG, a constituent is first introduced in a tree using its basic feature and then can be moved using its licensees. In MCG, a constituent will be introduced only when all its positions (which correspond to the basic feature and its licensees) have been marked in the proof by specific hypotheses. But we need to distinguish the type of the basic feature from the licensees features. That is why P is divided in two subsets P_1 and P_2. This sub-typing of formulae is used to well define lexicons of MCG.

The set E is Ph^*, and the set F, the set of formulae used to build *Lex*, is defined with the set P, the commutative product $\otimes$ and the two non-commutative implications $/$ and $\backslash$. Formulae of F are recognized by the non-terminal L of the following grammar:

$$L ::= (B) / P_1 \mid C$$
$$B ::= P_1 \backslash (B) \mid P_2 \backslash (B) \mid C$$
$$C ::= P_2 \otimes (C) \mid C_1$$
$$C_1 ::= P_1$$

In more details, MCG formulae start with a $/$ which is followed by a sequence of $\backslash$. This sequence contains operators allowing to compose the proof with another one (operators are the translation of selectors and licensors). Lexical formulae are ended by a sequence of $\otimes$. To sum up, these formulae have the structure $(c_m \backslash \ldots \backslash c_1 \backslash (b_1 \otimes \ldots \otimes b_n \otimes a))/d$, with $a \in P_1$, $b_i \in P_2$, $c_j \in P$ and $d \in P_1$. This structure corresponds to the two parts of the list of features we have mentioned in the previous section.

For the example *a man walks*, the MCG's lexicon is the following:

$$walks : case \backslash v / d$$
$$a : (case \otimes d)/n$$
$$man : n$$

Licensees, which express the need for an information, are there seen as a specific part of the basic feature (a part of the main sub-type). Licensors will be cancelled with an hypothesis to mark a position in the proof. Distinction between them is not written by an *ad hoc* marker but by structural relations inside the formula. Before we explain the *move* and *merge* rules, let us present the phonological tiers.

---

[1] In the following, *Lex* is a subset of $E \times F$. The semantic part is used for the syntax-semantics interface which is not detailed here.

2.3   Derivations

Labels. Derivations of MCG are labelled proofs of the mixed calculus. Before defining labelling, we define labels and operations on them.

Let V be an uncountable and finite set of variables such that: $Ph \cap V = \emptyset$. T is the union of Ph and V. We define the set Σ, called *labels set* as the set of triplets of elements of T^*. Every position in a triplet has a linguistic interpretation: they correspond to specifier/head/complement relations of minimalist trees. A label r will be considered as $r = (r_{spec}, r_{head}, r_{comp})$.

For a label in which there is an empty position, we adopt the following notation: $r_{-head} = (r_{spec}, \epsilon, r_{comp})$, $r_{-spec} = (\epsilon, r_{head}, r_{comp})$, and $r_{-comp} = (r_{spec}, r_{head}, \epsilon)$. We introduce variables in the string triplets and a substitution operation. They are used to modify a position inside a triplet by a specific material. Intuitively, this is the counterpart in the phonological calculus of the product elimination. The set of variables with at least one in r is denoted by $Var(r)$. The number of occurrences of a variable x in a string $s \in T^*$ is denoted by $|s|_x$, and the number of occurrences of x in r by $\varphi_x(r)$. A label is *linear* if for all x in V, $\varphi_x(r) \leqslant 1$.

A *substitution* is a partial function from V to T^*. For σ a substitution, s a string of T^* and r a label, we note $s.\sigma$ and $r.\sigma$ the string and the label obtained by the simultaneous substitution in s and r of the variables by the values associated by σ (variables for which σ is not defined remain the same).

If the domain of definition of a substitution σ is finite and equal to $x_1, \ldots, x_n$ and $\sigma(x_i) = t_i$, then σ is denoted by $[t_1/x_1, \ldots, t_n/x_n]$. Moreover, for a sequence s and a label r, $s.\sigma$ and $r.\sigma$ are respectively denoted $s[t_1/x_1, \ldots, t_n/x_n]$ and $r[t_1/x_1, \ldots, t_n/x_n]$. Every injective substitution which takes values in V is called *renaming*. Two labels r_1 and r_2 (respectively two strings s_1 and s_2) are equal modulo a renaming of variables if there exists a renaming σ such that $r_1.\sigma = r_2$ (*resp.* $s_1.\sigma = s_2$).

Finally, we need another operation on string triplets which allows to combine them together: the string concatenation of T^* is noted $\bullet$. Let *Concat* be the operation of concatenation on labels which concatenates the three components in the linear order: for $r \in \Sigma$, $Concat(r) = r_{spec} \bullet r_{head} \bullet r_{comp}$.

We then have defined a phonological structure which encodes specifier/complement/head relations and two operations: substitution and concatenation. These two operations will be counterparts in the phonological calculus of *merge* and *move*.

Labelled Proofs. Before exhibiting the rules of MCG, the concept of labelling on a subset of rules of the mixed logic is introduced. *Minimalist logic* is the fragment of mixed logic composed by the axiom rule, $\backslash_e$, $/_e$, $\otimes_e$ and $\sqsubset$.

For a given MCG $G = \langle N, \mathrm{P}, Lex, \Phi, C \rangle$, let a *G-background* be $x : A$ with $x \in V$ and $A \in F$, or $\langle G_1; G_2 \rangle$ or else (G_1, G_2) with G_1 and G_2 some *G-backgrounds* which are defined on two disjoint sets of variables. *G*-backgrounds are series-parallel orders on subsets of $V \times F$. They are naturally extended to the entropy rule, noted $\sqsubset$. A *G-sequent* is a sequent of the form: $\Gamma \vdash_G (r_s, r_t, r_c) : B$ where Γ is a G-background, $B \in F$ and $(r_s, r_t, r_c) \in \Sigma$.

A *G-labelling* is a derivation of a G-sequent obtained with the following rules:

$$\frac{\langle s, A \rangle \in Lex}{\vdash_G (\epsilon, s, \epsilon) : A} \, [Lex]$$

$$\frac{x \in V}{x : A \vdash_G (\epsilon, x, \epsilon) : A} \, [axiom]$$

$$\frac{\Gamma \vdash_G r_1 : A \, / \, B \quad \Delta \vdash_G r_2 : B \quad Var(r_1) \cap Var(r_2) = \emptyset}{\langle \Gamma; \Delta \rangle \vdash_G (r_{1s}, r_{1t}, r_{1c} \bullet Concat(r_2)) : A} \, [/_e]$$

$$\frac{\Delta \vdash_G r_2 : B \quad \Gamma \vdash_G r_1 : B \setminus A \quad Var(r_1) \cap Var(r_2) = \emptyset}{\langle \Gamma; \Delta \rangle \vdash_G (Concat(r_2) \bullet r_{1s}, r_{1t}, r_{1c}) : A} \, [\setminus_e]$$

$$\frac{\Gamma \vdash_G r_1 : A \otimes B \quad \Delta[x : A, y : B] \vdash_G r_2 : C \quad Var(r_1) \cap Var(r_2) = \emptyset \,\, A \in \mathrm{P}_2}{\Delta[\Gamma] \vdash_G r_2[Concat(r_1)/x, \epsilon/y] : C} \, [\otimes_e]$$

$$\frac{\Gamma \vdash_G r : A \quad \Gamma' \sqsubset \Gamma}{\Gamma' \vdash_G r : A} \, [\sqsubset]$$

Note that a G-labelling is a proof tree of the minimalist logic on which sequent hypotheses are decorated with variables and sequent conclusions are decorated with labels. Product elimination is used with a substitution on labels and implication connectors with concatenation (a triplet is introduced in another one by concatenating its three components).

If $\Gamma \vdash_G r : B$ is a derivable G-sequent, then r is linear, and $Var(r)$ is exactly the set of variables in Γ. Finally, for all renamings σ, $\Gamma.\sigma \vdash_G r.\sigma : B$ is a G-sequent differentiable.

Merge and Move Rules. are simulated by combinations of rules of the minimalist logic producing G-labeling.

Merge is the elimination of $/$ (*resp.* $\setminus$) immediately followed by an *entropy* rule. The meaning of this rule is joining two elements in regard to the left-right order (then non-commutative connectors are used) and, as mentioned earlier, all hypotheses must be accessible. To respect this, a commutative order between hypotheses is needed. Then an entropy rule immediately follows each implication elimination.

For the phonological tier, a label is concatenated in the complement (respectively specifier) position in another one. Note that a *merge* which uses $/$ must be realized with a lexical item, so the context is always empty.

$$\frac{\vdash (r_{spec}, r_{head}, r_{comp}) : A \mathbin{/} B \quad \Delta \vdash s : B}{\dfrac{\Delta \vdash (r_{spec}, r_{head}, r_{comp} \bullet Concat(s)) : A}{\Delta \vdash (r_{spec}, r_{head}, r_{comp} \bullet Concat(s)) : A} \, [\sqsubset]} \, [/e]$$

$$\frac{\Delta \vdash s : B \quad \Gamma \vdash (r_{spec}, r_{head}, r_{comp}) : B \backslash A}{\dfrac{\langle \Delta ; \Gamma \rangle \vdash (Concat(s) \bullet r_{spec}, r_{head}, r_{comp}) : A}{\Delta, \Gamma \vdash (Concat(s) \bullet r_{spec}, r_{head}, r_{comp}) : A} \, [\sqsubset]} \, [\backslash e]$$

These combinations of rules are noted $[mg]$.

For example, the proof of the utterance *a man walks* begins with the formulae of *walks*: $case\backslash v/d$. The first step of the calculus is to introduce two hypotheses, one for d and the other for $case$. The result is the following proof:

$$\frac{v : case \vdash (\epsilon, v, \epsilon) : case \quad \dfrac{\vdash (\epsilon, walks, \epsilon) : case\backslash v/d \quad u : d \vdash (\epsilon, u, \epsilon) : d}{u : d \vdash (\epsilon, walks, u) : case\backslash v} \, [mg]}{(v : case, u : d) \vdash (\epsilon, walks, u) : v} \, [mg]$$

In parallel, the derivation joins the determiner a and the noun *man*:

$$\frac{\vdash (\epsilon, a, \epsilon) : (case \otimes d)/n \quad \vdash (\epsilon, man, \epsilon) : n}{\vdash (\epsilon, a, man) : case \otimes d} \, [mg]$$

Note that the first proof contains two hypotheses which correspond to the type of the main formula in the second proof. The link between these two proofs will be made by a *move*, as we will show later.

Move is simulated by an elimination of a commutative product in a proof and, for the phonological calculus, is a substitution. We have structured the lexicons and the merge rule to delay to the move rule only the substitution part of the calculus.

$$\frac{\Gamma \vdash r_1 : A \otimes B \quad \Delta[u : A, v : B] \vdash r_2 : C}{\Delta[\Gamma] \vdash r_2[Concat(r_1)/u, \epsilon/v] : C} \, [\otimes e]$$

This rule is applied only if $A \in \text{P}2$ and B is of the form $B_1 \times \ldots B_n \times D$ where $B_i \in \text{P}2$ and $D \in \text{P}1$.

This rule is noted $[mv]$. *Move* uses hypotheses as resources. The calculus places hypotheses in the proof, and when all hypotheses corresponding to a constituent are introduced, this constituent is substituted. The hypothesis $\text{P}1$ is the first place of a moved constituent and hypotheses of $\text{P}2$ mark the different places where the constituent is moved or have a trace.

In recent propositions, Chomsky proposes to delay all moves after the realisation of all merges. MCG could not encode this but contrary to MG where a *move* blocks all the process, in MCG *merge* could happen, except in the case of hypotheses of a given constituent shared by two proofs which must be linked by a *move*.

In our example, we have two proofs:

- one for the verb: $(v : case, u : d) \vdash (\epsilon, walks, u) : v$
- one for the DP: $\vdash (\epsilon, a, man) : case \otimes d$

The first hypothesis corresponds to the entry position of the DP in MG and the second to the moved position. Here, we directly introduce the DP by eliminating the two hypotheses in the same step:

$$\frac{\vdash (\epsilon, a, man) : case \otimes d \quad (v : case, u : d) \vdash (\epsilon, walks, u) : v}{\vdash (a \ man, walks, \epsilon) : v} [mv]$$

The phonological result is *a man walks*. The proof encodes the same structure as the derivational tree of MG (modulo a small transduction on the proof).

For *cyclic move* (where a constituent is moved several times) all hypotheses inside this move must be linked together upon their introduction in the proof. For this, when a new hypothesis A is introduced, a $[mv]$ is applied with a sequent with hypothesis $A \otimes B \vdash A \otimes B$ where A is in P_2 and B is of the form $B_1 \otimes \ldots \otimes B_n \otimes D$ where $B_i \in P_2$ and $D \in P_1$.

$$\frac{x : A \otimes B \vdash (\epsilon, x, \epsilon) : A \otimes B \quad \Delta[u : A, v : B] \vdash r : C}{\Delta[A \otimes B] \vdash r[x/u, \epsilon/v] : C} [\otimes_e]$$

In the definition of *merge*, the systematic use of entropy comes from the definition of *move*. As it was presented, *move* consumes hypotheses of the proof. But, from a linguistic perspective, these hypotheses could not be supposed introduced next to each other. The non-commutative order inferred from $\backslash_e$ and $/_e$ blocks the *move* application. To avoid this, the entropy rule places them in commutative order. In MCG, all hypotheses are in the same relation, then to simplify the reading of proofs, the order is denoted only with ','.

The strong/weak move could be simulated with the localization of the substitution (if hypotheses are in P_1 or P_2).

$$\frac{s : \Gamma \vdash A \otimes B \quad r[u, v] : \Delta[u : A, v : B] \vdash C}{r[Concat(s)/u, \epsilon/v] : \Delta[\Gamma] \vdash C} [move_{strong}]$$

$$\frac{s : \Gamma \vdash A \otimes B \quad r[u, v] : \Delta[u : A, v : B] \vdash C}{r[\epsilon/u, Concat(s)/v] : \Delta[\Gamma] \vdash C} [move_{weak}]$$

This version of move is quite different from the one presented for MG, but is close to one developed for later MG such as [26].

The main difference between MG and MCG comes from *move*: in MCG, constituents do not move but use hypotheses marking their places. MCG uses commutativity properties of mixed logic and see hypotheses as resources. To sum up, the derivation rules of MCG is the following set of rules:

$$\frac{\langle s, A \rangle \in Lex}{\vdash_G (\epsilon, s, \epsilon) : A} \; [Lex] \qquad \frac{\vdash (r_{spec}, r_{head}, r_{comp}) : A \, / \, B \quad \Delta \vdash s : B}{\Delta \vdash (r_{spec}, r_{head}, r_{comp} \bullet Concat(s)) : A} \; [mg]$$

$$\frac{\Delta \vdash s : B \quad \Gamma \vdash (r_{spec}, r_{head}, r_{comp}) : B \setminus A}{\Delta, \Gamma \vdash (Concat(s) \bullet r_{spec}, r_{head}, r_{comp}) : A} \; [mg]$$

$$\frac{\Gamma \vdash r_1 : A \otimes B \quad \Delta[u : A, v : B] \vdash r_2 : C}{\Delta[\Gamma] \vdash r_2[Concat(r_1)/u, \epsilon/v] : C} \; [mv]$$

The set $\mathbb{D}_G$ of recognized derivations by a MCG G is the set of proofs obtained with this set of rules and for which the concluding sequent is $\vdash r : C$. The language generated by G is $L(G) = \{ Concat(r) | \vdash r : C \in \mathbb{D}_G \}$.

These derivations do not formally conserve the projection relation (nor the specifier, head and complement relations). These principles are reintroduced with strings. However, the head of a proof could be seen as the *principal formula* of mixed logic, and then by extension, the maximal projection is the proof for which a formula is the principal one. Specifier and complement are only elements on the right or left of this formula.

An interesting remark is that rules of MCG do not use the introduction rule of the mixed calculus. This way, they only try to combine together formulae extracted from a lexicon and hypotheses. As in MG where a derivation cancels features, the MCG system only consumes hypotheses and always reduces the size of the main formula (only the size of the context could increase). This corresponds to the cognitive fact that we stress the system in the analysis perspective. Introduction rules could be seen as captured by the given lexicon. But, because of the strong structure of the items, we directly associate formulae and strings.

We have presented all the MCG rules and lexicon, and illustrated them with a tiny example which encodes the main properties of this framework.

3 Conclusion

In this article, we propose new definitions of MG based on an algebraic description of trees. These definitions allow to check properties of this framework and moreover give a formal account to analyse links with other frameworks. Then, we give the definitions of MCG, a Type-Theoretic framework for MG. In this framework, *merge* and *move* are simulated by rules of the mixed logic (an extension of Lambek calculus to product and non-commutative connectors). The phonological calculus is added by labelling proofs of this logic.

The main contribution of MCG is certainly its syntax-semantics interface. This calculus is synchronized on proofs of MCG. But more technical details are needed to present this interface and the linguistic properties which it encodes. We delay the presentation of this interface to a future presentation.

Finally, the syntax-semantics interface of MCG should be used under the condition they keep properties of MG. This is the aim of another future article which will present the proof of inclusion of MG generated languages in MCG generated languages. To prove this property, two alternative representations of MG and MCG derivations are introduced: *alternative derived structures* and *split proofs* and the corresponding *merge* and *move*. These structures and rules make the gap between the two kinds of derivations. They need technical details and more space to be presented.

Definitions and proofs could be easily extended to refinements of *merge*: *Affix-Hopping* and *Head-Movement* because these operations derived the same strings in both structures. But we have not included these rules in this presentation. On another hand, the proof of inclusion presented here does not include the SMC. The interpretation of SMC in MCG must be better defined before being included in such perspective. The generative power of these grammars with shortest move condition is still open.

This article is a first step to several perspectives which make a strong link between a well defined framework with many linguistic properties and a new one which captures this framework and proposes a syntax-semantics interface.

Acknowledgements

The author would like to express his deep gratitude to his supervisors Alain Lecomte and Christian Retoré. In particular, discussions with Alain Lecomte was a source of supports and good advices which turn the author to this research.

The author also wants to thank the associated editors and the anonymous reviewers for their constructive remarks and suggestions, and finally Patrick Blackburn and Mathieu Morey for their careful readings.

References

1. Chomsky, N.: The Minimalist Program. MIT Press, Cambridge (1995)
2. Stabler, E.: Derivational minimalism. In: Retoré, C. (ed.) LACL 1996. LNCS (LNAI), vol. 1328, pp. 68–95. Springer, Heidelberg (1997)
3. Amblard, M.: Calcul de représentations sémantiques et suntaxe générative: les grammaires minimalistes catégorielles. Ph.D. thesis, université de Bordeaux 1 (Septembre 2007)
4. Muskens, R.: Language, Lambdas, and Logic. In: Kruijff, G.J., Oehrle, R. (eds.) Resource Sensitivity in Binding and Anaphora. Studies in Linguistics and Philosophy, pp. 23–54. Kluwer, Dordrecht (2003)
5. de Groote, P.: Towards abstract categorial grammars. Association for Computational Linguistics. In: Proceedings of the Conference on 39th Annual Meeting and 10th Conference of the European Chapter, Proceedings of the Conference (2001)
6. Mansfield, L., Martin, S., Pollard, C., Worth, C.: Phenogrammatical labelling in convergent grammar: the case of wrap (2009) (unpublished)
7. Berwick, R., Epstein, S.: On the convergence of 'minimalist' syntax and categorial grammars (1996)
8. Retoré, C., Stabler, E.: Reseach on Language and Computation, vol. 2(1). Christian Retoré and Edward Stabler (2004)

9. Lecomte, A.: Rebuilding the minimalist program on a logical ground. Journal of Research on Language and Computation 2(1), 27–55 (2004)
10. Cornell, T.: Lambek calculus for transformational grammars. Journal of Research on Language and Computation 2(1), 105–126 (2004)
11. Lecomte, A., Retoré, C.: Towards a logic for minimalist. In: Formal Grammar (1999)
12. Lecomte, A., Retoré, C.: Extending Lambek grammars: a logical account of minimalist grammars. In: Proceedings of the 39th Annual Meeting of the Association for Computational Linguistics, ACL 2001, pp. 354–361. ACL, Toulouse (2001), http://www.labri.fr/perso/retore
13. Lecomte, A.: Categorial grammar for minimalism. In: Language and Grammar: Studies in Mathematical Linguistics and Natural Language CSLI Lecture Notes, vol. (168), pp. 163–188 (2005)
14. Amblard, M., Lecomte, A., Retoré, C.: Syntax and semantics interacting in a minimalist theory. In: Prospect and Advance in the Syntax/Semantic Interface, pp. 17–22 (October 2003)
15. Amblard, M., Lecomte, A., Retoré, C.: Synchronization syntax semantic for a minimalism theory. Journée Sémantique et Modélisation (Mars 2004)
16. Huet, G.P.: The zipper. J. Funct. Program 7(5), 549–554 (1997)
17. Levy, J.J., Cori, R.: Algorithmes et Programmation. Ecole Polytechnique
18. Chomsky, N.: Conditions on transformations. In: Kiparsky, S.A.P. (ed.) A Festschrift for Morris Halle, pp. 232–286. Holt, Rinehart and Winston (1973)
19. Vermaat, W.: Controlling movement: Minimalism in a deductive perspective. Master's thesis, Universiteit Utrecht (1999)
20. Stabler, E.: Remnant movement and structural complexity. In: Constraints and Resources in Natural Language Syntax and Semantics pp. 299–326 (1999)
21. Koopman, H., Szabolcsi, A.: A verbal Complex. MIT Press, Cambridge (2000)
22. Kayne, R.S.: Overt vs covert movment. Syntax 1,2, 128–191 (1998)
23. Howard, W.A.: The formulae-as-types notion of construction. In: Hindley, J., Seldin, J. (eds.) To H.B. Curry: Essays on Combinatory Logic, λ-calculus and Formalism, pp. 479–490. Academic Press, London (1980)
24. de Groote, P.: Partially commutative linear logic: sequent calculus and phase semantics. In: Abrusci, V.M., Casadio, C. (eds.) Third Roma Workshop: Proofs and Linguistics Categories – Applications of Logic to the Analysis and Implementation of Natural Language, pp. 199–208. CLUEB, Bologna (1996)
25. Amblard, M., Retore, C.: Natural deduction and normalisation for partially commutative linear logic and lambek calculus with product. In: Computation and Logic in the Real World, CiE 2007 Quaderni del Dipartimento di Scienze Matematiche e Informatiche "Roberto Magari" (June 2007))
26. Kobele, G.: Generating Copies: An Investigation into Structural Identity in Language and Grammar. Ph.D. thesis, University of California, Los Angeles (2006)

Minimalist Grammars in the Light of Logic

Sylvain Salvati

INRIA Bordeaux-Sud Ouest
salvati@labri.fr

Abstract. In this paper, we aim at understanding the derivations of minimalist grammars without the shortest move constraint. This leads us to study the relationship of those derivations with logic. In particular we show that the membership problem of minimalist grammars without the shortest move constraint is as difficult as provability in Multiplicative Exponential Linear Logic. As a byproduct, this result gives us a new representation of those derivations with linear λ-terms. We show how to interpret those terms in a homomorphic way so as to recover the sentence they analyse. As the homorphisms we describe are rather evolved, we turn to a proof-net representation and explain how Monadic Second Order Logic and related techniques allow us both to define those proof-nets and to retrieve the sentence they analyse.

Since Stabler defined Minimalist Grammars[1] (MGs) as a mathematical account of Chomsky's minimalist program, an important effort of research has been dedicated to give a logical account of them. MGs use a feature checking system which guides the derivations and as those features behave similarly to resources, it seemed possible to represent those derivations in some substructural logic. There have been a lot of propositions (among others [1], [2], [3], [4], [5]), but we do not think that any of them establishes a relation between MGs and logic in a satisfactory way. These propositions are, in most cases, describing a way of building proofs in a certain logic so as to describe minimalist derivations. But they cannot be considered as a logical account of minimalist derivations since they use extra and non-logical constraints that rule out proofs that would not represent a minimalist derivation. Those propositions solve nevertheless some problem that is inherent to Stabler's formalism. Indeed, in Stabler's formalism, the derivations are ambiguous in the sense that they can be interpreted into different sentences that have different meanings. Thus when dealing with semantic interpretations, one needs to interpret derivations both syntactically and semantically so as to build the syntax/semantic relation.

In the present paper, we give a logical account of minimalist grammars as proofs in Multiplicative Exponential Linear Logic (MELL) [6]. We claim that this account is *accurate* and *of logical nature* for two reasons; first, because we prove that the membership problem for minimalist grammars is Turing-equivalent to provability in MELL; second, we define minimalist derivations as being all the

---

[1] Across the paper, unless stated otherwise, when we refer to Minimalist Grammars, we are referring to Stabler's Minimalist Grammars **without** the Shortest Move Constraint.

S. Pogodalla, M. Quatrini, and C. Retoré (Eds.): Lecomte Festschrift, LNAI 6700, pp. 81–117, 2011.
© Springer-Verlag Berlin Heidelberg 2011

proofs of a particular sequent (in the article we actually give the equivalent presentation in terms of closed linear λ-terms of a certain type). Nevertheless, even though linear logic is dealing with resources, in our approach, linear logic is not modeling the fact that features are treated as resources in MGs. While this is somehow a defect of our approach, it shows that MGs' derivations are dealing with other kinds of resources that we call *moving pieces*, but which correspond to the linguistic notion of *traces*.

The idea that has motivated this work is an idea that is not so wide-spread in the community of computational linguistics. It consists in making a clear distinction between derivations and surface realisations. This idea can be traced back to Curry [7], but is very common in compiling and has been recently reintroduced in computational linguistics by the works of Muskens [8] and de Groote [9]. So we start thinking about Minimalist Grammars only from the point of view of their derivations, trying to find a good representation and to understand how to build them. We continue by studying how to retrieve the surface form, or the string, that the derivation is analyzing. This step is harder than one would expect, but it also shows an interesting feature. Indeed, we have not been able to find a way to interpret our derivations without the use of a context which is quite similar to the context that de Groote proposes for semantics [10]. Finally since, so as to find a more satisfactory way of reading sentences out of derivations, we turn to Formal Language Theory and use techniques related to Monadic Second Order Logic (MSO). This leads us to a fairly simple account of both the structure of derivations and the way of interpreting them.

The paper is organized as follows. In Sect. 1 we introduce linear λ-calculus and minimalist grammars. We show that the languages defined by minimalist grammars are closed under intersection with recognizable sets. This allows us to prove the Turing-equivalence of the emptiness problem and of the membership problem for MGs. In Sect. 2 we show that the emptiness problem for MGs is Turing-equivalent to provability in MELL. We proceed in two steps, first we show that the emptiness problem for a particular class of automata, k-VATA, can be reduced to the emptiness problem for MGs. As the emptiness problem for k-VATA is as difficult as provability in MELL, this reduces provability in MELL to the emptiness of MGs. Second, we show an encoding of minimalist derivations as linear λ-terms and we study some consequences of that encoding. Section 3 shows how the representation of minimalist derivations as linear λ-terms can be interpreted into sentences and the limitations of this interpretation. Then Sect. 4, tries to overcome those limitations with Monadic Second Order Logic. Section 5 gives some conclusions on this work.

1   Preliminaries

In this section we introduce two technical notions the linear λ-calculus and minimalist grammars. The λ-calculus has been introduced so as to define a theory of functions. But it captures the notion of binding and has therefore been extensively used in formal semantics of natural languages. For the syntax of natural languages the linear λ-calculus can be seen as a representation of deduction of type logical grammars via the Curry-Howard isomorphism. A more explicit and systematic use of the linear λ-calculus in syntax is proposed by the Abstract Categorial Grammars [9] and the λ-grammars [8]. The interest of linear λ-calculus in modeling syntax is that it naturally extends the notion of syntactic tree by providing it with the possibility of representing *traces* with linear λ-abstraction. So even though there seems *a priori* to be very little relationships between minimalist grammars and linear λ-calculus, they can at least be related by the fact that traces occupy a central position in minimalist grammars and that linear λ-calculus offers the possibility to represent traces.

1.1 Linear λ-Calculus

We now present the linear λ-calculus. Linear types are built from a given finite set of atoms A by using the infix operator $\multimap$. The set of types built from A, $\mathcal{T}_{\multimap}(A)$, is constructed according to the following grammar:

$$\mathcal{T}_{\multimap}(A) ::= A | (\mathcal{T} \multimap \mathcal{T})$$

We adopt the convention that $\multimap$ associates to the right and that $\alpha_1 \multimap \cdots \multimap \alpha_n \multimap \beta$ represents the type $(\alpha_1 \multimap \cdots (\alpha_n \multimap \beta) \cdots)$. As usual $ord(\alpha)$, the order of a simple type α of $\mathcal{T}_{\multimap}(A)$, is defined to be 1 when α is atomic (*i.e.* α is an element of A), and $\max(ord(\alpha_1) + 1, ord(\alpha_2))$ when $\alpha = \alpha_1 \multimap \alpha_2$.

A higher order signature Σ, is a triple (A, C, τ) where A is a finite set of atoms, C is a finite set of constants and τ is a function from C to $\mathcal{T}_{\multimap}(A)$. A signature is said of nth order if $\max_{c \in C}(ord(\tau(c)) \leq n$. We use a type system *à la Church*, which means that variables explicitly carry their types. We adopt the notation x^α, to specify that x is a variable of type α. The family $(\Lambda^\alpha_\Sigma)_{\alpha \in \mathcal{T}_{\multimap}(A)}$ is defined by:

1. $c \in \Lambda^{\tau(c)}_\Sigma$ when $c \in C$,
2. $x^\alpha \in \Lambda^\alpha_\Sigma$,
3. $(t_1 t_2) \in \Lambda^\alpha_\Sigma$ if $t_1 \in \Lambda^{\beta \multimap \alpha}_\Sigma$, $t_2 \in \Lambda^\beta_\Sigma$ and $FV(t_1) \cap FV(t_2) = \emptyset$,
4. $\lambda x^\beta.t \in \Lambda^{\alpha \multimap \beta}_\Sigma$ if $t \in \Lambda^\beta_\Sigma$ and $x^\beta \in FV(t)$.

where $FV(t)$ is the set of free variables (defined as usual) of t. The λ-terms that are in Λ^α_Σ are said *linear*, because a variable may at most have one free occurrence in a term and because every bound variable has exactly one free occurrence below the λ that binds it.

When they are not relevant or when they can easily be infered from the context, we will omit the typing annotations on the variables. We also use the convention that $t_0 t_1 \ldots t_n$ denotes the term $(\cdots (t_0 t_1) \cdots t_n)$ and that $\lambda x_1 \ldots x_n.t$ denotes the term $\lambda x_1. \ldots \lambda x_n.t$. We take for granted the notions of α-conversion, β-contraction and η-contraction. We always consider λ-terms up to α-convertibility, and we respectively write (with $\gamma \in \{\beta; \eta; \beta\eta\}$) $\to_\gamma$, $\overset{*}{\to}_\gamma$, $=_\gamma$, the relation of γ-contraction, γ-reduction and γ-conversion. A term is *closed* when its set of free variables is empty.

Contexts are λ-terms with a hole which are written $C[]$. The operation of grafting a term N in the hole of a context $C[]$ is written $C[N]$. For example, if $C[] = \lambda x.[]$ and $N = x$ then $C[N] = \lambda x.x$.

The linear λ-calculus is a conservative extension of the notion of ranked trees. A signature $\Sigma = \langle A, C, \tau \rangle$ is said to be a *tree signature* when $A = \{o\}$ and for all $c \in C$, $\tau(c)$ is of the form $o \multimap \cdots \multimap o \multimap o$. We will in general write $o^n \multimap o$ for the type $\underbrace{o \multimap \cdots \multimap o}_{n \times} \multimap o$ (when $n = 0$, $o^n \multimap o$ simply denotes o). Trees are then denoted in the obvious way by closed linear λ-terms of type o in normal form. Tree signatures may also be called *ranked alphabets*. We may denote with $\Sigma^{(n)}$ the set of constants declared in Σ which have type $o^n \multimap o$. If $\Sigma_1 = \langle \{o\}, C_1, \tau_1 \rangle$ and $\Sigma_2 = \langle \{o\}, C_2, \tau_2 \rangle$ are two ranked alphabet such that $C_1 \cap C_2 = \emptyset$ we write $\Sigma_1 \cup \Sigma_2$ to refer to the ranked alphabet $\langle \{o\}, C_1 \cup C_2, \tau_1 \cup \tau_2 \rangle$. A *multi-sorted tree signature* or a *multi-sorted ranked alphabet* is simply a second order signature. When we deal with ranked trees, we assume that they are represented by linear λ-terms in normal form and we represent a subtree of a tree t as a pair $(C[], v)$ such that $C[v] = t$.

1.2   Minimalist Grammars

A *minimalist grammar* G is a tuple (V, B, F, C, c) where V is a finite set of *words*, B is a finite set of *selection features*, F is a finite set of *licensing features*, C is a *lexicon* (a finite set of *lexical entries* that are defined below) and $c \in B$. Features are used in two different forms, a positive form and a negative form. The positive form of a selection feature b (*resp.* licensing feature f) is denoted by $=b$ (*resp.* $+f$) while its negative form is denoted by b (*resp.* $-f$). The set of positive (*resp.* negative) features of G will be denoted by B^+ and F^+ (*resp.* B^- and F^-).

The elements of C, the *lexical entries*, are pairs (v, l) where $v \in V \cup \{\epsilon\}$ and l is a string built using symbols taken from $B^- \cup B^+ \cup F^- \cup F^+$. These strings are not arbitrary, they have a special structure, they are of the form $l_1 a l_2$ where:

1. $a \in B^-$,
2. l_1 is a string (possibly empty) of elements taken from $B^+ \cup F^+$ and which must start by an element of B^+ when it is not empty,
3. l_2 is a string (possibly empty) of elements taken only from F^-.

The set of *feature suffixes* of G is the set $\mathrm{Suff}(G) = \{l_2 | \exists (v, l_1 l_2) \in C\}$, the set of *moving suffixes* of G is the set $\mathrm{Move}(G) = \{l \in \mathrm{Suff}(G) | l \in (F^-)^*\}$. A *lexical construction* is a pair (w, l) such that $w \in V^*$ and $l \in \mathrm{Suff}(G)$; a *moving piece* is a lexical construction (w, l) such that $l \in \mathrm{Move}(G)$.

The *derivations* of minimalist grammars G are defined on a tree signature of the form: $\mathrm{Der}(G) = (\{o\}, \{\mathbf{merge}; \mathbf{move}\} \cup C, \rho)$ where $\rho(\mathbf{merge}) = o \multimap o \multimap o$, $\rho(\mathbf{move}) = o \multimap o$ and $\rho(c) = o$ when $c \in C$. The set of trees that can be built on $\mathrm{Der}(G)$ will be written $d(G)$.

In order to produce the strings that derivations are representing, we use a transformation $\mathcal{H}$ that interprets the elements of $d(G)$ as pairs $\langle s, L \rangle$ where:

1. s is a lexical construction, *the head* of the derivation, and,
2. L is a finite multiset of moving pieces.

We consider multisets built on a set A as functions from A to $\mathbb{N}$. Such a multiset L is said finite when $\sum_{a \in A} L(a)$ is finite. Given a and a multiset L we say that a has $L(a)$ occurrences in L. We will confuse a and the multiset L_a which contains one occurrence of a and no occurrence of elements different from a. We write $\emptyset$ to denote the multiset which contains no occurrence of any element. Given two multisets L_1 and L_2 we write $L_1 \cup L_2$ the multiset such that $(L_1 \cup L_2)(a) = L_1(a) + L_2(a)$. We may represent finite multisets L with a *list* notation $[e_1, \ldots, e_n]$, with the understanding that for each a there is exactly $L(a)$ e_i that are equal to a . The fact that we use multisets of moving pieces is a first hint for understanding the relation between MGs and MELL. Indeed, contexts of hypotheses in MELL are best represented as multisets of formulae.

The transformation $\mathcal{H}$ is defined as follows:

1. $\mathcal{H}(\mathbf{merge}\, t_1\, t_2) = \langle (w_2, l_2), (w_1, l_1) \cup L_1 \cup L_2 \rangle$ if $\mathcal{H}(t_1) = \langle (w_1, al_1), L_1 \rangle$, l_1 is not empty and $\mathcal{H}(t_2) = \langle (w_2, =al_2), L_2 \rangle$,
2. $\mathcal{H}(\mathbf{merge}\, t_1\, t_2) = \langle (w_1 w_2, l_2), L_1 \cup L_2 \rangle$ if $\mathcal{H}(t_1) = \langle (w_1, a), L_1 \rangle$, $\mathcal{H}(t_2) = \langle (w_2, =al_2), L_2 \rangle$ and t_2 is not an element of C
3. $\mathcal{H}(\mathbf{merge}\, t_1\, t_2) = \langle (w_2 w_1, l_2), L_1 \cup L_2 \rangle$ if $\mathcal{H}(t_1) = \langle (w_1, a), L_1 \rangle$, $\mathcal{H}(t_2) = \langle (w_2, =al_2), L_2 \rangle$ and t_2 is an element of C
4. let's assume $\mathcal{H}(t_1) = \langle (w, +al), (w', -al') \cup L \rangle$ then,

$$\mathcal{H}(\mathbf{move}\, t_1) = \begin{cases} \langle (w, l), (w', l') \cup L \rangle \text{ when } l' \text{ is not empty} \\ \langle (w'w, l), L \rangle \text{ otherwise} \end{cases}$$

5. in the other cases $\mathcal{H}(t)$ is undefined.

In this way G defines two languages:

1. the language of its derivations $\mathcal{D}(G) = \{t \,|\, \mathcal{H}(t) = \langle (w, c), \emptyset \rangle\}$,
2. the string language $\mathcal{L}(G) = \{w \in V^* \,|\, \exists t. \mathcal{H}(t) = \langle (w, c), \emptyset \rangle\}$

Example 1. In the course of this paper, we will use an example adapted from [11] with a grammar using the following lexical entries:

$$(\text{Maria}, d - \text{case}), (\text{speak}, =d\, =d\, v), (\text{will}, =v\, +\text{case}\, c), (\text{Nahuatl}, d)$$

With this grammar we can give an analysis of the sentence *Maria will speak Nahuatl* with the derivation t that is represented by the following term:

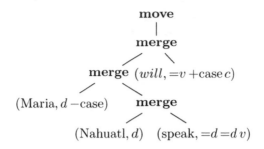

We here give the details of the computation of $\mathcal{H}(t)$:

1. let $u_1 = \mathbf{merge}\,(\text{Nahuatl}, d)(\text{speak}, =d=d\,v)$ then (case 3 of the definition)

$$\mathcal{H}(u_1) = \langle(\text{speak Nahuatl}, =d\,v), \emptyset\rangle$$

2. let now $u_2 = \mathbf{merge}\,(\text{Maria}, d-\text{case})\,u_1$ we have that (case 1 in the definition)

$$\mathcal{H}(u_2) = \langle(\text{speak Nahuatl}, v), [(\text{Maria}, -\text{case})]\rangle$$

3. let $u_3 = \mathbf{merge}\,u_2\,(will, =v+\text{case}\,c)$ and then (case 2 of the definition)

$$\mathcal{H}(u_3) = \langle(\text{will speak Nahuatl}, +case\,c), [(\text{Maria}, -\text{case})]\rangle$$

4. finally (case 4 of the definition) $\mathcal{H}(t) = \langle(\text{Maria will speak Nahuatl}, c), \emptyset\rangle$

An element t from $d(G)$ is said to satisfy the Shortest Move Constraint (SMC) if $\mathcal{H}(t)$ is defined and is of the form $\langle s, L\rangle$ where for each licensing feature f of G there is at most one occurrence in L of a moving piece of the form $(w, -fl)$. A term t is said to hereditarily satisfy the SMC when t and each of its subterm satisfy the SMC (we write that t is HSMC).

With the SMC, G defines two languages:

1. the language of its SMC-derivations $\mathcal{D}_{SMC}(G) = \{t|\mathcal{H}(t) = \langle(w, c), \emptyset\rangle$ and t is HSMC$\}$,
2. the string SMC-language $\mathcal{L}_{SMC}(G) = \{w \in W^*|\exists t \in \mathcal{D}_{SMC}(G).\mathcal{H}(t) = \langle(w, c), \emptyset\rangle\}$

In the general case (with derivations that do not satisfy the SMC), the mapping $\mathcal{H}$ cannot be seen as a homomorphism. Indeed, the interpretations of **merge** or **move** via $\mathcal{H}$ lead to functions which have to inspect their arguments in order to possibly compute a result. Moreover, the interpretation of **move** is not deterministic, since one can pick any element in the multiset of moving pieces which exhibits the required feature. There would be an easy way of turning $\mathcal{H}$ into a homomorphism, simply by:

- distinguishing the domains in which elements of $\mathcal{C}$ and complex expressions are interpreted by $\mathcal{H}$
- interpreting the term t as the set of pairs $\langle s, L\rangle$ in which $\mathcal{H}$ can interpret t

But, this technique does not help to grasp any interesting criterion, apart from the actual computation, that allows to understand in which cases $\mathcal{H}(t)$ gives an actual result. Thus this presentation of minimalist grammars does not give a satisfactory account of the mathematical nature of the derivations and can be seen as an algorithm that computes derived structures. Another reason why this technique of turning $\mathcal{H}$ into a homomorphism is not worthwhile is that in general minimalist grammars are not only concerned with syntax but also with the interface between syntax and semantics. And when $\mathcal{H}(t)$ outputs several results, these results should in general be put in relation with different semantic representations. Therefore, derivation terms do not determine completely the relation between syntax and semantics, this relation really depends on the actual computation $\mathcal{H}$ is doing on the terms. So that understanding the mathematical nature of the derivations of minimalist grammars should lead to the definition of derivations on which it would be both possible to check easily whether they denote a correct syntactic object and to relate this syntactic object uniquely to some semantic representation.

Example 2. We here give an artificial example of an ambiguous derivation. We use a grammar with the following lexical entries:

$$(\alpha, =a_1=a_2b), (\beta, =b+c+c+cb), (\gamma_1, =da_1-c-c), (\gamma_2, a_2-c), (\delta, d)$$

and we build the derivation t represented by the term:

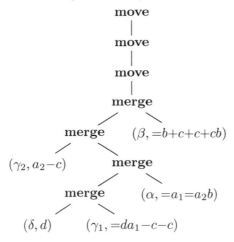

We can now compute the possible values of $\mathcal{H}(t)$:

1. let $u_1 = $ **merge**(**merge**$(\delta, d)(\gamma_1, =da_1-c-c))(\alpha, =a_1=a_2b)$ then $\mathcal{H}(u_1) = \langle(\alpha, =a_2b), [\gamma_1\delta, -c-c)]\rangle$,
2. let $u_2 = $ **merge** (**merge** (γ_2, a_2-c-c) (u_1)) $(\beta, =b+c+c+cb)$, we easily obtain that
$$\mathcal{H}(u_2) = \langle(\beta\alpha, +c+c+cb), [(\gamma_1\delta, -c-c), (\gamma_2, -c)]\rangle$$
3. let $u_3 = $ **move**(u_2) then we have two possible results for $\mathcal{H}(u_3)$:
$$\langle(\beta\alpha, +c+cb), [(\gamma_1\delta, -c), (\gamma_2, -c)]\rangle \text{ and } \langle(\gamma_2\beta\alpha, +c+cb), [(\gamma_1\delta, -c-c)]\rangle$$

4. let $u_4 = \mathbf{move}(u_3)$, there are two possible results for $\mathcal{H}(u_4)$:

$$\langle(\gamma_1\delta\beta\alpha, +cb), [(\gamma_2, -c)]\rangle \text{ and } \langle(\gamma_2\beta\alpha, +cb), [(\gamma_1\delta, -c)]\rangle$$

5. finally there are two possible results for $\mathcal{H}(t)$:

$$\langle(\gamma_2\gamma_1\delta\beta\alpha, b), \emptyset\rangle \text{ and } \langle(\gamma_1\delta\gamma_2\beta\alpha, b), \emptyset\rangle$$

We now show that the emptiness problem for minimalist grammars is Turing-equivalent to the membership problem. First, the emptiness problem can be reduced to the membership problem simply by replacing every element (v, l) in C by (ϵ, l), it is then trivial to check that the emptiness problem of the former grammar is equivalent to the membership of ϵ to the language of the new grammar. We can then state that:

Lemma 1. *If one can decide whether a sentense s belongs to the language of a minimalist grammar G then one can decide whether the language of a minimalist grammar is empty.*

In order to prove the converse property we show that the class of languages that can be defined with minimalist grammars is closed under intersection with recognizable sets of strings.

Lemma 2. *Given a minimalist grammar $G = (V, B, F, C, c)$ and a regular set of strings $Reg \subseteq V^*$, then there is a minimalist grammar G' whose language is the intersection of the language defined by G and Reg.*

Proof. Let us suppose that Reg is recognized by the following deterministic finite state automaton $\mathcal{A} = (V, Q, \delta, q_{\text{init}}, Q_f)$ where δ is the transition function from $V \times Q$ to Q (we make the confusion between δ and its homomorphic extension to the free monoid V^*, *i.e.* we consider that $\delta(\epsilon, q) = q$ and that, for w from V^*, $\delta(w, q)$ is the state that the automaton reaches when reading w from state q), $q_{\text{init}} \in Q$ is the initial state and $Q_f \subseteq Q$ is the set of final states.

We define $G' = (V, \{d\} \cup B', F', C', d)$ with $B' = B \times Q \times Q$, $F' = F \times Q \times Q$ and d not in $B'^- \cup B'^+ \cup F'^- \cup F'^+$. We let

$$C' = \{(\epsilon, =(c, q_{\text{init}}, q)d) | q \in Q_f\} \cup \bigcup_{(v,l)\in C} \varphi(v, l).$$

where $\varphi(v, l)$ is defined as follows[2]:

1. l is of the form $=b\epsilon_1 b_1 \ldots \epsilon_k b_k a - h_1 \ldots -h_{n+1}$ then we will have

$$\begin{aligned}\varphi(v, l) = \{(v, =(b, q_0, q)\epsilon_1(b_1, q_2, q_1)\ldots\epsilon_k(b_k, q_{k+1}, q_k)(a, q'_0, q'_0) \\ -(h_1, q'_1, q_1)\ldots-(h_n, q'_n, q'_n)-(h_{n+1}, q_{k+1}, q))| \\ q, q_0, \ldots, q_{k+1}, q'_0, \ldots q'_n \in Q \wedge \delta(v, q_1) = q_0\}\end{aligned}$$

---

[2] In the definition of φ, we adopt the convention that ϵ_i is $=$ when b_i is in B and $+$ when b_i is in F.

2. l is of the form $=b\epsilon_1 b_1 \ldots \epsilon_k b_k a$ then we will have

$$\varphi(v, l) = \{(v, =(b, q_0, q)\epsilon_1(b_1, q_2, q_1) \ldots \epsilon_k(b_k, q_{k+1}, q_k)a(q_{k+1}, q))| \\ q, q_0, \ldots, q_{k+1} \in Q \wedge \delta(v, q_1) = q_0\}$$

3. l is of the form $a - h_1 \ldots - h_{n+1}$ the we let:

$$\varphi(v, l) = \{(v, (a, q_0', q_0')-(h_1, q_1', q_1') \ldots -(h_n, q_n', q_n')-(h_{n+1}, q_1, q_0))| \\ q_0, q_1, q_0', \ldots, q_n' \in Q \wedge \delta(v, q_1) = q_0\}$$

4. l is of the form a then we let:

$$\varphi(v, l) = \{(v, (a, q_1, q_0))|q_0, q_1 \in Q \wedge \delta(v, q_1) = q_0\}$$

We here give an rough explanation about the definition $\varphi(v, l)$. If we look at a lexical entry produced as in the first case of that definition, it will be used to build a lexical construction of the form

$$\langle(w_k w_{k-1} \ldots w_1 v w_0, (a, q_0', q_0')-(h_1, q_1', q_1') \ldots -(h_n, q_n', q_n')-(h_{n+1}, q_k, q)), M\rangle$$

where the word w_0 (possibly the empty string) comes from the lexical construction to which the lexical entry is first merged and the w_i (possibly empty strings) are the words that are put in front of the lexical construction through successive **merge** and **move** operations. The construction we give guaranties that $\delta(w_i, q_{i+1}) = q_i$ when $i > 0$ and $\delta(w_0, q_0) = q$ so that, knowing that $\delta(v, q_1) = q_0$, we have that $\delta(w_k w_{k-1} \ldots w_1 v w_0, q_{k+1}) = q$. This can help to understand how the states are related to each other in the positive part of the list of features of the lexical entry. Afterwards, this lexical construction can be merged and then moved several times in another lexical construction leaving the head of this construction unchanged until the final **move** operation. Thus in the negative part of the list of features, the first negative features just contain pairs of identical states because they correspond the fact that the head of the lexical construction in which it is a moving piece is left unchanged. Then, when the last **move** operation happens, the string $w_k w_{k-1} \ldots w_1 v w_0$ will be put in front of the head and the fact that when reading it the automaton goes from state q_k to state q must be consistently used.

Let's now follow this intuition and turn to a sketch of a proof that $\mathcal{L}(G')$ is equal to $\mathcal{L}(G) \cap Reg$.

In each of the cases of the definition $\varphi(v, l)$, if s is in $\varphi(v, l)$ (we suppose that s is written as in the cases defining the set $\varphi(v, l)$) then we write $range(s)$ for the pair of states (q_1, q_0).

Given a list of features l from $\mathrm{Suff}(G')$ we define $rg(l)$ as follows[3]:

1. if l starts with a positive feature and $l = \epsilon(b, q, q_1)l'\epsilon'(f, q', q_0)$ (l' being a list of features and $\epsilon'(f, q', q_0)$ a negative feature), then $rg(l) = (q_1, q_0)$

_____

[3] We adopt the convention that ϵ is either $=$ or $+$ and ϵ' is either $-$ or empty (when the feature $\epsilon'b$ is a negative base feature).

2. if l does not start with a positive feature, then $l = l'\epsilon'(f, q_1, q_0)$ and $rg(l) = (q_1, q_0)$.

Given an element t of $\text{Der}(G')$, such that $\mathcal{H}(t) = \langle (w, l), M \rangle$ we write range(t) for the pair of states defined as follows:

1. if t is of the form s where s is in C' then range$(t) = range(s)$,
2. otherwise range$(t) = rg(l)$.

For a list of features l of G', we write $\bar{l}$ for the list of features of G such that $\epsilon(b, q, q')l' = \epsilon b \bar{l'}$.

An easy induction on t' in $d(G')$ proves that if the following properties are verified:

1. $\mathcal{H}(t') = \langle (w, l), [(w_1, l_1), \dots, (w_n, l_n)] \rangle$, and
2. range$(t') = (q, q')$, $rg(l_1) = (q_1, q_1')$, $\dots$, $rg(l_n) = (q_n, q_n')$

then we have:

1. $\delta(w, q) = q'$, $\delta(w_1, q_1) = q_1'$, $\dots$, $\delta(w_n, q_n) = q_n'$,
2. there is t in $d(G)$ such that $\mathcal{H}(t) = \langle (w, \bar{l}), [(w_1, \bar{l_1}), \dots, (w_n, \bar{l_n})] \rangle$.

Another simple induction on t in $d(G)$ shows that whenever

$$\mathcal{H}(t) = \langle (w, l), [(w_1, l_1), \dots, (w_n, l_n)] \rangle$$

then for every pairs of states (q, q'), (q_1, q_1'), $\dots$, (q_n, q_n') such that $\delta(w, q) = q'$, $\delta(w_1, q_1) = q_1'$, $\dots$, $\delta(w_n, q_n) = q_n'$ and every l', l_1', $\dots$, l_n' from $\text{Suff}(G')$, such that range$(l') = (q, q')$ and $\bar{l'} = l$, range$(l_1') = (q_1, q_1')$ and $\bar{l_1'} = l_1$, $\dots$, range$(l_n') = (q_n, q_n')$ and $\bar{l_n'} = l_n$ there is t' in $d(G')$ such that $\mathcal{H}(t') = \langle (w, l'), [(w_1, l_1'), \dots, (w_n, l_n')] \rangle$.

These two properties have the consequence that a term t' from $d(G')$ verifies $\mathcal{H}(t') = \langle (w, (c, q_{\text{init}}, q_f)), \emptyset \rangle$ with q_f in Q_f if and only if w is in $\mathcal{L}(G) \cap Reg$. Thus a sentence w is in $\mathcal{L}(G')$ (i.e. there is t' in $d(G)$ such that $\mathcal{H}(t') = \langle (w, d), \emptyset \rangle$) if and only if w is in $\mathcal{L}(G) \cap Reg$.

Thus the class of languages defined by minimalist grammars is closed under intersection with regular sets.

Note that this proof gives an actual construction of G' and has therefore the next lemma as a consequence.

Lemma 3. *If the emptiness problem for minimalist grammars is decidable then the membership problem for those grammars is decidable.*

Proof. If we want to know whether w belongs to the language defined by G, since $\{w\}$ is a regular set, we construct G' the minimalist grammar whose language is the intersection of the language of G and of $\{w\}$. The language of G' is empty if and only if w belongs to the language defined by G.

Theorem 1. *The emptiness problem and the membership problem for minimalist grammars are Turing-equivalent.*

2   Minimalist Grammars and MELL

We are now going to show that provability in MELL is Turing-equivalent to the emptiness problem for minimalist grammars. We prove each direction of the equivalence separately.

First we reduce the provability in MELL to the emptiness of MGs. For this purpose we use a class of tree automata, k-VATA, introduced in [12], and which generalizes the notion of Vector Addition Systems (VAS) which are equivalent to Petri nets. It is proved in [12] that the decidability of the emptiness problem for k-VATA is equivalent to the decidability of the provability of sequents in MELL.

Second we show how to represent derivations in MGs as linear λ-terms built over a certain signature. It is well-known [12] that deciding provability in MELL is equivalent to deciding the existence of such linear λ-terms.

2.1   Emptiness of k-VATAs Reduced to Emptiness of MGs

A k-VATA is a tuple (Σ, Q, δ, C_f) where:

1. Σ is a tree signature,
2. Q is a finite set of states,
3. δ is a finite set of rules of the form:

$$f(q_1, \mathbf{x}_1) \ldots (q_n, \mathbf{x}_n) \longrightarrow \left(q, \sum_{i \in 1}^{n} (\mathbf{x}_i - \mathbf{z}_i) + \mathbf{z} \right)$$

   where f is a constant of Σ and $\mathbf{x}_i$ are variables and $\mathbf{z}_i$ and $\mathbf{z}$ are elements of $\mathbb{N}^k$.
4. C_f is a finite subset of $Q \times \mathbb{N}^k$, the *accepting configurations*

For a k-VATA, a configuration is an element of $Q \times \mathbb{N}^k$, a k-VATA is rewriting terms built on the tree signature Σ and that can have as leaves configurations. Thus given a rule of the considered k-VATA, a tree t which is equal to $C[f(q_1, \mathbf{p}_1) \ldots (q_n, \mathbf{p}_n)]$ and a rule

$$f(q_1, \mathbf{x}_1) \ldots (q_n, \mathbf{x}_n) \longrightarrow \left(q, \sum_{i=1}^{n} (\mathbf{x}_i - \mathbf{z}_i) + \mathbf{z} \right)$$

then it rewrites t to $t' = C[(q, \sum_{i=1}^{n} (\mathbf{p}_i - \mathbf{z}_i) + \mathbf{z})]$ provided that for all i in $[1; n]$, $\mathbf{p}_i - \mathbf{z}_i$ is an element of $\mathbb{N}^k$. In such a case, we write $t \longrightarrow_{\mathcal{A}} t'$ and $\xrightarrow{*}_{\mathcal{A}}$ denotes the reflexive and transitive closure of $\longrightarrow_{\mathcal{A}}$. The language of a k-VATA $\mathcal{A} = (\Sigma, Q, \delta, C_f)$ is the set $\mathcal{L}(\mathcal{A}) = \{ t \in \mathcal{T}(\Sigma) | t \xrightarrow{*}_{\mathcal{A}} (q, \mathbf{p}) \wedge (q, \mathbf{p}) \in C_f \}$.

For a given k, we write 0 (*resp.* $\mathbf{e}_i$) to denote the element of $\mathbb{N}^k$ whose components are all zero (*resp.* except the ith which is 1). A k-VATA is in *normal form* if it has only one accepting configuration which is of the form $(q, 0)$ and if all its rules are in one of the following form:

1. $c \longrightarrow (q, \mathbf{e}_i)$ for some i in $[1; k]$,
2. $f(q_0, \mathbf{x}) \longrightarrow (q, \mathbf{x} - \mathbf{e}_i)$ for some i in $[1; k]$,
3. $f((q_1, \mathbf{x}_1), (q_2, \mathbf{x}_2)) \longrightarrow (q, \mathbf{x}_1 + \mathbf{x}_2)$

As it is showed in [12], the emptiness problem for k-VATA in normal form is as difficult as for general k-VATA. Furthermore, the theorem is proved by giving an effective construction.

Theorem 2. *Given a k-VATA $\mathcal{A}$, there is a k-VATA $\mathcal{B}$ in normal form such that $\mathcal{L}(\mathcal{A})$ is empty if and only if $\mathcal{L}(\mathcal{B})$ is empty.*

We can now reduce the emptiness problem of a k-VATA in normal form to the emptiness of a minimalist grammar. Suppose that we are given a k-VATA in normal form $\mathcal{A} = (\Sigma, Q, \delta, \{(q_f, 0)\})$, we construct the following MG $G_{\mathcal{A}} = (\emptyset, Q, [1; k], C, q_f)$ where C contains the following entries:

- $(\epsilon, q{-}i)$ when there is a rule of the form $c \longrightarrow (q, \mathbf{e}_i)$ in δ
- $(\epsilon, {=}q_1{=}q_2 q)$ when there is a rule of the form $f((q_1, \mathbf{x}_1), (q_2, \mathbf{x}_2)) \longrightarrow (q, \mathbf{x}_1 + \mathbf{x}_2)$ in δ
- $(\epsilon, {=}q_0{+}iq)$ when there is a rule of the form $f(q_0, \mathbf{x}) \longrightarrow (q, \mathbf{x} - \mathbf{e}_i)$ in δ

We are going to prove that $\mathcal{L}(G_{\mathcal{A}})$ is empty if and only if $\mathcal{L}(\mathcal{A})$ is empty by giving an interpretation of the derivations of $G_{\mathcal{A}}$ as configurations of $\mathcal{A}$. Given t from $d(G_{\mathcal{A}})$, t can be interpreted as an element of $\mathbb{N}^k$ when $\mathcal{H}(t)$ is defined, then the ith component of that vector is the number of occurrences of the feature $-i$ in $\mathcal{H}(t)$. We write $\mathcal{V}(t)$ for the vector denoted by t when it is defined. The state of t, denoted by $\mathcal{Q}(t)$, is the element of Q such that $\mathcal{H}(t) = ((v, ql), L)$. Note that $\mathcal{Q}(t)$ is not defined when $\mathcal{H}(t) = ((v, lql'), L)$ and l is not empty. Thus t in $d(G_{\mathcal{A}})$ is interpreted as a configuration of $\mathcal{A}$ by $\text{conf}(t) = (\mathcal{Q}(t), \mathcal{V}(t))$. This configuration is defined only when $\mathcal{Q}(t)$ is defined (note that when $\mathcal{Q}(t)$ is defined, obviously $\mathcal{H}(t)$ is defined and thus so is $\mathcal{V}(t)$).

Lemma 4. *Given $\mathbf{v} \in \mathbb{N}^k$ and $q \in Q$, there is t in $d(G_{\mathcal{A}})$ such that $\text{conf}(t) = (q, \mathbf{v})$ if and only if there is a term t' such that $t' \xrightarrow{*}_{\mathcal{A}} (q, \mathbf{v})$.*

Proof. We first remark that whenever $\text{conf}(t)$ is defined, then t is in one of the three following forms:

1. $t = (\epsilon, q{-}i)$, where $(\epsilon, q - i)$ is in C,
2. $t = \mathbf{merge}\, t_2(\mathbf{merge}\, t_1(\epsilon, {=}q_1{=}q_2 q))$ where $\mathcal{H}(t_1) = ((\epsilon, q_1 l_1), L_1)$ and where $\mathcal{H}(t_2) = ((\epsilon, q_2 l_2), L_2)$,
3. $t = \mathbf{move}(\mathbf{merge}\, u\, ({=}q_0{+}iq))$ where $\mathcal{H}(u) = ((\epsilon, q_0 l), L)$ and the ith component of $\mathcal{V}(u)$ is strictly positive.

We now prove the existence of t' by induction on t.

In case $t = (\epsilon, q{-}i)$, then, by definition of $G_{\mathcal{A}}$ there is a rule in δ which is of the form $c \longrightarrow (q, \mathbf{e}_i)$. Then it suffices to take $t' = c$.

In case $t = \mathbf{merge}\, t_2(\mathbf{merge}\, t_1(\epsilon, {=}q_1{=}q_2 q))$ then, by induction hypothesis, we have the existence of t_1' and t_2' such that $t_i' \xrightarrow{*}_i \text{conf}(t_i)$. Moreover, by definition of C, there is a rule of the form $f((q_1, \mathbf{x}_1), (q_2, \mathbf{x}_2)) \longrightarrow (q, \mathbf{x}_1 + \mathbf{x}_2)$ in C. We then let t' be $f t_1' t_2'$.

In case $t = \mathbf{move}(\mathbf{merge}\, u\, ({=}q_0{+}iq))$, then, by induction hypothesis, there is u' such that $u' \xrightarrow{*}_{\mathcal{A}} \text{conf}(u)$. Furthermore, we know that the ith component of

$\mathcal{V}(u)$ is strictly positive, and that, by definition of C, there is in δ a rule of the form $f(q_0, \mathbf{x}) \longrightarrow (q_0, \mathbf{x} - \mathbf{e}_i)$. We can then choose t' to be $f(u')$.

The proof of the converse property is using a similar induction.

The parallel that is drawn between minimalist grammars and k-VATA allows us to give a negative answer to the conjecture raised in [13] that MGs (without SMC) define only semi-linear languages. To prove it we use the notion of k-VAS (k- Vector Addition Systems). A k-VAS can be seen as a k-VATA whose signature contains only nullary and unary operators, and, given a state q, the sets of vectors that are accessible at q for a k-VAS $\mathcal{A}$ is $\mathrm{Acc}(\mathcal{A}, q) = \{\mathbf{v} | \exists t.t \xrightarrow{*}_{\mathcal{A}} (q, \mathbf{v})\}$. It is known that the sets of the form $\mathrm{Acc}(\mathcal{A}, q)$ may not be semi-linear [14]. As for k-VATA, there is a normal form for k-VAS, where the rules are of the following form:

1. $c \longrightarrow (q, \mathbf{0})$
2. $f(q_1, \mathbf{x}) \longrightarrow (q_2, \mathbf{x} - \mathbf{e}_i)$ for some i in $[1; k]$,
3. $f(q_1, \mathbf{x}) \longrightarrow (q_2, \mathbf{x} + \mathbf{e}_i)$ for some i in $[1; k]$

The important property is that if $\mathcal{A}$ is a k-VAS, and q is a state of $\mathcal{A}$, then there is a k-VAS in normal form $\mathcal{B}$ and a state q' of $\mathcal{B}$ such that $\mathrm{Acc}(\mathcal{A}, q) = \mathrm{Acc}(\mathcal{B}, q')$.

So given a k-VAS in normal form $\mathcal{A}$ and its final state p, we can define the following MG $G_{\mathcal{A}} = ([1; k], Q \cup d, [1; k], C, d)$:

1. (ϵ, q) if there is a rule $e \longrightarrow (q, \mathbf{0})$ is in δ,
2. $(\epsilon, =q_1 + iq_2)$ if there is a rule $f(q_1, \mathbf{x}) \longrightarrow (q_2, \mathbf{x} - \mathbf{e}_i)$ in δ,
3. $(\epsilon, =q_1 q_2 - i)$ if there is a rule $f(q_1, \mathbf{x}) \longrightarrow (q_2, \mathbf{x} + \mathbf{e}_i)$ in δ,
4. $(\epsilon, =pd)$
5. $(i, =d + id)$ for all i in $[1; k]$

Similarly to the proof of Lemma 4, it can be showed that whenever $\mathbf{v}$ is accessible at q in $\mathcal{A}$ then there is t such that $\mathrm{conf}(t) = (q, \mathbf{v})$. Then the lexical entries $(\epsilon, =pd)$ and $(i, =d + id)$ (where i is in $[1; k]$) transform the vector $\mathbf{v}$ into a word of $[1; k]^*$ such that, for all i in $[1; k]$, it contains exactly $\mathbf{v}_i$ occurrences of i (if $\mathbf{v}_i$ is the ith component of $\mathbf{v}$) so that the language defined by $G_{\mathcal{A}}$ is the set of elements of $[1; k]^*$ whose Parikh image is $\mathrm{Acc}(\mathcal{A}, q)$. Thus the language of $G_{\mathcal{A}}$ is semi-linear if and only if the set of vectors accessible by $\mathcal{A}$ form a semi-linear set. Thus, we have the following theorem.

Theorem 3. *The class of languages defined by MGs is not semi-linear.*

2.2   Representing MG Derivations as Proofs in MELL

We here give an account of the derivations of an MG with the linear λ-terms built over a certain signature. It is known (*c.f.* [12]) that finding such λ-terms is in general Turing-equivalent to provability in MELL. This encoding thus completes the proof that the membership problem for MGs is Turing-equivalent to provability in MELL.

For a given MG, $G = (B, F, W, C, c)$, we define Σ_G which declares the following set of atomic types:

1. $e(l)$ if there is (w, l) in C,
2. $d(l)$ if l is an element of $\mathrm{Suff}(G)$,
3. $h(l)$ if l is an element of $\mathrm{Move}(G)$

Even though we use a predicate-like notation, note that since C, $\mathrm{Suff}(G)$ and $\mathrm{Move}(G)$ are finite, there are finitely many types that are declared in Σ_G. The type $e(l)$ represents the type of a lexical entry, $d(l)$ represents the type of a derivation whose head is of the form (w, l) and $h(l)$ is the type of a moving piece of the form (w, l). We make the distinction between $e(l)$ and $d(l)$ so as to know how to interpret **merge** in a homomorphic way.

Σ_G also declares the following constants:

1. $(w, l) : e(l)$ if (w, l) is in C,
2. $merge[k(al_1), k'(=al_2)] : k(al_1) \multimap k'(=al_2) \multimap h(l_1) \multimap d(l_2)$ where l_1 is not empty and with k, k' in $\{d; e\}$
3. $merge[k(a), k'(=al_2)] : k(a) \multimap k'(=al_2) \multimap d(l_2)$ with k, k' in $\{d; e\}$
4. $move[h(-al_1), d(+al_2)] : (h(-al_1) \multimap d(+al_2)) \multimap h(l_1) \multimap d(l_2)$ where l_1 is not empty,
5. $move[h(-a), d(+al)] : (h(-a) \multimap d(+al)) \multimap d(l)$

We will show that there are closed terms of type $k(c)$ (with k in $\{d; e\}$) if and only if $\mathcal{L}(G)$ is not empty. Terms of $d(G)$ that can be interpreted with the function $\mathcal{H}$ are represented as terms built on Σ_G whose types are $d(l)$ or $e(l)$ and whose free variables have types of the form $h(l)$.

Lemma 5. *There is $t \in \Lambda_{\Sigma_G}^{k(l)}$ (with k being either d or e) such that $FV(t) = \{x_1^{h(l_1)}; \ldots; x_n^{h(l_n)}\}$ is derivable if and only if there is t' in $d(G)$ such that $\mathcal{H}(t') = \langle(w, l), [(w_1, l_1) \ldots (w_n, l_n)]\rangle$.*

Proof. We first construct t' by induction on t. We suppose without loss of generality that t is in normal form.

If $t = (w, l)$ then it suffices to take $t' = (w, l)$.

If $t = merge[k(al_1), k'(= al_2)]t_1 t_2 t_3$, then because there is no constant that has the type $h(l_1)$ as a conclusion and because free variables all have a type of the form $h(l)$, it is necessary that, for some i, $t_3 = x_i^{h(l_i)}$ and $h(l_i) = h(l)$. Thus, we have that $t_1 \in \Lambda_{\Sigma_G}^{k(al)}$ with $FV(t_1) = \{x_{i_1}^{h(l_{i_1})}; \ldots; x_{i_p}^{h(l_{i_p})}\}$, $t_2 \in \Lambda_{\Sigma_G}^{k'(=al_2)}$ with $FV(t_2) = \{x_{j_1}^{h(l_{j_1})}; \ldots; x_{j_p}^{h(l_{j_p})}\}$ and $\langle\{i_1; \ldots; i_p\}, \{j_1; \ldots; j_q\}, \{i\}\rangle$ forms a partition of $[1; n]$. By induction hypothesis, we get the existence of t_1' and t_2' verifying the right properties and it suffices to take $t' = \textbf{merge}\, t_1'\, t_2'$.

If $t = merge[k(a), k'(= al_2)]t_1 t_2$, then we proceed similarly to the previous case.

If $t = move[h(-al), d(+al')](\lambda x^{h(-al)}.t_1)t_2$ then, similarly to the previous case, we have that t_2 must be one of the $x_i^{h(l_i)}$. We suppose without loss of generality, that $t_2 = x_1^{h(l_1)}$ and then we have that $t_1 \in \Lambda_{\Sigma_G}^{d(+al')}$ with $FV(t_1) = \{x_2^{h(l_2)}; \ldots; x_n^{h(l_n)}; x^{h(-al)}\}$. Then we obtain a t_1' from t_1 by using the induction hypothesis and it suffices to take $t' = \mathbf{move}(t_1')$ by assuming that $\mathbf{move}$ is operating on a moving piece of the form $(v, -al)$ which by induction hypothesis must exist.

If $t = move'[h(-a), d(+al)] \, \lambda x.t_1$ then we proceed in a way similar to the previous case.

The converse does not present more difficulty and is then left to the reader.

This Lemma together with Lemma 4 answers the question of the mathematical nature of the derivations of minimalist grammars. It shows that these derivations can be seen as closed linear λ-terms of type $d(c)$ or $e(c)$. Thus, with such a representation, checking whether such a derivation is correct does not amount to compute whether it can be interpreted as a string, but merely amounts to type checking.

Example 3. We show here the representation of the derivation of Example 1 as a linear λ-term:

$$move[h(-case), d(+case\,c)]$$
$$|$$
$$\lambda x.\, merge[d(v), e(=v +\text{case}\,c)]$$

$$merge[e(d -\text{case}), d(=d\,v)] \qquad (will, =v +\text{case}\,c)$$

$$(\text{Maria}, d -\text{case}) \qquad merge[e(d), e(=d =d\,v]) \qquad x$$

$$(\text{Nahuatl}, d) \quad (\text{speak}, =d =d\,v)$$

On the other hand, the derivation of Example 2 can be represented by three different linear λ-terms (for the sake of concision we erase the squared brackets $[\alpha, \beta]$ of the constants $move[\alpha, \beta]$ and $merge[\alpha, \beta]$):

1.

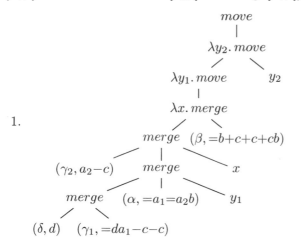

$$move$$
$$|$$
$$\lambda y_2.\, move$$

$$\lambda y_1.\, move \qquad y_2$$
$$|$$
$$\lambda x.\, merge$$

$$merge \qquad (\beta, =b+c+c+cb)$$

$$(\gamma_2, a_2-c) \qquad merge \qquad x$$
$$|$$
$$merge \qquad (\alpha, =a_1=a_2b) \qquad y_1$$

$$(\delta, d) \quad (\gamma_1, =da_1-c-c)$$

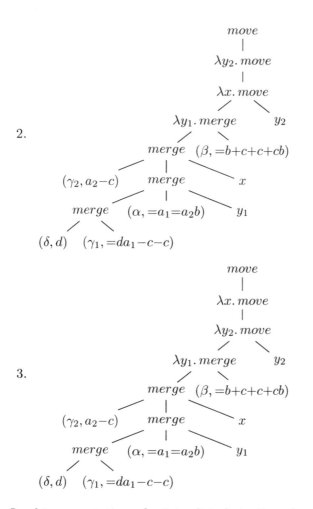

In this presentation of minimalist derivations λ-variables represent the moving pieces of a derivation. When a derivation t_1 is merged to another derivation t_2 and must be moved afterwards then the new derivation is of the form $merge\, t_1\, t_2\, x$ where the λ-variable x materialises t_1 as a moving piece.

Each time a **move** operation is applied, it is applied to a third-order term of the form $\lambda x.t$ where x indicates which moving piece is actually moved. When a constant of the form $move[\alpha, \beta]$ has two arguments, it means that the moving piece that the **move** operation has moved still has to be moved and then the second argument is a λ-variable that materialises the actualisation of this moving piece.

In the representation of minimalist derivations we propose, it becomes explicit that the **move** operation corresponds to binding some variable, but we can go a little further in the logical interpretation of **move**. Indeed, it would be possible to define a signature Π_G which only contains constants representing the lexical entries of G and no operator representing **move** or **merge**. The types used by Π_G are: $d(la)$ where la is such that there is $(w, l_1 l a l_2)$ in C and l is either starting with an element of F^+ or is empty. For every entry $(w, la-f_1 \ldots -f_n)$ in C, Π_G contains constants of type

$$((\ldots(((g(la) \multimap d(+f_1 l_1)) \multimap g(l_1) \multimap d(+f_2 l_2)) \multimap g(l_2)) \ldots) \multimap d(+f_n l_n)) \multimap g(l_n)$$

for every possible atomic type of the form $d(+f_i l'_i)$ and where $g(l)$ is equal to $d(a_1) \multimap \cdots d(a_k) \multimap d(l'b)$ if l is of the form $=a_1 \ldots =a_k l'b$ and l' if either starting with some element of F^+ or is empty. The idea is that the $d(+f_i l'_i)$ and e_i represent the features that the head has to licence when the ith movement of the entry happens.

Example 4. If we applied such a transformation to the grammar we used in our examples then we would get the following type assignment for the lexical entries for the derivations we showed:

$$
\begin{aligned}
(Maria, d -case) &: (d(d) \multimap d(+case\, c)) \multimap d(c) \\
(will, =v +case\, c) &: d(v) \multimap d(+case\, c) \\
(Nahuatl, d) &: d(d) \\
(speak, =d =d\, v) &: d(d) \multimap d(d) \multimap d(v)
\end{aligned}
$$

Then the derivation is represented by the linear λ-term:

$$(Maria, d -case)$$
$$|$$
$$\lambda x.\,(will, =v +case\, c)$$
$$|$$
$$(speak, =d =d\, v)$$
$$\diagup \qquad \diagdown$$
$$(Nahuatl, d) \qquad x$$

For the second example, we may represent the derivations given as examples with the following constants:

$$
\begin{aligned}
\gamma_2^1 &: (((d(a_2) \multimap d(+c+cb)) \multimap d(+c\,b)) \multimap d(+c)) \multimap d(b) \\
\gamma_2^2 &: (((d(a_2) \multimap d(+c+c+cb)) \multimap d(+c+cb)) \multimap d(+c)) \multimap d(b) \\
\gamma_2^3 &: (((d(a_2) \multimap d(+c+c+cb)) \multimap d(+c+cb)) \multimap d(+c+c)) \multimap d(+cb) \\
\gamma_1^1 &: ((d(d) \multimap d(a_1)) \multimap d(+c+c+cb)) \multimap d(+c+c\,b) \\
\gamma_1^2 &: ((d(d) \multimap d(a_1)) \multimap d(+c+cb)) \multimap d(+c\,b) \\
\gamma_1^3 &: ((d(d) \multimap d(a_1)) \multimap d(+cb)) \multimap d(b) \\
\beta &: d(b) \multimap d(+c+c+cb) \\
\alpha &: d(a_1) \multimap d(a_2) \multimap d(b) \\
\delta &: d(d)
\end{aligned}
$$

With these constants, the derivations can be represented by the linear λ-terms:

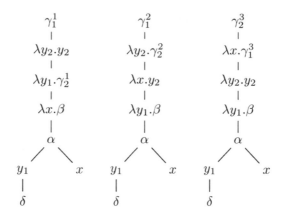

We can now understand the technical contributions of **move** and **merge** by comparing Σ_G and Π_G. First, we remark that in Π_G each entry conveys explicitly the context in which it is used; in particular it specifies the characteristics of the head at each step of its movements. It has the inconvenience that Π_G has a size that is a $\mathcal{O}(|G|^{n+1})$ where n is the maximum number of movements that a moving piece can do whereas Σ_G is much more compact and has a size in $\mathcal{O}(|G|^2)$. Furthermore, by making the types of the constants $merge[k(al_1), k'(= al_2)]$, $move[h(-al_1), d(+al_2)]$ and $move[h(-a), d(+al)]$ be polymorphic in a, l_1, l_2 or l we obtain a grammar whose size is linear with respect to the size of G. This polymorphism has also the advantage that we can add new entries without having to change the grammar in any respect. We can also use a notion of polymorphism to Π_G, but it needs to be stronger a notion. Indeed, while in Σ_G, polymorphism instantiates differently atomic types, in Π_G, because we use a function $g(l)$ that gives a complex type depending on the shape of l, this polymorphism requires to have a notion of functions from feature string to types.

A more interesting remark concerning the difference between Π_G and Σ_G concerns their respective order. Indeed Σ_G is a third order signature whereas Π_G is a signature whose order is between $n + 1$ and $n + 2$ where n is the maximum number of movements a moving piece can do. If G did not contain any moving feature then both Σ_G and Π_G would be second order signatures. Thus movement is responsible for the higher order types in Σ_G and Π_G. We can see the **move** operation as being responsible of transforming higher order into third order. Transforming higher order into third order is quite usual in intuitionistic implicative logics. Indeed, in minimal logic as well as in intuitionisitic implicative linear logic, a sequent $\Gamma \vdash \alpha$ which may contain formulae of any order can be transformed in a sequent $\Delta \vdash \beta$ which contains only formulae that are at most third order and which is provable if and only if $\Gamma \vdash \alpha$ is provable. But interestingly if we use the construction that underpins this property on Π_G we will not obtain Σ_G as a result. This is due to the fact that **move** and **merge** also break down the complexity of the polymorphism that would be necessary to make Π_G be of a reasonable size. The interesting thing about comparing Π_G and Σ_G is to show how the linguistic ideas that lead to **merge** and **move** operations make drastic simplifications in the mathematical objects used to represent derivations. It also gives an opening towards the understanding of the mathematical nature of these simplifications.

3   Interpreting Minimalist Derivations

In this section we show how to interpret the terms of the signature Σ_G so as to obtain the string that they analyse. In the previous section we have already remarked that these terms were explicitly representing via variable binding which moving piece is actually moved when a **move** operation is used. This allows us to give a homomorphic interpretation of these terms that yield the unique strings that they represent. Thus this representation of derivations makes the linearisation of the derivations become independent from their semantic interpretation. This should make it easier to describe the interface between syntax and semantics for MGs.

We have already seen that interpreting trees of $d(G)$, for an MG G, requires that we have a list of moving pieces. In our homomorphic interpretation of the terms built on Σ_G, we will also need such a list. This list will be used very similarly to the context that is introduced in [10] for semantic purposes. This shows that the mapping from minimalist derivations to the surface structure is far from being trivial.

In order to define our context we need to work in a system with at least as much computational power as Gödel's system T. We do not give all the implementation details because they are not of much interest. We wish to convince the reader that the homomorphic interpretation of minimalist derivations requires a rather sophisticated implementation and technical details would obfuscate the reasons why it is so. A *syntactic context* is defined as a pair $\langle L, n \rangle$ where:

1. L is a list of pairs (w, p) with w belonging to W^* and p being an integer,
2. n is an integer.

Integers are used here so as to *give a name to* moving pieces. They allow to make the distinction between several moving pieces. Thus, L is a list that associates specific integers to moving pieces so as to retrieve them and n is a fresh integer so as to be able to extend and search the list. We use the following constants and operations on *syntactic contexts*:

- the empty list is $[]$,
- concatenation $(L_1, p_1) \bullet (L_2, p_2) = (L_1@L_2, \max(p_1, p_2))$, where @ is the operation of list concatenation
- adding an element $push(e, (L, p)) = (e :: L, p)$, where :: is the operation that adds an element to a list,
- incrementation $incr(L, p) = (L, p + 1)$,
- getting a fresh name $fresh(L, p) = p + 1$,
- selection $sel(k, (L, p))$ which sends the string associated to k in L.

We now give the interpretation of the types of Σ_G

- $e(l)$ et $d(l)$ are interpreted as being of type $str \times \gamma$ where str is the type of strings and γ that of syntactic contexts.
- $h(l)$ is interpreted as being the type $\mathbb{N}$, the type of integers.

For the sake of simplicity, we write $\lambda(x_1, x_2).t$ and use some **let. . . and . . . in** constructions instead of the usual projection operators π_1 and π_2. Furthermore as we are interested in the language of an MG and as derivations are interpreted as a pair of type $str \times \gamma$ we introduce two new constants in the signature: $realise_1$ of type $d(c) \multimap s$ and $realise_2$ of type $e(c) \multimap s$ and whose purpose is to get the string part of a valid derivation. When t represents a derivation of the MG G as a term built on the signature Σ_G, the resulting string is obtained using a homomorphism $\mathcal{I}$ on the term $realise_1(t)$ or $realise_2(t)$ depending on whether t have type $d(c)$ or $e(c)$. In what follows, as we will need to concatenate strings, we will write $w \cdot w'$ the concatenation of two terms that are strings in order to avoid confusion with term application.

The interpretation of the constants of Σ_G is (in what follows $k(l)$ and $k'(l)$ may denote either $d(l)$ or $e(l)$):

1. for $realize_1 : d(c) \multimap s$ we have $\mathcal{I}(realize_1) = \lambda(w, L).w$
2. for $realize_2 : e(c) \multimap s$ we have $\mathcal{I}(realize_2) = \lambda(w, L).w$
3. for $(w, l) : e(l)$, we have $\mathcal{I}((w, l)) = (w, ([], 0))$
4. for $merge[k(al_1), k'(=al_2)] : k(al_1) \multimap k'(=al_2) \multimap h(l_1) \multimap d(l_2)$ where l_1 is not empty we have:

$$\mathcal{I}(merge[k(al_1), k'(=al_2)]) = \lambda(w_1, \mathbf{s}_1)(w_2, \mathbf{s}_2)p.(w_2, (push\,(w_1, p)\,(\mathbf{s}_1 \bullet \mathbf{s}_2)))$$

5. for $merge[k(a), d(=al_2)] : k(a) \multimap d(=al_2) \multimap d(l_2)$ we have:

$$\mathcal{I}(merge[k(a), d(=al_2)]) = \lambda(w_1, \mathbf{s}_1)(w_2, \mathbf{s}_2).(w_1 \cdot w_2, (\mathbf{s}_1 \bullet \mathbf{s}_2))$$

6. for $merge[k(a), e(=al_2)] : k(a) \multimap e(=al_2) \multimap d(l_2)$ we have:

$$\mathcal{I}(merge[k(a), d(=al_2)]) = \lambda(w_1, \mathbf{s}_1)(w_2, \mathbf{s}_2).(w_2 \cdot w_1, (\mathbf{s}_1 \bullet \mathbf{s}_2))$$

7. for $move[h(-al_1), d(+al_2)] : (h(-al_1) \multimap d(+al_2)) \multimap h(l_1) \multimap d(l_2)$ (by definition l_1 is not empty) we have:

$$\mathcal{I}(move[h(-al_1), d(+al_2)]) = \lambda fp.fp$$

8. for $move[h(-a), d(+al_2)] : (h(-a) \multimap d(+al_2)) \multimap d(l_2)$ we have:

$$\mathcal{I}(move[h(-al_1), d(+al_2)]) = \lambda f.\mathbf{let}\ (\_, \mathbf{s}) = (f\,0)$$
$$\mathbf{and}\ n = fresh(\mathbf{s})$$
$$\mathbf{and}\ (w, \mathbf{s}') = (fn)$$
$$\mathbf{in}\ ((sel(n, \mathbf{s}')) \cdot w, (incr(\mathbf{s}')))$$

The only operation that is complicated is the $\mathcal{I}(move[h(-a), d(+al_2)])$, because this is the one where a moving piece stops moving and is incorporated to the head. First we retrieve the context $\mathbf{s}$, by giving 0 as a dummy argument to f, this allows us to obtain n as a *fresh name* to give to the moving piece, we then apply f to n and we get the string of the head and a context $\mathbf{s'}$ which associates n to the moving piece that will be incorporated to the head. The operation $sel(n, \mathbf{s'}))$ retrieves the string of that moving piece and the context is incremented so that in a next use of the context, that moving piece won't be chosen. We could have deleted it from the list, but it is not necessary here. Deletion in list is in general a more complex operation than selection in the λ-calculus.

This usage of the context of type γ is typical of the continuation passing style of programming. Even though it is technical, it is quite easy to prove that the set

$$\{w | \exists t \in \Lambda_{\Sigma_G}^{d(c)}.t \text{ is closed and } \mathcal{I}(realise_1 \, t) = w\}$$
$$\bigcup$$
$$\{w | \exists t \in \Lambda_{\Sigma_G}^{e(c)}.t \text{ is closed and } \mathcal{I}(realise_2 \, t) = w\}$$

is equal to $\mathcal{L}(G)$; the induction is very similar to the one we used to prove Lemma 4.

In this paper, for clarity reasons, we deliberately use the simplest notion of minimalist grammars as possible. In particular, we omitted weak features that are necessary in most reasonable linguistic models. At the level of the derivation structures, the addition of weak features almost does not change anything; changes occur at the level of the interpretation. We will not enter in the details of a possible homomorphic interpretation of derivations with weak features, but we can say that it is much more evolved than the homomorphism $\mathcal{I}$.

3.1   The Shortest Move Constraint

Now we can see that the shortest move constraint can be expressed on minimalist derivations represented as terms built on Σ_G as the constraint that in any subterm of such a term there is at most one free variable having a type of the form $h(-al)$ for each licencing feature a. With the Curry-Howard isomorphism, we can see linear λ-terms as proofs in implicative linear logic which establishes judgments of the form $\Gamma \vdash \alpha$ where Γ is a multiset of linear types and α is a linear type. The restriction that there is at most one free variable having a type of the form $h(-al)$ is interpreted in implicative linear logic as constraining the possible judgement as being of the form $\Gamma \vdash \alpha$ where Γ contains at most one occurrence of a formula of the form $h(-al)$. This means that the possible Γ may only contain a number of type that is bounded by the number of movement features, the size of $\mathcal{F}$. And thus, there are finitely many possible Γ that obey this constraint. This is the key property that makes minimalist grammars with the shortest move constraint languages of multiple context free grammars (MCFL).

Indeed, because of the finiteness of the possible Γ and of the subformula property, there are only finitely many possible judgements that may have to be proved. We can therefore represent the set of all proofs in an algebraic setting; it suffices to take all the possible instances of the *elimination rules* and of the *introduction rules* of the intuitionistic implicative linear logic. For a given signature Σ_G, we do this by building the following multi-sorted tree signature $\mathrm{SMC}(\Sigma_G)$:

1. the types are $[h(-a_1l_1), \ldots, h(-a_nl_n) \vdash \alpha]_I$ and $[\Gamma \vdash \alpha]_E$ where $-a_il_i$ is in $\text{Move}(G)$, the a_i are pairwise distinct and α is a subformula of the type of a constant in Σ_G
2. $c : [\vdash \alpha]_E$ for each constant $c : \alpha$ of the signature (c can be either a lexical entry or one of the constants representing the **move** and **merge operations**.
3. $E_1 : [\Gamma \vdash \alpha \multimap \beta]_E \multimap [\Delta \vdash \alpha]_E \multimap [\Gamma, \Delta \vdash \beta]_E$ if α is atomic,
4. $E_2 : [\Gamma \vdash \alpha \multimap \beta]_E \multimap [\Delta \vdash \alpha]_I \multimap [\Gamma, \Delta \vdash \beta]_E$ if α is not atomic,
5. $I_1 : [\Gamma, \alpha \vdash \beta]_E \multimap [\Gamma \vdash \alpha \multimap \beta]_I$ if β is atomic,
6. $I_2 : [\Gamma, \alpha \vdash \beta]_I \multimap [\Gamma \vdash \alpha \multimap \beta]_I$ if β is not atomic.

To be rigorous, we should have, similarly to the definitions of the constants representing **merge** and **move** in the signature Σ_G, several versions of the constants E_1, E_2, I_1 and I_2 for their various possible typing. But for the sake of the simplicity of the notations, we simply use those four constants and consider that they have several types.

In order to have a unique representation of each proof we have annotated types with I or E, types with an I as subscript are types of proofs that finish with an introduction rule, whereas the one with an E are the other cases. The representation we have chosen corresponds to β-normal and η-long terms built on Σ_G.

We now give the interpretation of the terms built on $\text{SMC}(\Sigma_G)$ with an homomorphism $\mathcal{D}$ that retrieves the λ-term of Σ_G that is represented:

1. $\mathcal{D}([\alpha_1, \ldots, \alpha_n \vdash \alpha]_E) = \mathcal{D}([\alpha_1, \ldots, \alpha_n \vdash \alpha]_I) = \alpha_1 \multimap \cdots \multimap \alpha_n \multimap \alpha$
2. $\mathcal{D}(c) = c$
3. $\mathcal{D}(E_1) = \lambda f g x_1 \ldots x_n y_1 \ldots y_p . f x_1 \ldots x_n (g y_1 \ldots y_p)$
4. $\mathcal{D}(E_2) = \lambda f g x_1 \ldots x_n y_1 \ldots y_p . f x_1 \ldots x_n (g y_1 \ldots y_p)$
5. $\mathcal{D}(I_1) = \lambda f . f$
6. $\mathcal{D}(I_2) = \lambda f . f$

We can also define a homomorphism $\mathcal{J}$ that transforms a tree t of $\text{SMC}(\Sigma_G)$ in the same string as $\mathcal{D}(\mathcal{I}(t))$ but with the property that every constant is interpreted as an affine λ-term. The idea behind the definition of $\mathcal{J}$ is that we can represent a p-tuple of strings $(s_1, \ldots, s_p)$ that are used to build a string by a term of the form $P = \lambda f . f s_1 \ldots s_p$, then, as an example, we can use P to form a string $w_1 s_1 \cdots w_p s_p w_{p+1}$ simply with the following λ-term: $P(\lambda x_1 \ldots x_p . w_1 \cdot x_1 \cdot \ldots \cdot w_p \cdot x_p \cdot w_{p+1})$.

1. let's suppose that the number of licencing features of G is p, then types of the form $[\Gamma \vdash k(l)]_M$ or $[\Gamma \vdash h(l') \multimap k(l)]_M$ with k in k in $\{d; e\}$ and M in $\{I; E\}$ is interpreted as the type $\gamma = (str^{p+1} \multimap str) \multimap str$. We furthermore assume that the set of licensing features is $\{a_1; \ldots; a_p\}$ so that they are implicitly ordered.
2. the types of the form $[\vdash \alpha]_E$, where α is a the type of a **move** constant, are interpreted as $\gamma \multimap \gamma$.
3. the types of the form $[\vdash \alpha]_E$ where α is a the type of a **merge** constant, are interpreted as $\gamma \multimap \gamma \multimap \gamma$.

4. then $\mathcal{J}((w,l)) = \lambda g.g\, w\, \underbrace{\epsilon \ldots \epsilon}_{p\times}$

5. $\mathcal{J}(merge[k(b-a_k l_1), k'(=bl_2)]) =$
   $\lambda D_1 D_2 g.D_1(\lambda s_1 x_1 \ldots x_p.$
   $\quad D_2(\lambda s_2 y_1 \ldots y_p.$
   $\quad\quad g\, s_2\, (x_1 \cdot y_1) \ldots (x_{k-1} \cdot y_{k-1})(s_1) \ldots (x_p \cdot y_p)))$

6. $\mathcal{J}(merge[k(b), d(=bl_2)]) =$
   $\lambda D_1 D_2 g.D_1(\lambda s_1 x_1 \ldots x_p.$
   $\quad D_2(\lambda s_2 y_1 \ldots y_p.g(s_1 \cdot s_2)\,(x_1 \cdot y_1) \ldots (x_p \cdot y_p)))$

7. $\mathcal{J}(merge[k(b), e(=bl_2)]) =$
   $\lambda D_1 D_2 g.D_1(\lambda s_1 x_1 \ldots x_p.$
   $\quad D_2(\lambda s_2 y_1 \ldots y_p.g(s_2 \cdot s_1)\,(x_1 \cdot y_1) \ldots (x_p \cdot y_p)))$

8. $\mathcal{J}(move[h(-a_k-a_j l_1), d(+a_k l_2)]) =$
   $\lambda Dg.D(\lambda s x_1 \ldots x_p g.g\, s\, x_1 \ldots x_{k-1}\epsilon \ldots x_{j-1} x_k \ldots x_p)$

9. $\mathcal{J}(move[h(-a_k), d(+a_k l_2)]) =$
   $\lambda Dg.D(\lambda s x_1 \ldots x_p g.g\,(x_k \cdot s)\, x_1 \ldots x_{k-1}\epsilon \ldots x_p))$

10. $\mathcal{J}(E_1) = \lambda f x.f\, x$ and $\mathcal{J}(E_2) = \lambda f x.f\, x$

All together, SMC(Σ_G) and $\mathcal{J}$ define an affine second order string Abstract Categorial Grammar in the sense of [15] which also shows that the language of such a grammar is the language of a *linear* second order string Abstract Categorial Grammar. But it is showed in [16] that such grammars can only define MCFLs.

This construction of an MCFL from an MG with the SMC is not essentially different from the one given in [17], but the transformation we propose preserves in an obvious way (thanks to the homomorphism $\mathcal{D}$) the structure of the derivation, so that it preserves the interface between syntax and semantics. Furthermore, the use of tuples can also replace the complex *semantic contexts* that would be necessary without the SMC so that it would become very similar to Montague semantics.

3.2   Saving Computation

One of the interest of representing the derivation by using the signature Σ_G is that it enables to separate the syntactic interpretation of the derivations from their semantic interpretation. Indeed, as in [18], the semantic interpretation of minimalist grammars has to be done in parallel to its syntactic interpretation. Nevertheless, this parallel computation shows that if we want to give a semantic interpretation of the derivations of minimalist grammars, then we will need to implement a context that is at least as complicated as the one we have defined for the syntactic interpretation. In order to avoid similar computations that need to be accomplished both for the syntactic and the semantic interpretations, we can compute an intermediate structure in which all the computations that are necessary for both the syntactic interpretation and the semantic one are already performed.

This intermediate structure is built on a rather simple signature Int_G whose types are the set of features of the minimalist grammar G plus a fresh type $\mathbf{d}$ for complete derivations, $B \cup F \cup \{\mathbf{d}\}$. The constants are defined as follows:

1. $(w, \epsilon_1 b_1 \ldots \epsilon_n b_n a - f_1 \ldots - f_p) : ((a \multimap f_1 \multimap \cdots \multimap (b_1 \multimap \cdots \multimap b_n \multimap f_p) \multimap \mathbf{d}) \multimap \mathbf{d}$ for every lexical entry $(w, \epsilon_1 b_1 \ldots \epsilon_n b_n a - f_1 \ldots - f_p)$ in C, where $p > 0$,

2. $(w, \epsilon_1 b_1 \ldots \epsilon_n b_n a) : ((b_1 \multimap \cdots \multimap b_n \multimap a) \multimap \mathbf{d}) \multimap \mathbf{d}$ for every lexical entry $(w, \epsilon_1 b_1 \ldots \epsilon_n b_n a)$ in C,

3. $r : c \multimap \mathbf{d}$

In this signature derivations are represented by closed terms of the form:

$$e_1(\lambda y_1^1 \ldots y_{p_1}^1 x_1 \ldots e_n(\lambda y_1^n \ldots y_{p_n}^n x_n . r\, t)$$

where the e_i are constants and where t is a term built only with the variables x_i and y_j^i. The x_i represent the last place where e_i is moved and it is glued there with the components that have licenced its features; whereas the y_j^i represent the traces of e_i in the derivation after it has been moved several times. Of course, if we take every closed terms of this form, many of them will not correspond to an actual minimalist derivation. Moreover, this presentation has some shortcomings since it may have several representations of a single derivation. Indeed, without any further constraint, if

$$e_1(\lambda x_1 y_1^1 \ldots y_{p_1}^1 \ldots e_n(\lambda x_n y_1^n \ldots y_{p_n}^n . r\, t)$$

represents a minimalist derivation then, so is

$$e_{\tau(1)}(\lambda x_{\tau(1)} y_1^{\tau(1)} \ldots y_{p_{\tau(1)}}^{\tau(1)} \ldots e_{\tau(n)}(\lambda x_{\tau(n)} y_1^{\tau(n)} \ldots y_{p_{\tau(n)}}^{\tau(n)} . r\, t)$$

for any permutation τ of $[1; n]$. In order to eliminate these *spurious ambiguities* we can constrain the e_i to appear in the same order as in the surface interpretation of the derivation.

Example 5. A representation of the derivation of Example 1 as an intermediate structure can be given using the constants:

1. $(Maria, d - case) : (d \multimap case \multimap \mathbf{d}) \multimap \mathbf{d}$
2. $(will, =v + case\, c) : ((v \multimap case \multimap c) \multimap \mathbf{d}) \multimap \mathbf{d}$
3. $(speak, =d = d\, v) : ((d \multimap d \multimap v) \multimap \mathbf{d}) \multimap \mathbf{d}$
4. $(Nahuatl, d) : (d \multimap \mathbf{d}) \multimap \mathbf{d}$

With those constants the derivation is represented by the following λ-terms (only the first one respects the constraint that eliminates spurious ambiguities):

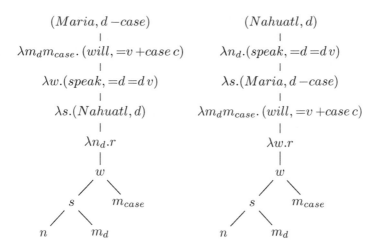

For Example 2, the derivations can be represented using the constants types as:

1. $(\alpha, =a_1=a_2 b) : ((a \multimap a \multimap b) \multimap d) \multimap d$
2. $(\beta, =b+c+c+cb) : ((b \multimap c \multimap c \multimap c \multimap b) \multimap d) \multimap d$
3. $(\delta, d) : (d \multimap d) \multimap d$
4. $(\gamma_1, =da_1-c-c) : (a_1 \multimap c \multimap c \multimap d) \multimap d$
5. $(\gamma_2, a_2-c) : (a_2 \multimap c \multimap d) \multimap d$

With this constants, including $r : b \multimap d$, we can represent the three derivations given in Example 3 with the following λ-terms (here we only give the terms obeying the constraint that avoids spurious ambiguities):

$$
\begin{array}{ccc}
(\gamma_2, a_2-c) & (\gamma_1, =da_1-c-c) & (\gamma_1, =da_1-c-c) \\
| & | & | \\
\lambda x_2 y_2.(\gamma_1, =da_1-c-c) & \lambda x_1 y_1 z_1.(\delta, d) & \lambda x_1 y_1 z_1.(\delta, d) \\
| & | & | \\
\lambda x_1 y_1 z_1.(\delta, d) & \lambda v.(\gamma_2, a_2-c) & \lambda v.(\gamma_2, a_2-c) \\
| & | & | \\
\lambda v.(\beta, =b+c+c+cb) & \lambda x_2 y_2.(\beta, =b+c+c+cb) & \lambda x_2 y_2.(\beta, =b+c+c+cb) \\
| & | & | \\
\lambda f.(\alpha, =a_1=a_2 b). & \lambda f.(\alpha, =a_1=a_2 b). & \lambda f.(\alpha, =a_1=a_2 b). \\
| & | & | \\
\lambda g.r & \lambda g.r & \lambda g.r \\
| & | & | \\
f & f & f \\
\end{array}
$$

Interestingly the variable v that represent the position of the lexical entry (δ, d), is the argument of the variable z_1 which is the variable that represents the last position the moving piece built around $(\gamma_1, =da_1-c-c)$ occupies after movement. This has to be contrasted with the terms built in Example 4 where the lexical entry (δ, d) is placed as an argument of the variable y_1 that represents the first position occupied by $(\gamma_1, =da_1-c-c)$. So with this representation of derivations every movement has already been performed.

Remark that the order in which y_1, z_1 and z_2 appear as arguments of f accounts for the order in which the licencing feature $-c$ of (γ_1, a_1-c-c) and (γ_2, a_2-c) are checked against the $+c$ feature of $(\beta, =b+c+c+cb)$. In particular, this enforces a particular order amongst y_1 and z_1 that represent the two places where (γ_1, a_1-c-c) is moving, y_1 being the first and z_1 being the second. With the choices we made about representing movement order, the following λ-term, even though it is well-typed, does not represent a derivation since it would mean that the second movement of (γ_1, a_1-c-c) has been performed before its first:

$$(\gamma_1, =da_1-c-c)$$
$$|$$
$$\lambda x_1 y_1 z_1.(\delta, d)$$
$$|$$
$$\lambda v.(\gamma_2, a_2-c)$$
$$|$$
$$\lambda x_2 y_2.(\beta, =b+c+c+cb)$$
$$|$$
$$\lambda f_b.(\alpha, =a_1=a_2 b).$$
$$|$$
$$\lambda g.r$$
$$|$$
$$f$$
$$\diagup | \backslash\backslash$$
$$g \quad y_2 \ z_1 \ y_1$$
$$\diagup\backslash \qquad |$$
$$x_1 \ x_2 \qquad v$$

There are several things to remark about this representation of minimalist derivations. First of all, contrary to our proposal in MELL, the features are treated explicitly as resources by the logic since they are represented as atomic formulae. The positive or negative versions are represented by the very same atomic type, the way to retrieve whether they are negative or positive amounts to find their polarity in the formula. As polarity in linear logic corresponds to the fact that a formula provides or requires some other formula as resource, the feature checking system of minimalist grammars is adequately modeled that way. This fact has been observed in previous works on logical accounts of minimalist grammars where people have tried to use polarities to elegantly render the feature checking system of minimalist grammars. As we have showed in the example, multiplicative linear logic does not seem to give enough control on the structure of the proofs so as to define derivations as being all the closed terms of a particular type, it explains the reason why those attempts have used logics similar to Lambek calculus. But, since this line of research has not succeeded in defining minimalist derivations uniquely by logical means, it seems to be a difficult problem to define in logical terms exactly the terms that represent minimalist derivations in a signature similar to as Int_G.

Another nice property of the representation of derivations in Int_G, is that, as we wished, the homomorphism that interpret those terms into sentences is quite simple. Indeed, $(w, \epsilon_1 b_1 \ldots \epsilon_n b_n a - f_1 \ldots - f_p)$ would be interpreted as:

$$\lambda g.g \underbrace{\epsilon \ldots \epsilon}_{p\times} (\lambda z_1 \ldots z_n . z_n \cdot \ldots \cdot z_2 \cdot w \cdot z_1)$$

For the semantic interpretation this would also yield to such simple homomorphisms. Thus being able to compute these intermediate representations factors out the computation that is common to both the syntactic and semantic interpretations of the derivations.

Since it does not seem possible yet to define by logical means the element built on Int_G that are representing minimalist derivations, we must use language theoretic means and define these elements with a homomorphism from Σ_G to Int_G. The definition of the homomorphism computing this intermediate representation from the derivation requires a technique very similar to the one used for the definition of $\mathcal{I}$ which is transforming derivations into sentences. The actual implementation is a little more complex, because we need to handle lists of traces, but it can be represented using the same computational power as for $\mathcal{I}$ (*i.e.* Gödel system T). Due to space limitations, we cannot give here the technical details of the transformation.

4   The Point of View of Monadic Second Order Logic

We have seen that linear λ-terms represent adequately minimalist derivations. But we have also seen that the interpretation of those terms is not trivial. This leads us to the conclusion that terms are not an adequate representation of proofs so as to interpret them as strings. We therefore switch to a proof-net representation of those proofs. We could use the proof-nets that represent the λ-terms we have defined in the previous section. We will however not do so and use the proof-nets introduced by Stabler in [19]. Stabler's proof-nets are tailor-made for representing minimalist derivations and are therefore more concise than the ones we would obtain by a direct representation of the proofs built on Σ_G. We then give the syntactic interpretation of those proof-nets with an MSO-transduction which is fairly simple when compared to the previous homomorphisms. This shows that graph transformations are more natural than homomorphisms when dealing with interpretation of minimalist derivations. This comes from the fact that dealing with graphs has the advantage of avoiding the top-down rigidity of terms. As there is no directionality, we can easily find the right place where to put things. This suggests that MSO-transductions of proof-nets should also be used to deal with the semantic interpretation of minimalist derivations.

We first start by defining Stabler's proof-nets as relational structures. Given a ranked alphabet Ω, an Ω-relational structure, is a tuple $(S, (R_a)_{a \in \Omega})$ where S is a finite set, the *carrier* of the Ω-relational structure, and R_a is a subset of S^n (n being the arity of a). Thus we define Stabler's proof-nets as $R(G)$-relational structures where, given a minimalist grammar G, $R(G)$ is the ranked alphabet whose constants are the lexical entries of G and the arity of such a constant (w, l) is the length of l. Given an $R(G)$-relational structure $\Pi = (S, (R_{(w,l)})_{(w,l) \in R(G)})$, a tuple $(x_1, \ldots, x_{|l|})$ that is in $R_{(w,l)}$ is called a (w, l)-link or a link. We say that x_i *belongs* to that link; the type of x_i in that link is the ith feature of l. Of course, not every possible $R(G)$-relational structure is going to represent a derivation of G and as usual we need a correctness criterion to discriminate structures representing an actual derivation from those that do not. If the tuple $(x_1, \ldots, x_{|l_1|}, z_0, z_1, \ldots, z_{|l_2|})$ is a $(w, l_1 a l_2)$-link then, x_i is its ith *argument* and z_j is its jth *trace*, z_0 is its *initial trace* and $z_{|l_2|}$ is its *actual trace*. We say that a link l_1 dominates a link l_2 if the initial trace of l_2 is an argument of l_1, we then write $l_2 \lhd l_1$ ($\overset{*}{\lhd}$ is the reflexive transitive closure of $\lhd$). Then the correctness criterion can be stated as:

1. there is a unique element r, the *conclusion* of the proof-net which belongs to exactly one link, its type is c,
2. every element y different from x, belongs to exactly two links p_y and n_y. y is a trace of p_y and an argument of n_y and if the type of y in p_y is a (*resp.* $-f$) then its type in n_y is $=a$ (*resp.* $+f$),
3. on links the relation $\lhd$ forms a tree whose root is p_r,
4. if y_1 and y_2 are respectively the j_1^{th} and the j_2^{th} traces of a link l and if $j_1 < j_2$ then $n_{y_1} \overset{*}{\lhd} n_{y_2}$ and in case $n_{y_1} = n_{y_2}$, y_1 being its i_1^{th} argument and y_2 being its i_2^{th} argument, we have $i_1 < i_2$.

The relational structures that satisfy all those properties are called *proof-nets*. It is easy to prove a property similar to sequentialization so as to show the correspondence between those proof-nets and the closed terms of Σ_G of type $d(c)$. We do not give the formal proof here as it would not bring anything of interest to our exposition.

Intuitively the first condition expresses that proof-net form a derivation of the correct type. The second condition expresses that fact that every feature has to be licensed in proof-nets. The third condition enforces the hierarchical construction of the derivation. Finally the last condition makes the movements of a *moving piece* be performed in the right order so that the licensing features are licenced in the linear order in which they appear in the list of features.

Example 6. We will give a graphical representation of proof-nets. The links of a lexical entry like $(\gamma_1, =da_1 - c - c)$ will be represented as a hyperedge like:

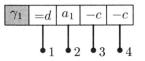

The vertices (the elements of the carrier of the relational structure) are represented with black dots. As in this example, where they are labeled 1, 2, 3 and 4, we will use label in order to designate certain elements of the carrier. Here the $(\gamma_1, =da_1-c-c)$-link that is graphically represented is $(1, 2, 3, 4)$, this link on has one argument 1 it has three traces, 2, 3 and 4, the actual trace of the link being 4; 1, 2, 3 and 4 respectively have type $=d$, a_1, $-c$ and $-c$ in this link. This information is graphically represented in the intuitive way by the origins of the tentacles on the hyperedge.

The derivation of Example 1 is graphically represented by the following proof-net:

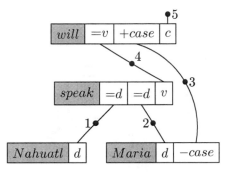

It is easy to check that this proof-structure verifies the two first requirements for being a proof-net. Concerning the third condition, it is fulfilled since we have that the sole $(will, =v+casec)$-link dominates the sole $(speak, =d=dv)$-link which dominates the $(Nahuatl, d)$-link and the $(Maria, d-case)$-link, and there is no other domination relation. Finally the fourth condition has to be checked only of the vertices 2 and 3 which are traces of the $(Maria, d-case)$-link, we can see that 2 is an argument of the $(speak, =d=dv)$-link and that 3 is an argument of the $(will, =v+casec)$-link and that there domination relation agrees with the fourth condition.

The derivation of Example 2 are represented with the following proof-nets:

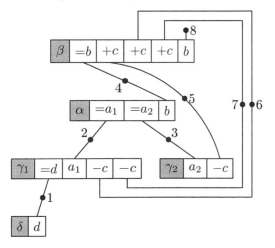

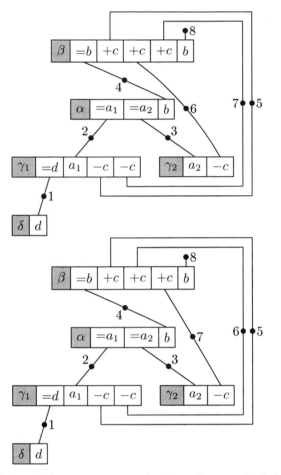

The fourth condition of the correctness criterion rules out the following structure as being a proof-net:

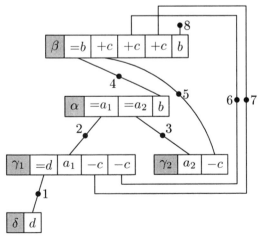

In order to give the syntactic interpretation of those proof-nets, we are going to use the notion of MSO-transduction (see [20]). An MSO-transduction is transforming a Ω-relational structure into a Δ-relational structure as follows:

1. first a finite number of copies of the carrier of the initial relational structure is done,
2. for each copy an MSO-formula specifies which elements of the carrier are kept,
3. then for each relation in Δ, some MSO-formulae specify which tuples of the remaining points verify this relation.

For the sake of simplicity, the MSO-transduction that gives the syntactic interpretation of proof-nets is specified as the composition of two MSO-transductions. A first transduction transforms the proof-nets into a string represented as a relational structure. This string may contain some occurrences of ϵ, the empty string. The second transduction is simply removing these occurrences of ϵ. This second transduction is quite simple and we will not enter into the details of its implementation.

Thus, the first transduction transforms $R(G)$-relational structures $\mathcal{R}$ that are proof-nets into a $W(G)$-relational structures $\mathcal{W}$ where $W(G)$ is the set of binary relations $W \cup \{\epsilon\}$. We first take two copies of the elements of $\mathcal{R}$ and we keep every vertex of each copy in the new structure. We write $fst(x)$ and $snd(x)$ two respectively denote the first and second copy of x in the new structure. In the new structure, we add a relation $\epsilon(fst(x), snd(x))$ if x is not the actual trace of p_x and $w(fst(x), snd(x))$ if x is the actual trace of p_x which is a (w, l)-link.

So as to explain the transduction, we will use the following derivation as a running example.

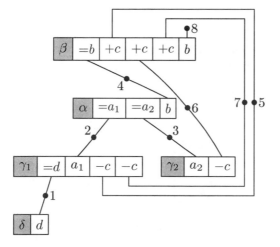

The first step of the MSO-transduction that we have just described transforms this derivation structure into the following structure. We keep the same label for the vertices of the first copy of the carrier and we use primed labels for the second copy, furthermore we have put an arrow on one of the tentacle which symbolise the right of the represented letter (the second argument in the represented relation):

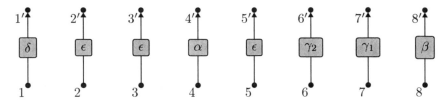

We now have all the ingredients that are necessary to construct the string we want. It just remains to concatenate them suitably. This concatenation will be performed simply by putting epsilon relations where needed. If we want to concatenate the words in which x and y are transformed in $\mathcal{W}$, it suffices to put a relation $\epsilon(snd(x), fst(y))$ in $\mathcal{W}$. This concatenation will be possible only if we can express in MSO the relation $x < y$ which is the linear order of the chain we want to build. If we look at the level of a $(w, l_1 a l_2)$-link $(x_1, \ldots, x_{|l_1|}, z_0, z_1, \ldots, z_{|l_2|})$ in order to build the string around $z_{|l_2|}$, the actual trace, we need to build the string $s_{|l_1|} \ldots s_2 w s_1$ if s_i is the string that is constructed around x_i. To do so, we need to be able to find the elements of $\mathcal{R}$ that start or end the string that is built around an element x. To achieve this, we introduce two binary predicates $\texttt{follow}(x, y)$ and $\texttt{precede}(x, y)$:

1. $\texttt{follow}(x, y)$ if and only if x is the actual trace of the link p_x, p_x has at least one argument, and y is the first argument of p_x,
2. $\texttt{precede}(x, y)$ holds if and only if x is the actual trace of the link p_x, p_x has at least two arguments and y is the last argument of p_x.

The relations $\texttt{follow}(x, y)$ and $\texttt{precede}(x, y)$ hold in a proof-net when y is the element in p_x whose start or end is also the start or the end of the string built around x when x is the actual trace of some link. In the example, if we represent pictorially the relations $\texttt{follow}$ and $\texttt{precede}$ (the arrow is pointing at the second element of the predicate) then we would obtain:

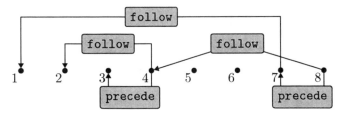

It is obvious that $\texttt{follow}(x, y)$ and $\texttt{precede}(x, y)$ are MSO-definable predicates. We note $\texttt{follow}^*(x, y)$ and $\texttt{precede}^*(x, y)$ the respective reflexive and transitive closures of $\texttt{follow}(x, y)$ and $\texttt{precede}(x, y)$. These relations are also MSO-definable since transitive closures of MSO-definable relations are also MSO-definable. We then define the relations $\texttt{start}(x, y)$ and $\texttt{end}(x, y)$ as being:

$$\mathtt{start}(x,y) \equiv \mathtt{precede}^*(x,y) \wedge \forall z.\mathtt{precede}^*(y,z) \Rightarrow y = z$$
$$\mathtt{end}(x,y) \equiv \mathtt{follow}^*(x,y) \wedge \forall z.\mathtt{follow}^*(y,z) \Rightarrow y = z$$

On a proof-net the relation $\mathtt{start}$ and $\mathtt{end}$ define functions, *i.e.* for every x there is exactly one y_s and exactly one y_e such that $\mathtt{start}(x, y_s)$ and $\mathtt{end}(x, y_e)$. According to the definition, we obtain the following table to describe these relations:

x	y_s	y_e		x	y_s	y_e
1	1	1		5	5	5
2	2	2		6	6	6
3	3	3		7	7	1
4	3	2		8	7	2

We are now in position to define the relation $x < y$ which says that the trace introduced by x appears just before the trace introduced by y.

If $(x_1, \ldots, x_n, z_0, \ldots, z_p)$ is a $(w, =b_1 \ldots \epsilon_n b_n, z_0, \ldots, z_p)$-link then we have that $x < y$ if and only if one of the following holds:

1. if $n > 0$, $\mathtt{start}(x_1, x) \wedge y = z_p$,
2. if $n > 1$, $\mathtt{end}(x_2, x) \wedge y = z_p$
3. for some $1 < i < n$, $\mathtt{end}(x_{i+1}, x) \wedge \mathtt{start}(x_i, y)$

This is enough to define the precedence relation. It is provable that the transitive closure of $<$ is a total order when $\mathcal{R}$ is a proof-net. On our example the relation $<$ would order the set $\{1; \ldots; 8\}$ as follows:

$$7 < 1 < 6 < 5 < 8 < 3 < 4 < 2$$

Indeed, if we look at 8 the conclusion of the proof-net, it is the actual trace of the $(\beta, =b+c+c+cb)$-link of the proof-net and, respectively, the first second third and fourth arguments of the link are 4, 5, 6 and 7. As we have $\mathtt{start}(4, 3)$, we have $8 < 3$, and as we have $\mathtt{end}(7, 1)$ and $\mathtt{start}(6, 6)$ we have $1 < 6$, as we have $\mathtt{end}(6, 6)$ and $\mathtt{start}(5, 5)$, we have $6 < 5$ and as we have $\mathtt{end}(5, 5)$ we have $5 < 8$. Similarly, by looking at every vertex that is the actual trace of some link we can complete the relation $<$ as above. Since $\mathtt{follow}^*$, $\mathtt{precede}^*$ are MSO-definable relations, then $\mathtt{start}$ and $\mathtt{end}$ are MSO-definable, and thus $<$ is an MSO-definable relation.

As mentioned previously the relation $<$ describes the way the words represented by binary relations must be concatenated in order to produce the resulting string. As we describe the transduction as the composition of two transductions, the first one building the resulting string interspersed with empty strings and the second one deleting the empty strings, we represent concatenation of two nodes as putting x and y as putting an empty string between the second copy of x, and the first copy of y. So if we add this concatenation requirement to the definition of ϵ, we have that $\epsilon(fst(x), snd(x))$ holds if and only if x is not the actual trace of any link and $\epsilon(snd(x), fst(y))$ holds if and only if $x < y$. In our example concatenating 5 and 8 amounts to add the pair $(5', 8)$ to the relation ϵ. So after the MSO-transduction we have defined is applied to the derivation we have taken as an example we obtain the following relational structure that represents the string $\gamma_1 \epsilon \delta \epsilon \gamma_2 \epsilon \epsilon \epsilon \beta \epsilon \epsilon \epsilon \alpha \epsilon \epsilon$:

Then a simple string homomorphism can suppress the occurrences of ϵ. In the example we would then obtain the relational structure representing, as expected, the string $\gamma_1 \delta \gamma_2 \beta \alpha$. Such string to string transformations can be defined with MSO-transductions. As MSO-transductions are closed under composition, we have showed that the interpretation of proof-nets into strings can be computed using MSO-transductions.

Now if we are concerned with the shortest move constraint, we first need to remark that proof-nets are MSO-definable in $R(G)$-relational structure and then we can easily see that the shortest move constraint gives proof-nets with a bounded treewidth. These proof-nets can therefore be represented as the language of a hyperedge replacement grammar (HR-languages). As HR-languages are closed under MSO-transduction we get that the languages of MGs with shortest move are HR-languages. But it is known that the string languages of HR grammars coincide with MCFLs [21].

5   Conclusion

This work is mainly aiming at clarifying the status of derivations in minimalist grammars without the shortest move constraint. It also tries to promote a certain attitude towards formalisms describing natural languages. This attitude consists in trying to identify and study the abstract syntax of the formalisms. Abstract syntax plays a central role in formalisation because it is the particular place where the connection between syntax and semantics can be made. It is also at the level of abstract syntax that linguistic ideas like **move** and **merge** have the greatest influence. We have emphasized this role from a mathematical point of view by showing that these two operations dramatically reduce the complexity of generating syntactic structure by allowing a rather powerful polymorphism and also by taming variable binding using only third order types.

From the mathematical side, this careful study of the derivations in connection with some simple ideas coming from formal language theory has lead us to several new results. First we have showed that the membership problem for MGs is as difficult as the problem of proof-search in MELL. This result shows that it is not obvious at all that the membership problem for MGs is decidable or not. Second we have obtained the unintuitive result that the languages of MGs may not be semi-linear contradicting a conjecture by [13]. Finally we have obtained a rather interesting and new logical characterization of these derivations as closed linear λ-terms of a certain type. This characterization can be said as being logical since, with the Curry-Howard isomorphism, closed linear λ-terms correspond proofs in implicative linear logic with proper axioms (they play the role of the exponentials) and since we do not appeal to extra constraints in order to rule out terms that would not represent derivations. Furthermore, this way of representing derivations is made even more natural by the aforementioned Turing-equivalence of the membership problem for MGs and proof-search in MELL.

From a linguistic point of view, this careful study also has some outcomes. Indeed, the representation of the derivations of MGs we propose are unambiguous in the sens that, contrary to Stabler's proposal, they only represent the syntactic analysis of one sentence. Furthermore, since the ambiguity of Stabler's proposal makes sentences that have different meanings have the same derivation, the disambiguation we propose should allow a simpler interface between syntax and semantics. Our proposal makes it also clear that movement and traces are adequately rendered by variable binding. It also gives a methodological way of extending MGs. Indeed, the linear λ-calculus and typing theory offers a good framework for devising sensible improvements of MGs.

Nevertheless, our proposal has several defects. First of all, contrary to what would be expected, the feature checking system of MGs is not rendered by using the resource sensitivity of linear logic but it is rather modeled by the particular management of types that we use. Moreover, the linearisation of those structures to string uses a non-trivial homomorphism and most of the computation that are induced by the **move** operation is common to both the syntactic linearisation and the semantic interpretation. This can be fixed by transforming derivations with a homomorphism into intermediate structures. Interestingly at the level of these intermediate structures the feature checking system of MGs is rendered by the resource sensitivity of linear logic, unfortunately we would need extra logical constraints so as to rule out certain terms that do not represent MG derivations and to avoid some spurious ambiguities.

Finally combining proof-nets and MSO related techniques we are able to give a simple interpretation of derivation structures using MSO-transductions. The main problem of this approach is the fact that a proof-net is actually transformed into a string needs to be proved while this is guaranteed by type-checking in the homomorphic approach that maps λ-terms to strings. But, this approach is rather new in mathematical linguistic, so that maybe there could be certain way of guarantying certain properties easily. It would also be interesting to see how this approach could be used for semantic interpretation of derivations.

This work appeals to various techniques from formal language theory. A rule-based one that is rendered by our representation of derivations as linear λ-terms and the homomorphic interpretation of those terms. A descriptive one that resembles Model Theoretic Syntax [22] that uses MSO to describe and interpret derivations. This variety of techniques allows us to appeal to many results in the literature to retrieve results like [17] from results on rule-based techniques or from results on MSO related techniques. These two points of view are complementary. The first one helps to understand computational difficulty, to design parsing algorithm. The second one simplifies greatly the overall description of the formalism.

This duality in formalization helps us to understand in a better way the gap that separates computational linguists from descriptive linguists. While the first are interested in accounting for the way sentences are constructed by designing some generation process, the second are mostly describing linguistic data, explaining how constituents are related in certain circumstances. This opposition seems very similar to the one that opposes MTS to Context Free Grammars.

References

1. Lecomte, A., Retoré, C.: Towards a minimal logic for minimalist grammars: a tranformational use of lambek calculus. In: Formal Grammar 1999 (1999)
2. Lecomte, A., Retoré, C.: Extending lambek grammars: a logical account of minimalist grammars. In: Proceedings of the 39th Meeting of the Association for Computational Linguistics, ACL 2001, pp. 354–361 (2001)
3. Lecomte, A.: A computational approach to minimalism. In: Proceedings of ICON 2003, International Conference on Natural Language. Central Institute of Indian Languages, pp. 20–31 (2003)
4. Lecomte, A.: Derivations as proofs: a logical approach to minimalism. In: Proceedings of CG 2004 (2004)
5. Amblard, M.: Calculs de représentations s'emantique et syntaxe générative: les grammaires minimalistes catégorielles. PhD thesis, Université de Bordeaux 1 (2007)
6. Girard, J.Y.: Linear logic. Theoretical Computer Science 50, 1–102 (1987)
7. Curry, H.B.: Some logical aspects of grammatical structure. In: Jakobson, R. (ed.) Structure of Language and Its Mathematical Aspects, pp. 56–68. AMS Bookstore (1961)
8. Muskens, R.: Lambda Grammars and the Syntax-Semantics Interface. In: van Rooy, R., Stokhof, M. (eds.) Proceedings of the Thirteenth Amsterdam Colloquium, Amsterdam, pp. 150–155 (2001)
9. de Groote, P.: Towards abstract categorial grammars. In: Association for Computational Linguistics, Proceedings 39th Annual Meeting and 10th Conference of the European Chapter, pp. 148–155. Morgan Kaufmann Publishers, San Francisco (2001)
10. de Groote, P.: Towards a montagovian account of dynamics. In: Proceedings of Semantics in Linguistic Theory, vol. XVI. CLC Publications (2007)
11. Stabler, E.: Derivational minimalism. In: Retoré, C. (ed.) LACL 1996. LNCS (LNAI), vol. 1328, pp. 68–95. Springer, Heidelberg (1997)
12. de Groote, P., Guillaume, B., Salvati, S.: Vector addition tree automata. In: de Groote, P., Guillaume, B., Salvati, S. (eds.) 19th IEEE Symposium on Logic in Computer Science, pp. 63–74 (2004)
13. Gärtner, H.M., Michaelis, J.: Locality conditions and the complexity of minimalist grammars: a preliminary survey. In: Rogers, J. (ed.) Workshop on Model Theoretic Syntax (MTS@10), Dublin, Ireland, pp. 89–100 (2007)
14. Hopcroft, J.E., Pansiot, J.J.: On the reachability problem for 5-dimensional vector addition systems. Theoretical Computer Science 8(2), 135–159 (1979)
15. Yoshinaka, R.: Linearization of affine abstract categorial grammars. In: Proceedings of the 11th Conference on Formal Grammar (2006)
16. Salvati, S.: Encoding second order string acg with deterministic tree walking transducers. In: Wintner, S. (ed.) Proceedings FG 2006: the 11th Conference on Formal Grammars. FG Online Proceedings, pp. 143–156. CSLI Publications, Stanford (2007)

17. Michaelis, J.: Derivational minimalism is mildly context-sensitive. In: Moortgat, M. (ed.) LACL 1998. LNCS (LNAI), vol. 2014, pp. 179–198. Springer, Heidelberg (2001)
18. Kobele, G.M.: Generating Copies: An Investigation into Structural Identity in Language and Grammar. PhD thesis, University of California Los Angeles (2006)
19. Stabler, E.P.: Remnant movement and structural complexity. In: Constraints and Resources in Natural Language, Studies in Logic, Language and Information, pp. 299–326. CSLI, Stanford (1999)
20. Courcelle, B.: Monadic second-order definable graph transductions: A survey. Theoritical Computer Science 126(1), 53–75 (1994)
21. Weir, D.J.: Linear context-free rewriting systems and deterministic tree-walking transducers. In: ACL, pp. 136–143 (1992)
22. Pullum, G.K., Scholz, B.C.: On the distinction between model-theoretic and generative-enumerative syntactic frameworks. In: de Groote, P., Morrill, G., Retoré, C. (eds.) LACL 2001. LNCS (LNAI), vol. 2099, pp. 17–43. Springer, Heidelberg (2001)

Good Types Are Useful for Learning

Isabelle Tellier and Daniel Dudau-Sofronie

LIFO - université d'Orléans
6 rue Léonard de Vinci, BP 6759
45 067 Orléans cedex 2, France
isabelle.tellier@univ-orleans.fr
http://www.univ-orleans.fr/lifo/Members/Isabelle.Tellier

Abstract. This paper presents learnability results from Typed Examples for some classes of Lambek Grammars, in the context of Gold's model of identification in the limit. Typed Examples are semantic information and we show that, as soon as syntax and semantics are connected by some compositional morphism, they allow to learn rich syntactic formalisms. A learning strategy is also presented and exemplified.

1 Introduction

Although categorial grammars have been known for a long time, the question of their learnability is a recent issue. In the nineties, Kanazawa [17] opened new ways of research in this domain. He proved that, even if the class of every AB-Categorial Grammars [2] (or CG) is trivially not learnable from positive examples in Gold's model [14], large subclasses are. The most interesting classes are called k-valued: they are defined as the sets of CG assigning at most k distinct categories to each member of their vocabulary. Thanks to his work, we now know that for any $k \geq 1$, the class of k-valued CG is learnable from Structural Examples (i.e. syntactic analysis structures where rules are preserved but intermediate categories are deleted) and from strings (or sentences). These theoretical results are associated with learning algorithms, inspired by the pioneer work of Buszkowski and Penn [7]. Unfortunately, the only tractable (polynomial) case is the learning of rigid (i.e. 1-valued) CG from Structural Examples. The problem that naturally arose from these first results was to adapt them to known variants of k-valued Lambek Grammars [18] (or LG). But it appeared not to be a very easy issue. As a matter of fact, it has been proved that it is possible to learn the class of rigid LG from proof structures of a certain normal form [6] but, on the contrary, this class is not learnable from strings alone [12]. Thus, for LG, learnability results crucially rely on the available input data. Another known learnability result on rigid LG relies on additional restrictions on grammars [4].

We have introduced the concept of learnability from Typed Examples in the context of CG [10]. It has also been adapted to Pregroup Grammars [5] and other formalisms [13]. Typed Examples are sentences where each word is associated with a lexicalized type derived from its category in the target grammar by a morphism. Typed Examples can be considered as intermediary input data, richer

S. Pogodalla, M. Quatrini, and C. Retoré (Eds.): Lecomte Festschrift, LNAI 6700, pp. 118–137, 2011.

than strings but less informative than Structural Examples. They can also be interpreted as coming from semantic information, as the types used are inspired by Montague's semantics [19]. In a cognitive perspective, it is relevant to consider that *semantics is acquired before syntax* [24]. So, providing semantically typed examples to help learning grammars is also cognitively relevant [26,3]. We have identified interesting subclasses of CG learnable from Typed Examples [11]. But, in this case, the learnability result itself was a trivial consequence of the learnability of rigid CG from strings. For LG, the situation is different as rigid LG are learnable from Structural Examples but not from strings. In this article, we show that large subclasses of LG are in fact learnable from Typed Examples. Furthermore, the learnability result for CG from Typed Examples was associated with an original learning algorithm inspired by syntactic analysis procedures. While Kanazawa's learning algorithm implements a generalisation strategy, ours is a *specialisation strategy* [27]. This is also in favor of a better cognitive relevance [15]. We show here that this specialisation strategy can also be applied to LG.

After some preliminary definitions, the paper focuses on the notion of learnability from Typed Examples in Gold's model. It is proved that interesting subclasses of LG are learnable from Typed Examples and an original inference algorithm (which is nevertheless not a full learning algorithm in the sense of Gold) is provided. This global strategy is illustrated on examples. The properties of our algorithm, some implementation details and extensions are also discussed.

2 Preliminaries

2.1 Categorial Grammars

In categorial grammars, the syntax is *lexicalized*. The syntactic categories assigned to each word carry its combinatorial potential. Every kind of categorial grammar share the same notion of categories.

Definition 1 (Categories). *Let $\mathcal{B}$ be a countably infinite set of basic categories containing a distinguished category $S \in \mathcal{B}$, called the axiom. We note $Cat(\mathcal{B})$ the term algebra built over the two binary symbols $/$, $\backslash$ which is the smallest set such that $\mathcal{B} \subset Cat(\mathcal{B})$ and for any $A, B \in Cat(\mathcal{B})$ we have: $/(A, B) \in Cat(\mathcal{B})$ and $\backslash(A, B) \in Cat(\mathcal{B})$*[1].

Definition 2 (AB-Categorial Grammars and Lambek Grammars). *For every finite vocabulary Σ and for every set of basic categories $\mathcal{B}$ ($S \in \mathcal{B}$), a **categorial grammar** is a finite relation G over $\Sigma \times Cat(\mathcal{B})$. We note $\langle u, A \rangle \in G$ the assignment of the category $A \in Cat(\mathcal{B})$ to the element of the vocabulary $u \in \Sigma$. The family of categorial grammars is composed of two main subclasses: AB-Categorial Grammars (CG) and Lambek Grammars (LG).*

---

[1] For reasons that will become clear further, we give up here the classical notations B/A and $A\backslash B$: in our notation, terms $/(A, B)$ and $\backslash(A, B)$ are both functors whose first component A is the argument and whose second component B is the result.

AB-Categorial Grammars (CG) are categorial grammars where the syntactic rules take the form of two rewriting schemes: $\forall A, B \in Cat(\mathcal{B})$

- *FA (Forward Application)* : $/(A, B) \; A \to B$
- *BA (Backward Application)* : $A \; \backslash(A, B) \to B$

The language generated by a CG G is:
$L(G) = \{u_1 \ldots u_n \in \Sigma^+ \mid \forall i \in \{1, \ldots, n\}, \exists A_i \in Cat(\mathcal{B}) \text{ such that } \langle u_i, A_i \rangle \in G$
and $A_1, \ldots, A_n \to^* S\}$.
Lambek Grammars (LG) are categorial grammars in which the syntactic analysis is described by a logical calculus defined by:

- *axioms:*

$$[ID] \; A \vdash A$$

- *inference rules:*

$$[/R] \; \frac{\Gamma, A \vdash B}{\Gamma \vdash /(A, B)} \qquad\qquad [\backslash R] \; \frac{A, \Gamma \vdash B}{\Gamma \vdash \backslash(A, B)}$$

$$[/L] \; \frac{\Gamma \vdash A \quad \Delta, B, \Pi \vdash C}{\Delta, /(A, B), \Gamma, \Pi \vdash C} \; [\backslash L] \; \frac{\Gamma \vdash A \quad \Delta, B, \Pi \vdash C}{\Delta, \Gamma, \backslash(A, B), \Pi \vdash C}$$

where $A, B, C \in Cat(\mathcal{B})$ and Γ, Δ, Π are finite sequences of categories from $Cat(\mathcal{B})$, $\Gamma \neq \emptyset$. The language $L(G)$ generated by a LG G is:
$L(G) = \{u_1 \ldots u_n \in \Sigma^+ \mid \forall i \in \{1, \ldots, n\}, \exists A_i \in Cat(\mathcal{B}) \text{ such that } \langle u_i, A_i \rangle \in G$
and $A_1, \ldots, A_n \vdash S\}$.
In the following, elements of Σ will be called *words* and elements of $L(G)$ will be called *sentences*.

Of course, the rewriting schemes allowed in CG are valid sequents of LG (see the rules $[/R]$ and $[\backslash R]$). So, for a given assignment of categories, every sentence belonging to the language of a CG also belongs to the language of the corresponding LG. The variant of the Lambek calculus considered in this paper is non-commutative, associative, without product and without empty antecedent. This variant is the one which has received the greatest linguistic and logical attention [21,25]. The Lambek calculus can also be expressed in the context of natural deduction, but here we only use the sequent calculus which can be easily linked with parse algorithms.

Example 1. Let $\mathcal{B} = \{S, T, N\}$ be a set of basic categories (T stands for "term" and N for "common noun") and $\Sigma = \{$a, lecture, teaches, Alain$\}$ a vocabulary. Let G be the Lambek Grammar over $\Sigma \times Cat(\mathcal{B})$ defined by the following assignments: $\{\langle a, /(N, \backslash(/(T, S), S)) \rangle, \langle lecture, N \rangle, \langle Alain, T \rangle, \langle teaches, \backslash(T, S) \rangle,$ $\langle teaches, /(T, \backslash(T, S)) \rangle\}$. G recognizes sentences like "Alain teaches" or "Alain teaches a lecture", as displayed by the following proof (the notation [ID] is omitted for readability):

$$[/L]\dfrac{N \vdash N \quad [\backslash L]\dfrac{[/R]\dfrac{[/L]\dfrac{T \vdash T \quad [\backslash L]\dfrac{T \vdash T \quad S \vdash S}{T, \backslash(T,S) \vdash S}}{T, /(T, \backslash(T,S)), T \vdash S}}{T, /(T, \backslash(T,S)) \vdash /(T,S)} \quad S \vdash S}{T, /(T, \backslash(T,S)), \backslash(/(T,S), S) \vdash S}}{T, \quad /(T, \backslash(T,S)), /(N, \backslash(/(T,S), S)), \quad N \vdash S}$$

$$\text{Alain} \qquad \text{teaches} \qquad\qquad a \qquad\quad \text{lecture}$$

It is easy to observe that this sentence is not recognized by the CG with the same assignment of categories. To to so, it would be necessary to assign an extra category to the word "teaches": $\backslash(T, /(T, S))$. The inference rules of the Lambek calculus simulate multiple category assignments, but at the price of a higher complexity for parsing [23].

We denote by $\mathcal{G}$ the class of CG and by $\mathcal{LG}$ the class of LG. For every integer $k \geq 1$, the set of CG (resp. LG) assigning at most k distinct categories to each word is the class of k-valued CG (resp. LG) denoted by $\mathcal{G}_k$ (resp. $\mathcal{LG}_k$).

2.2   Semantic Types

Montague [19] was one of the first to propose a typed logic to represent natural language semantics. The associated notion of semantic type became so forth classical. It is this (slightly generalised) notion of type that will be used here. These types can also be assigned to words, according to their lexical semantics. Like categories, types characterize a combinatorial potential, but at the semantic level.

Definition 3 (Semantic Types). *Let Θ be a finite set of basic types containing a distinguished type $t \in \Theta$. We note Types(Θ) the set of all possible types, which is the smallest set such that: $\Theta \subset$ Types(Θ) and for any $u, v \in$ Types(Θ), $(u, v) \in$ Types(Θ). The type (u, v) is assigned to a functor expecting an argument of type u and providing a result of type v[2].*

Example 2. The usual set of basic types is $\Theta = \{e, t\}$, where e is the type of elementary entities and t the type of truth values. In a logical-based semantic representation, identifiers for individuals like "Alain" can be represented by a logical constant of type e (Montague prefered a more complicated type) while common nouns and intransitive verbs can be associated with one place predicates, of type (e, t). Transitive verbs are denoted by two-place predicates, of type $(e, (e, t))$. Verbs like "teaches" can have both a transitive and an intransitive use, and thus receive both assignments of types.

There is a close connection between categories of categorial grammars and semantic types. Both are binary terms. This connection can be formalized by the notion of Typing Function.

---

[2] In Montague's tradition, this type would be noted $\langle u, v \rangle$, or $u \longrightarrow v$, but we prefer a notation closer to the one of categories.

Definition 4 (Typing Function). *For any set of basic categories* $\mathcal{B}$ $(S \in \mathcal{B})$ *and any set of basic types* Θ $(t \in \Theta)$, *a Typing Function h is a morphism from* $Cat(\mathcal{B})$ *to* $Types(\Theta)$ *satisfying the following conditions:*

1. $h(S) = t$;
2. $\forall A, B \in \mathcal{B}$: *if* $h(A) = h(B) \in \Theta$ *then* $A = B$. *Note that this does not imply that h is injective on $\mathcal{B}$ because of the condition that both images must belong to* Θ, *i.e. be basic types.*
3. $\forall A, B \in Cat(\mathcal{B})$: $h(/(A, B)) = h(\backslash(A, B)) = (h(A), h(B))$.

As h is a morphism and $Cat(\mathcal{B})$ is built over the set $\mathcal{B}$, it is enough to define h on $\mathcal{B}$ to deduce its values on $Cat(\mathcal{B})$. This definition justifies the notation chosen for categories, where the operators (/ or \\) playing the role of functors in a term, are simply deleted by the Typing Function.

Example 3. If we set: $h(T) = e, h(S) = t, h(N) = (e, t)$, we define a Typing Function for the categories of the grammar in Example 1 perfectly compatible with their semantics in Example 2. Note that a basic category (N in our example) can be associated with a non-basic type and that two distinct (non-basic, otherwise it would contradict condition (2)) categories can be associated with an identical type as: $h(\backslash(T, S)) = (h(T), h(S)) = (e, t) = h(N)$. As a matter of fact, both common nouns and transitive verbs semantically behave as one-place predicates, but they are not syntactically equivalent: so, they share the same semantic types but not the same syntactic categories.

The Principle of Compositionality asserts that the meaning of a sentence only depends of the meaning of its parts and of its syntactic structure [22,16] (where the "parts" are usually identified with words). This principle is at the heart of the correspondence between syntax and semantics in Montague's work, and in the categorial grammar framework in general. In this framework, it is usually translated by a similarity of structure between syntactic and semantic trees (or proofs). But categories and types are *lexicalized structures* linked by a Typing Function. The Typing Function can thus be seen as the *lexicalized version of the Principle of Compositionality*. If semantics is acquired before syntax, it means that semantic types may be available to a learner who has to acquire the syntactic categories of his mother tongue. So, the inputs available to this learner are sentences labelled by semantic types: this is what we call h-Typed Examples.

Definition 5 (The h-Typed Language of a Lambek Grammars). *For any sets* Σ, $\mathcal{B}$ *and* Θ, *any LG G over* $\Sigma \times Cat(\mathcal{B})$ *and any Typing Function h from* $Cat(\mathcal{B})$ *to* $Types(\Theta)$, *the h-Typed Language of G is defined by:* $\langle u_1, \tau_1 \rangle ... \langle u_n, \tau_n \rangle \in TL_h(G)$ *if* $\forall i \in \{1, ..., n\}$ $\exists A_i$ *so that* $\langle u_i, A_i \rangle \in G, \tau_i = h(A_i)$ *and* $A_1, ..., A_n \vdash S$. *An element of $TL_h(G)$ is called a h-Typed Example of G.*

Example 4. The h-Typed Example corresponding with the sentence analysed in Example 1 and the Typing Function of Example 3 is the following:
$\langle Alain, e \rangle \langle teaches, (e, (e, t)) \rangle \langle a, ((e, t), ((e, t), t)) \rangle \langle lecture, (e, t) \rangle$.

Definition 6 (Lengths). *For any category $A \in Cat(\mathcal{B})$ (resp. for any type $\tau \in Types(\Theta)$), the length of A, noted $|A|$ (resp. the length of τ noted $|\tau|$) is the number of basic categories (resp. of basic types) it contains:*

- *if $A \in \mathcal{B}$ (resp. $\tau \in \Theta$) then $|A| = 1$ (resp. $|\tau| = 1$);*
- *$\forall A, B \in Cat(\mathcal{B})$ (resp. $\forall u, v \in Types(\Theta)$) $|/(A,B)| = |\backslash(A,B)| = |A| + |B|$ (resp. $|(u,v)| = |u| + |v|$).*

Lemma 1. *(trivial) For any set of basic categories $\mathcal{B}$, any set of basic types Θ and any Typing Function h from $Cat(\mathcal{B})$ to $Types(\Theta)$ we have:*
$\forall C \in Cat(\mathcal{B}), |C| \leq |h(C)|$.

2.3 Grammar Systems and Learnability Theory

To deal with questions of learnability, Kanazawa [17] introduced the notion of Grammar System, allowing a reformulation of the classical Gold's model of *identification in the limit from positive examples* [14]. We recall this notion here and some known learnability results concerning categorial grammars.

Definition 7 (Grammar System). *A **Grammar System** is a triple $\langle \Omega, \Lambda, L \rangle$:*

- *Ω is the hypothesis space (here, Ω will be a set of grammars),*
- *The sample space Λ is a recursive subset of A^*, for some fixed alphabet A (elements of Λ are sentences and subsets of Λ are languages);*
- *$L : \Omega \to pow(\Lambda)$ is a naming function. The question of whether $w \in L(G)$ which holds between $w \in \Lambda$ and $G \in \Omega$, is supposed to be computable.*

The main Grammar System we deal with in the following of this paper is $\langle \mathcal{LG}, (\Sigma \times Types(\Theta))^*, TL_h \rangle$. It means that we are going to study how to learn a Lambek Grammar from Typed Examples, that is from sentences where each word is associated with its semantic type.

Definition 8 (Learnability Criterion). *Let $\langle \Omega, \Lambda, L \rangle$ be a Grammar System and $\phi : \bigcup_{k \geq 1} \Lambda^k \to \Omega$ be a computable function. We say that ϕ **converges** to $G \in \Omega$ on a sequence $\langle s_i \rangle_{i \in \mathbb{N}}$ of elements of Λ if $G_i = \phi(\langle s_0, ..., s_i \rangle)$ is defined and equal to G for all but finitely many $i \in \mathbb{N}$ - or equivalently if there exists $n_0 \in \mathbb{N}$ such that for all $i \geq n_0$, G_i is defined and equal to G. Such a function ϕ is said to **learn** $\mathcal{G} \subseteq \Omega$ if for every language L in $L(\mathcal{G}) = \{L(G) | G \in \mathcal{G}\}$ and for every infinite sequence $\langle s_i \rangle_{i \in \mathbb{N}}$ that enumerates the elements of L (i.e. such that $\{s_i | i \in \mathbb{N}\} = L$), there exists some G in $\mathcal{G}$ such that $L(G) = L$ and ϕ converges to G on $\langle s_i \rangle_{i \in \mathbb{N}}$.*

Kanazawa [17] proved that for every $k \geq 1$, the class $\mathcal{G}_k$ of CG assigning at most k distinct categories to each of its words is learnable in the Grammar System $\langle \mathcal{G}, \Sigma^*, L \rangle$. So, any CG which is known to be k-valued for a given k is learnable from plain sentences. As a consequence, subclasses of CG are also learnable with more information, such like Typed Examples. These classes can thus trivially be learned in the Grammar System $\langle \mathcal{G}, (\Sigma \times Types(\Theta))^*, TL_h \rangle$ [11].

For LG, we also know that the class of rigid LG is learnable from Structural Examples where the structure is provided by a normal form of proofs [6], but is not learnable in the Grammar System $\langle \mathcal{LG}, \Sigma^*, L \rangle$ [12] i.e. from strings alone. We will now focus on the learnability of subclasses of LG in the Grammar System $\langle \mathcal{LG}, (\Sigma \times Types(\Theta))^*, TL_h \rangle$, i.e. from Typed Examples, which are h-Typed Examples where h is not known.

3   Learning Lambek Grammars from Typed Examples

In this section, we first prove learnability results for subclasses of LG from Typed Examples. We then describe an original algorithm which provides the set of LG compatible with a set of Typed Examples.

3.1   Learnability Theorems

The classes of LG we are interested in are those for which types are enough to characterize categories. The condition we introduce thus means that each time a single word is associated with two distinct categories, then the corresponding semantic types are also distinct.

Definition 9 (Typed Lambek Grammars). *For every vocabulary Σ, every set of basic categories $\mathcal{B}$, every set of basic types Θ, the class of Typed LG $\mathcal{LG}_{type}$ is the set of LG G over $\Sigma \times Cat(\mathcal{B})$ such that there exists a Typing Function h from $Cat(\mathcal{B})$ to $Types(\Theta)$ satisfying the condition:*
$\forall u \in \Sigma, \forall \langle u, A \rangle \in G$ and $\langle u, A' \rangle \in G, A \neq A' \Rightarrow h(A) \neq h(A')$.

The class $\mathcal{LG}_{type}$ is very similar to the one studied in the context of CG called $\mathcal{G}_{type}$[11]. We have proved interesting language theoretical results concerning $\mathcal{G}_{type}$ for the special case where $h = h_0$, defining a one to one correspondence between $\mathcal{B}$ and Θ (i.e. h_0 only deletes operators without modifying anything else). As a matter of fact, for every CG, there exists a member of this class with $h = h_0$ recognizing the same structure language. We do not have any similar result for LG and the class $\mathcal{LG}_{type}$ but note that $\mathcal{LG}_{type}$ contains every rigid LG and intersects every set of k-valued LG. For example, the LG of Example 1 is 2-valued and in $\mathcal{LG}_{type}$ because for any h, the two distinct categories assigned to the word "teaches" are associated with distinct types. Nevertheless the restriction expressed in Definition 9 prohibits to assign both $/(N, \backslash (/(T, S), S))$ and $/(N, /(\backslash (T, S), S))$ to determiners (classically, the first one is assigned to determiners introducing direct objects, the second one to determiners introducing subjects) because both always lead to the same type (the type $((e, t), ((e, t), t))$ in our example). We will see in the following how to treat such cases.

Theorem 1. *The class $\mathcal{LG}_{type}$ is learnable from Typed Examples, i.e. in the Grammar System $\langle \mathcal{LG}, (\Sigma \times Types(\Theta))^*, TL_h \rangle$.*

The main idea of the proof is that there exists a finite number of possible categories which are compatible with a given semantic type, and so a finite number of possible grammars (and of possible h) compatible with any given sample of Typed Examples. This property is detailed in the following lemma.

Lemma 2. *For every vocabulary Σ, every set $\mathcal{B}$ and Θ, every $G \in \mathcal{LG}_{type}$ without useless category (i.e. without any category assignment never used in any syntactic analysis) associated with the Typing Function h from $Cat(\mathcal{B})$ to $Types(\Theta)$, there exists an integer $N \in \mathbb{N}$ and a finite sample $\langle s_i \rangle_{i \leq N} \subseteq TL_h(G)$, such that from this sample it is possible to compute:*

- *the least integer k such that G is k-valued;*
- *a bound on the maximal length of the categories assigned to the words of G;*
- *a bound on the maximal number of distinct basic categories used to define the categories assigned to the words of G.*

Proof (proof of Lemma 2). For any given $G \in \mathcal{LG}_{type}$, the required characteristic sample just needs to contain some Typed Examples such that at least one occurrence of every couple $\langle word, type \rangle$ appears somewhere. By definition of $G \in \mathcal{LG}_{type}$, it is enough to take the Typed Examples corresponding with sentences such that at least one occurrence of every couple $\langle word, category \rangle$ is rquired for parsing. From such a sample set, let us compute each of the values:

- To compute the least integer k such that G is k-valued, it is enough to note that the condition for G to belong to $\mathcal{LG}_{type}$ is precisely that there are exactly the same number of distinct couples $\langle word, category \rangle$ in G as there are corresponding distinct couples $\langle word, type = h(category) \rangle$ in elements of $TL_h(G)$. After all such couples have been presented at least once in the sample set, k is available.
- To compute a bound on the maximal length of categories assigned to the words of G it is, similarly, enough to take the maximal length of types appearing in elements of the sample set. Lemma 1 ensures that the bound on the lengths of types is also a bound on the lengths of categories. Let us call L such a bound.
- Finally, to compute a bound on the maximal number of distinct basic categories used to define the categories assigned to the words of G, it is enough to take advantage of both previous results. This number is bounded by $k \times L \times |\Sigma|$ where $|\Sigma|$ stands for the number of distinct words in G, available as soon as each word has been presented at least once.

Proof (proof of Theorem 1). The theorem is a direct consequence of Lemma 2. As a matter of fact, the lemma implies that there exists a finite computable number of LG without useless categories (up to a renaming of basic categories) compatible with any sequence enumerating the elements of some $TL_h(G)$ and that this set is recursively enumerable. This situation classically implies [1,17] the learnability of the class $\mathcal{LG}_{type}$ in the Grammar System $\langle \mathcal{LG}, (\Sigma \times Types(\Theta))^*, TL_h \rangle$.

It is now easy to generalize this result to the case of multiple category assignments to the same word, corresponding with a unique type.

Definition 10 (m-distinct Typed LG). *For every vocabulary Σ, every set of basic categories $\mathcal{B}$, every set of basic types Θ and every $m \geq 1$, the class of*

m-distinct Typed LG noted $\mathcal{LG}^m_{type}$ *is the set of LG G over* $\Sigma \times Cat(\mathcal{B})$ *such that there exists a Typing Function h from* $Cat(\mathcal{B})$ *to* $Types(\Theta)$ *satisfying:*

$$\max_{\langle u, A \rangle \in G} (Card\{A' | \langle u, A' \rangle \in G \text{ and } h(A) = h(A')\}) \leq m$$

When $m = 1$, this condition is equivalent with Definition 9, so we keep the notation: $\mathcal{LG}_{type} = \mathcal{LG}^1_{type}$. If, for example, $G \in \mathcal{LG}$ contains two assignments for determiners associated with the same type (e.g with $\langle a, /(N, \backslash(/(T, S), S)) \rangle \in G$ for introducing direct objects and $\langle a, /(N, /(\backslash(T, S), S)) \rangle \in G$ for introducing subjects) then $G \in \mathcal{LG}^2_{type}$ but $G \notin \mathcal{LG}^1_{type}$.

Theorem 2. *(obvious)*

$$\forall m \geq 1, \ \mathcal{LG}^m_{type} \subseteq \mathcal{LG}^{m+1}_{type} \text{ and } \mathcal{LG} = \bigcup_{m \geq 1} \mathcal{LG}^m_{type}$$

The hierarchy of m-distinct Typed Lambek Grammars plays the same role here as the one played by the hierarchy of k-valued CG in [17]. Similarly, the results obtained for the class $\mathcal{LG}_{type}$ can easily be generalized to the classes $\mathcal{LG}^m_{type}$ for any $m \geq 1$.

Theorem 3. *For any $m \geq 1$, the class $\mathcal{LG}^m_{type}$ is learnable from Typed Examples, i.e. in the Grammar System $\langle \mathcal{LG}, (\Sigma \times Types(\Theta))^*, TL_h \rangle$.*

Proof (of Theorem 3). The known number m is a new multiplicative factor to be applied on the previous computation of the number of distinct LG compatible with a set of Typed Examples, but this set of grammars is still finite.

The proofs of these theorems suggest enumerative learning algorithms. This is not, of course, a tractable strategy. We define in the following another way to identify the set of LG compatible with a given set of Typed Examples.

3.2   Learning Strategy

We first focus on the class $\mathcal{LG}_{type}$ (i.e. $m = 1$) and propose a strategy to infer LG in this class from Typed Examples. The key point of this strategy is to observe that types provide indications about the functor or argument nature of the words they are associated with, even if the direction of the operators (/ or \) are lost. Types are "degraded versions" of the categories they derive from by h and the goal of the learning strategy is to "rebuild" the categories from the types. This will be acheived in three steps described below: *variabilisation, constraint inference* and *category deduction*.

Variabilisation. First, a step of *variabilisation* is necessary to introduce variables in type expressions at operator positions, i.e. before every opening parenthesis of every type. This step is applied once for all Typed Examples in the input, respecting the following constraint: *every occurrence of the same word* *with the same associated type receives the same variables.* This constraint is a direct consequence of the target class of grammars: for every grammar in $\mathcal{LG}_{type}$, each time the same couple $\langle word, type \rangle$ occurs in a Typed Example, we know that it refers to a unique couple $\langle word, category \rangle$.

Definition 11 (types with variables). *Let $\mathcal{X}$ be an infinite countable set of variables. The set of types with variables over the set of basic types[3] Θ is denoted $VarType(\Theta)$ and is defined as the smallest set such that: $\Theta \subset VarType(\Theta)$ and for any $u, v \in VarType(\Theta)$ and $x_i \in \mathcal{X} \cup \{/, \backslash\}$, $x_i(u, v) \in VarType(\Theta)$.*

The variables in $\mathcal{X}$ are mapped to $\mathcal{X} \cup \{/, \backslash\}$. Note that this variabilisation step is defined relatively to a *set* of Typed Examples.

Example 5. The variabilisation step applied to the Typed Example of Example 4 gives:

Alain	teaches	a	lecture
e	$x_0(e, x_1(e, t))$	$x_2(x_3(e, t), x_4(x_5(e, t), t))$	$x_6(e, t)$

In fact, as explained in [27] for CG, such a variabilisation implicitly specifies *a set of grammars*: the set of every grammar in $\mathcal{LG}_{type}$ sharing the same semantic type assignments. As already seen, this set of grammars is always finite. Among them, we now want to select the grammar(s) for which there exists h such that their h-Typed language contains a given set of Typed Exampes. To characterise these grammars, we will need to constraint the possible values of the introduced variables.

Constraint Inference. This step consists in deducing constraints over the variables introduced. These constraints will be stored into substitutions.

Definition 12. *A **substitution** is a mapping from $\mathcal{X}$ to $\mathcal{X} \cup \{/, \backslash\}$. For any substitution σ, σ is extended over $VarType(\Theta)$ as follows:*

1. $\forall u \in Types(\Theta) \cup \{/, \backslash\}$, $\sigma(u) = u$;
2. $\sigma(x_i(u, v)) = \sigma(x_i)(\sigma(u), \sigma(v))$.

For any substitution σ, we define an adapted σ-dependent Lambek-inspired sequent calculus:

- axioms : $[ID]^\sigma \dfrac{\sigma(A) = \sigma(A')}{A \Vdash_\sigma A'}$ for any $A, A' \in VarType(\Theta)$;
- inference rules :

$$[/R]^\sigma \frac{\Gamma, A \Vdash_\sigma B \quad \sigma(x) = /}{\Gamma \Vdash_\sigma x(A, B)} \qquad [\backslash R]^\sigma \frac{A, \Gamma \Vdash_\sigma B \quad \sigma(x) = \backslash}{\Gamma \Vdash_\sigma x(A, B)}$$

$$[/L]^\sigma \frac{\Gamma \Vdash_\sigma A \quad \Delta, B, \Pi \Vdash_\sigma C \quad \sigma(x) = /}{\Delta, x(A, B), \Gamma, \Pi \Vdash_\sigma C} \quad [\backslash L]^\sigma \frac{\Gamma \Vdash_\sigma A \quad \Delta, B, \Pi \Vdash_\sigma C \quad \sigma(x) = \backslash}{\Delta, \Gamma, x(A, B), \Pi \Vdash_\sigma C}$$

---

[3] For the examples in this presentation of the learning strategy we always use the set of basic types $\Theta = \{e, t\}$.

where $A, B, C \in VarType(\Theta)$ and Γ, Δ, Π are sequences of types with variables in $VarType(\Theta)$, $\Gamma \neq \emptyset$. In this calculus, a derivation is constrained by conditions on types with variables but also by conditions on σ. Making a proof in this system thus assigns values to σ on $\mathcal{X}$.

To deduce constraints on category assignments from a given Typed Example, it is enough to prove that the sequent having the corresponding sequence of types with variables as antecedent and t as consequent is valid in a σ-sequent calculus. Searching such proofs by backward chaining, as for parsing, provides sets of constraints on σ. Solutions of these sets of constraints are the resulting substitutions. If the sequence of types with variables comes from a h-Typed Example (i.e. is the result of applying some h to a sequence of categories which can be proved to derive S in the Lambek calculus), it is easy to see that there exists at least one σ such that the sequent can be proved in this σ-sequent calculus (σ can be obtained from h).

Example 6. Applied to the variabilised Typed Example of Example 5, the search for a proof in a σ-sequent calculus gives rise to the search tree of Fig. 1, where only the branches leading to valid proofs are displayed. In ovals are given the constraints applying on substitutions and in rectangles the sequents obtained after applying the rules (not themselves represented in the Figure). 7 substitutions are obtained, among which only 5 are distinct (we have: $\sigma_2 = \sigma_3 = \sigma_4$). They are summed-up in Table 1.

Table 1. The substitutions inferred for Example 5

Variables	σ_1	σ_2	σ_5	σ_6	σ_7
x_0	\	\	/	\	\
x_1	$\sigma_1(x_3)$	$\sigma_2(x_5)$	\	/	\
x_2	\	/	\	\	\
x_3	$\sigma_1(x_1)$	$\sigma_2(x_6)$	/	/	\
x_4	/	\	/	/	/
x_5	$\sigma_1(x_6)$	$\sigma_2(x_1)$	$\sigma_5(x_6)$	$\sigma_6(x_6)$	$\sigma_7(x_6)$
x_6	$\sigma_1(x_5)$	$\sigma_2(x_3)$	$\sigma_5(x_5)$	$\sigma_6(x_5)$	$\sigma_7(x_5)$

Each substitution selects a subset of grammars associated with their Typing Fonctions among the set $\mathcal{LG}_{type}$. In this sense, our algorithm is a *specialisation strategy* at the *set level*: every new constraint reduces the search space.

But in Gold's model, the learning function takes as input a *set of examples*, not a single one. Each Typed Example is treated one after the other. At each step are kept only the substitutions that are compatible with the new Typed Example being analysed. The compatibility relation is a composition denoted by $\ominus$. For any substitutions σ_1 and σ_2 we define:

$$\forall u \in Types(\Theta) \cup \{/, \backslash\}, (\sigma_1 \ominus \sigma_2)(u) = u,$$

$$\forall x_i \in \mathcal{X}, (\sigma_1 \ominus \sigma_2)(x_i) = \begin{cases} \sigma_1(x_i) \text{ if } \sigma_1(x_i) = \sigma_2(x_i) \\ \sigma_1(x_i) \text{ if } \sigma_2(x_i) = x_i \\ \sigma_2(x_i) \text{ if } \sigma_1(x_i) = x_i \\ \text{not defined if } \sigma_1(x_i), \sigma_2(x_i) \in \{/, \backslash\} \text{ and } \sigma_1(x_i) \neq \sigma_2(x_i) \end{cases}$$

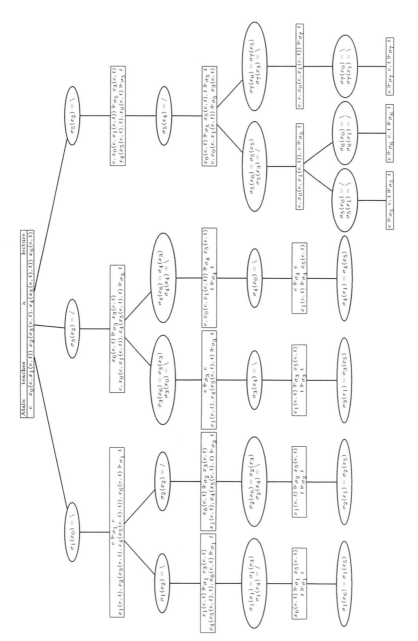

Fig. 1. The substitution searching tree

Note that the composition $\ominus$ between substitutions can be seen in terms of the classical notion of "most general unifier" (mgu) between substitutions, taking into account the domain of these substitutions. The composition of two sustitutions can introduce new equality constraints between variables (first line of the definition). It does not exist when the two substitutions are not compatible on at least one variable because substitutions are functions and thus cannot take both values $/$ and $\backslash$ for this variable. The other conditions of the definition rely on the fact that the set of substitutions is initialized with the Identity function on $VarType(\Theta)$.

Example 7. Let us consider compositions between the subtitutions defined in Table 1. The composition $\sigma_1 \ominus \sigma_2$ is undefined on $\mathcal{X}$ because $\sigma_1(x_2) \neq \sigma_2(x_2)$ but $\sigma_1 \ominus \sigma_6$ is defined by: $(\sigma_1 \ominus \sigma_6)(x_0) = \backslash$, $(\sigma_1 \ominus \sigma_6)(x_1) = \sigma_1(x_3) = /$, $(\sigma_1 \ominus \sigma_6)(x_2) = \backslash$, $(\sigma_1 \ominus \sigma_6)(x_3) = \sigma_1(x_1) = /$, $(\sigma_1 \ominus \sigma_6)(x_4) = /$, $(\sigma_1 \ominus \sigma_6)(x_5) = \sigma_1(x_6) = \sigma_6(x_6)$, $(\sigma_1 \ominus \sigma_6)(x_6) = \sigma_1(x_5) = \sigma_6(x_5)$.

Category Deduction. Finally, after every Typed Example has been treated, each distinct remaining substitution will give rise to a distinct LG G, associated with its specific Typing Function h. To obtain G and h from a substitution σ, the first thing to do is to apply σ to each type with variables appearing at least once in the variabilised Typed Examples. A step of category deduction is necessary because a non-basic type can derive by h from a basic category (remember $h(N) = (e, t)$). The deduction of categories is performed as follows:

1. the type t, in the axiom $t \Vdash_\sigma t$, is associated with the basic category S;
2. every other class of distinct subtypes with variables linked by axioms $[ID]^\sigma$ in a proof (i.e. each class of subtypes with variables equal up to the substitution σ) is associated with a new basic category.

The definition of each Typing Function h naturally follows from these definitions.

Example 8. The application of the substitution σ_1 (obtained in the leftmost branch of Fig. 1) to the types with variables appearing in the Typed Example of Example 5 gives the following assignments: $\langle Alain, e\rangle$, $\langle teaches, \backslash(e, x_1(e, t))\rangle$, $\langle lecture, x_5(e, t)\rangle$ and $\langle a, \backslash(x_1(e, t), /(x_5(e, t), t))\rangle$. By convention, when a substitution integrates several equality constraints between variables, its value on these variables is the variable of least index. In the leftmost branch of Fig. 1, the axiom $e \Vdash_\sigma e$ induces the definition of a basic category A_1 (with $h(A_1) = e$). The axioms $x_1(e, t) \Vdash_\sigma x_3(e, t)$ and $x_6(e, t) \Vdash_\sigma x_5(e, t)$ induce the definitions of A_2 and A_3 respectively (with $h(A_2) = (e, t) = h(A_3)$). As long as variables x_1 and x_5 remain distinct (we have not obtained a constraint of the form $\sigma_1(x_1) = \sigma_1(x_5)$), A_2 and A_3 also remain distinct, which illustrates that h is not necessarily inductive. The final LG obtained is: $G = \{\langle Alain, A_1\rangle, \langle teaches, \backslash(A_1, A_2)\rangle, \langle a, \backslash(A_2, /(A_3, S))\rangle, \langle lecture, A_3\rangle\}$.

Note that if a semantic distinction is made, for example, between "animated" and "not animated" nouns, associated with two distinct types (for example e_1 and e_2), this would lead to a distinction between two syntactic categories for common nouns (for example some N_1 and N_2 respectively). But note also that having the same (not basic) semantic type does not at all necessarily means having the same syntactic category: for example, common nouns and intransitive verbs, are both of type (e, t), but they will nevertheless most of the time receive distinct syntactic categories. As a matter of fact, this type will be variabilised into as many distinct $x_i(e, t)$ as there are distinct words associated with the initial type. Then, it is expected that the variable x_i will sometimes unify with \ (for example in a sentence like "Alain teaches", where (e, t) is the type of "teaches"), and some other times stay unspecified because common nous are usually not used as functors. This distinction is enough to provide two distinct syntactic category.

The final global inference strategy applied to a set of Typed Examples is given in Algorithm 1.

Algorithm 1. Global inference strategy for a set of Typed Examples

---

Require: $TE = \{te_1, \ldots, te_n\}$ a set of Typed Examples;
1: $\mathcal{U} = \{Id_{VarTypes(\Theta)}\}$ the initial set of substitutions;
2: **for** every Typed Example $te_i \in TE$ **do**
3:     introduce variables respecting the condition of Sect. 3.2 to obtain tv_i;
4: **end for**
5: **for** every sequence of types with variables tv_i **do**
6:     prove the sequent $tv_i \Vdash_\sigma t$ in the σ-sequent calculus to obtain a set of substitutions $\mathcal{U}_i$;
7:     $\mathcal{U} := \{\sigma \ominus \sigma_i | \sigma \in \mathcal{U}, \sigma_i \in \mathcal{U}_i\}$;
8: **end for**
9: **for** every substitution σ_i from $\mathcal{U}$ **do**
10:     apply σ_i over types with variables;
11:     apply rules (1) and (2) of deducing categories to obtain $\langle G_i, h_i \rangle$
12: **end for**
Ensure: $\mathcal{G}_r(TE) = \{\langle G_i, h_i \rangle | \sigma_i \in \mathcal{U}\}$

Exemple of the Global Strategy. Let us apply the previous algorithm to a pair of Typed Examples.

Alain	teaches	a	lecture
e	$(e, (e, t))$	$((e, t), ((e, t), t))$	(e, t)
e	$x_0(e, x_1(e, t))$	$x_2(x_3(e, t), x_4(x_5(e, t), t))$	$x_6(e, t)$
Isabelle	writes	a	paper
e	$(e, (e, t))$	$((e, t), ((e, t), t))$	(e, t)
e	$x_7(e, x_8(e, t))$	$x_2(x_3(e, t), x_4(x_5(e, t), t))$	$x_9(e, t)$

For this sample of Typed Examples, the variabilisation (third line of each example) has been performed according to the constraint of Sect. 3.2. So, both occurrences of the determiner "a" receive the same variables. After treating the first Typed Example, the resulting substitutions are those given in Table 1.

The second Example "Isabelle writes a paper" is treated exactly the same way as the first one and also gives rise to 5 different substitutions (replace x_0 by x_7, x_1 by x_8 and x_6 by x_9 in Table 1 to obtain their values). Among the 25 possible compositions between one σ_i and one of these new substitutions, only 13 are defined, and 7 distinct. The 7 distinct LG of the following table are finally obtained:

	Alain	teaches	a	lecture	Isabelle	writes	paper
G_1	A_1	$\backslash(A_1,\backslash(A_1,S))$	$\backslash(\backslash(A_1,S),/(A_2,S))$	A_2	A_1	$\backslash(A_1,\backslash(A_1,S))$	A_2
G_2	A_1	$\backslash(A_1,A_2)$	$\backslash(A_2,/(A_3,S))$	A_3	A_1	$\backslash(A_1,A_2)$	A_3
G_3	A_1	$\backslash(A_1,A_2)$	$/(A_3,\backslash(A_2,S))$	A_3	A_1	$\backslash(A_1,A_2)$	A_3
G_4	A_1	$\backslash(A_1,/(A_1,S))$	$\backslash(/(A_1,S),/(A_2,S))$	A_2	A_1	$\backslash(A_1,/(A_1,S))$	A_2
G_5	A_1	$\backslash(A_1,/(A_1,S))$	$\backslash(/(A_1,S),/(A_2,S))$	A_2	A_1	$/(A_1,\backslash(A_1,S))$	A_2
G_6	A_1	$/(A_1,\backslash(A_1,S))$	$\backslash(/(A_1,S),/(A_2,S))$	A_2	A_1	$/(A_1,\backslash(A_1,S))$	A_2
G_7	A_1	$/(A_1,\backslash(A_1,S))$	$\backslash(/(A_1,S),/(A_2,S))$	A_2	A_1	$\backslash(A_1,/(A_1,S))$	A_2

Among these grammars, the last three are "real" Lambek Grammars in the sense that the same assignment of categories in a CG would not allow the analysis of at least one of the two initial sentences.

Note that every solution grammar assigns the same basic category A_1 to "Alain" and "Isabelle". This is a direct consequence of their assignment to the same basic type and of condition (2) of Definition 4. More interestingly, every solution grammar also assigns the same basic category to "lecture" and "paper". This results from an equality condition between the values of every final substitution on x_6 and x_9. Fundamentally, it is because both words are introduced by the same determiner "a", whose type is variabilised only once. But the various subtypes (e, t) occurring in initial types gave rise to various categories, basic or not (for example in G_1, $h_1(A_2) = (e, t) = h_1(\backslash(A_1, S))$). In fact, grammatical categories can be defined as equivalence classes between subtypes that have the same combinatorial behaviour. The substitutability at the "type with variables" level is the criterion our algorithm uses to infer grammatical categories.

It can also be noted that the 7 grammars obtained can be reduced to 3 classes, on the basis on their expressive power. G_1 is clearly apart. G_2 and G_3 are such that, up to a renaming of basic categories, $h_2 = h_3$ and $\forall w \in \Sigma$, $\exists C_2, C_3 \in Cat(\mathcal{B})$ with: $\langle w, C_2 \rangle \in G_2$, $\langle w, C_3 \rangle \in G_3$, $C_2 \vdash C_3$ and $C_3 \vdash C_2$. It is easy to prove (using the Cut rule in the Lambek calculus, not presented here) that this condition implies that $\forall h$, $TL_h(G_2) = TL_h(G_3)$. So, G_2 and G_3 are equivalent with respect to the convergence criterion of learnability in the limit and it is enough to keep memory of only one of them. The same situation occurs for the four grammars G_4, G_5, G_6 and G_7. Unfortunately, the previous condition is only a sufficient one for Typed Languages to be equal.

3.3   Properties of the Algorithm

In this section, we discuss the main properties of the algorithm: it is correct and complete, in the sense that it is able to identify every LG without useless category -and up to a renaming of basic categories- and its associated Typing Function, compatible with a given set of Typed Examples. Nevertheless, it is not in itself a learning algorithm in the sense of Gold.

Theorem 4. *For every sets Σ, $\mathcal{B}$ and Θ, every $G \in \mathcal{LG}_{type}$ and every set TE of Typed Examples of G, the result $\mathcal{G}_r(TE)$ of our algorithm contains every possible couple $\langle G_i, h_i \rangle$ -up to a renaming of basic categories- such that G_i is without useless category, h_i is a Typing Function from $Cat(\mathcal{B})$ to $Types(\Theta)$ and $TE \subset TL_{h_i}(G_i)$.*

The complete proof of this correctness and completeness theorem is a direct adaptation of the one for CG [8]. The key point consists in the following lemma:

Lemma 3. *For every Σ, $\mathcal{B}$, Θ and h, every non empty finite sequence of categories Γ from $Cat(\mathcal{B})$ and every category $C \in Cat(\mathcal{B})$ we have: $\Gamma \vdash C$ in the Lambek calculus if and only if there exists a substitution σ on $VarType(\Theta)$ such that $\Delta \vDash_\sigma C'$ in the σ-dependent Lambek calculus, where $\Delta \in VarType(\Theta)$ is the variabilisation of $h(\Gamma)$ and $C' \in VarType(\Theta)$ is the variabilisation of $h(C)$, the variabilisation step being performed according to Sect. 3.2.*
Note that h is naturally extended to finite sequences of categories, i.e. if $\Gamma = A_1 \ldots A_n$ then $h(\Gamma) = h(A_1) \ldots h(A_n)$.

Proof (sketch of proof of Lemma 3). Two things must be proved:

- if $\Gamma \vdash C$, we can define σ from h by using the variabilisation step (trivial);
- if $\exists \sigma\ \Delta \vDash_\sigma C'$ then an induction on the length of the proof must be done:
  - if only an axiom $[ID]^\sigma$ is used, i.e. $\sigma(\Delta) = \sigma(C')$ then apply the category deduction phase in Sect. 3.2: a new category A is introduced, with $h(A)$ equals the un-variabilised version of Δ and C'. Either $\Delta = C' \in \Theta$ and this is consistent with Definition 4 (2), either Δ and C' are not basic and σ defines equality conditions between variables. In any case, we have $\Gamma = C = A$ with $A \vdash A$ an axiom of the Lambek calculus.
  - each time a rule in the σ-dependant Lambek calculus is used in the proof, the corresponding rule in the Lambek calculus will be applicable on the categories introduced by the category deduction phase. This step of deduction also prevents from deducing useless categories.

The main difference between the lemma and the theorem is the fact that a real input is made of several Typed Examples and not of only one. So everything relies on the correct definition of the composition $\ominus$ between substitutions.

But the previous theorem is not enough to make our algorithm a learning algorithm in the sense of Gold, as it does not allow to select a unique solution grammar, as required by the "learnability in the limit" criterion. Note that the same problem occurred for Kanazawa's strategy to learn CG from strings[17]. But the problem is even stronger for LF, because it is possible that $\exists \langle G_i, h_i \rangle$, $\langle G_j, h_j \rangle \in \mathcal{G}_r(TE)$ such that $TL_{h_i}(G_i) \subsetneq TL_{h_j}(G_j)$ (see Example 9). This situation never occurred for CG. When it occurs, to avoid over-generalisation, the least general grammar G_i should be chosen. It is not even known whether the inclusion of Typed Languages is computable. This inclusion can nevertheless be checked for every Typed Example of bounded length: this is, again, Kanazawa's strategy for learning CG from strings. It is computable but not tractable in practice.

Example 9. Let $\Sigma = \{a, b, c, d, e, f\}$ be a vocabulary, $\mathcal{B} = \{A, B, S\}$ the set of basic categories and $\Theta = \{\alpha, t\}$ the set of basic types. We define $G \in \mathcal{LG}$ by:
$G = \{\langle a, /(A, A)\rangle, \langle b, /(B, A)\rangle, \langle c, B\rangle, \langle d, A\rangle, \langle e, \backslash(A, \backslash(A, A))\rangle, \langle f, \backslash(A, \backslash(A, S))\rangle\}$.
G is rigid, so $\forall h, G \in \mathcal{LG}_{type}$. Let h be the following Typing Function: $h(A) = \alpha$, $h(B) = (\alpha, \alpha)$ and let the following sequence of h-Typed Examples:

(1) $\langle a, (\alpha, \alpha)\rangle \langle b, ((\alpha, \alpha), \alpha)\rangle \langle c, (\alpha, \alpha)\rangle \langle d, \alpha\rangle \langle e, (\alpha, (\alpha, \alpha))\rangle \langle d, \alpha\rangle \langle f, (\alpha, (\alpha, t))\rangle$.
(2) $\langle b, ((\alpha, \alpha), \alpha)\rangle \langle c, (\alpha, \alpha)\rangle \langle b, ((\alpha, \alpha), \alpha)\rangle \langle c, (\alpha, \alpha)\rangle \langle e, (\alpha, (\alpha, \alpha))\rangle \langle d, \alpha\rangle$
$\langle f, (\alpha, (\alpha, t))\rangle$.
(3) $\langle d, \alpha\rangle \langle d, \alpha\rangle \langle d, \alpha\rangle \langle e, (\alpha, (\alpha, \alpha))\rangle \langle f, (\alpha, (\alpha, t))\rangle$.

Applying Algorithm 1 to this set provides several solutions $\langle G_i, h_i\rangle$ among which are the following two ones:

$\langle G_1, h_1\rangle$	$\langle G_2, h_2\rangle$
$\langle a, /(A_1, A_1)\rangle$ with $h_1(A_1) = \alpha$	$\langle a, /(A_2, A_2)\rangle$ with $h_2(A_2) = \alpha$
$\langle b, /(A_0, A_1)\rangle$ with $h_1(A_0) = (\alpha, \alpha)$	$\langle b, /(/(A_2, A_2), A_2)\rangle$
$\langle c, A_0\rangle$	$\langle c, /(A_2, A_2)\rangle$
$\langle d, A_1\rangle$	$\langle d, A_2\rangle$
$\langle e, \backslash(A_1, \backslash(A_1, A_1))\rangle$	$\langle e, \backslash(A_2, \backslash(A_2, A_2))\rangle$
$\langle f, \backslash(A_1, \backslash(A_1, S))\rangle$	$\langle f, \backslash(A_2, \backslash(A_2, S))\rangle$

The two grammars G_1 and G_2 are such that $TL_{h_1}(G_1) \subsetneq TL_{h_2}(G_2)$. The inclusion of Typed Languages is obvious (every derivation in G_1 can be transformed into a derivation in G_2, replacing A_0 by $/(A_2, A_2)$ and A_1 by A_2). The non equality is exemplified by the following Typed Example, element of $TL_{h_2}(G_2)$ but not of $TL_{h_1}(G_1)$: $\langle c, (\alpha, \alpha)\rangle \langle d, \alpha\rangle \langle d, \alpha\rangle \langle f, (\alpha, (\alpha, t))\rangle$.

3.4   Implementation

We have specified the heart of our strategy (the constraint inference phase) in terms of sequent deduction, without specifying any implementation details. In fact, every algorithm able to perform a syntactic analysis within the Lambek calculus can be adapted to a constraint inference algorithm and integrated at step 6 of our Algorithm 1. It is known that the complexity of such a parsing algorithm is at least exponential in the number of words in a sentence [23], so is the step 6 of Algorithm 1. Furthermore, we have already explained in [10] that the number of distinct CG compatible with a given Typed Example of n words could reach $C(n, 2n)$. This result is all the more true for LG (with the same example): it means that for a given sequence tv_i of n types with variable, the set $\mathcal{U}_i$ may contain $C(n, 2n)$ distinct substitutions.

To implement the strategy in practice, a valid heuristics based on the *Count* function defined in [28] can be used. Applied to (sequence of) categories, this function computes the exponent of a basic category in this sequence. A necessary condition for a sequent to be valid in the Lambek calculus is that, for every basic category, the value of *Count* must be equal on each side of this sequent. This criterion applies as well on (sequences of) types. In this case, let *Count* be defined for elements of $VarType(\Theta)$ as follows:

1. $Count_\tau(\tau) = 1, \forall \tau \in \Theta$
2. $Count_\tau(\rho) = 0$ if $\tau \neq \rho, \forall \tau, \rho \in \Theta$
3. $Count_\tau(x_i(\alpha_1, \alpha_2)) = Count_\tau(\alpha_2) - Count_\tau(\alpha_1), \forall x_i \in \mathcal{X} \cup \{/, \backslash\}$ and $\forall \tau \in \Theta, \forall \alpha_1, \alpha_2 \in VarType(\Theta)$.

It is naturally extended to sequences: $Count_\tau(\tau_1 \ \tau_2) = Count_\tau(\tau_1) + Count_\tau(\tau_2)$. It is easy to prove that for any sequence of types with variables Γ and Δ and every substitution σ: if $\Gamma \Vdash_\sigma \Delta$ then $\forall \tau \in \Theta, Count_\tau(\Gamma) = Count_\tau(\Delta)$. This equality can be checked in linear time and allows to prune unfruitful branches during the search for a proof.

3.5 Extensions

It remains to see how our learning strategy could be adapted to learn the class $\mathcal{LG}_{type}^m$ (see Definition 10) from Typed Examples. Two approaches are possible.

The first one consists in changing the variabilisation phase, by giving up the condition of Sect. 3.2. In this case, all introduced variables are distinct and the phase of constraint inference is performed as described. But the category deduction phase must be modified, to take into account the fact that every couple ⟨word, category⟩ can give rise to at most m distinct couples ⟨word, type⟩.

The second possible approach starts preserving the variabilisation phase as described in Sect. 3.2 and the constraint deduction phase, but allowing that substitutions are no longer functions but relations (allowing different possible values for some $\sigma(x)$). The definition of the composition $\ominus$ between substitutions in Sect. 3.2 is thus changed, to allow at most m distinct values for every *set* of variables appearing in a unique type. For examples, if the target LG belongs to $\mathcal{LG}_{type}^2$, the *set* of variables $\{\sigma(x_2), \sigma(x_3), \sigma(x_4), \sigma(x_5)\}$ (i.e. the variables introduced in the type of the determiner "a") is allowed to have two different extensions. The category deduction phase is then not modified.

We haven't precisely proved the completeness and validity of these approaches but they are natural extensions of the basic one. Whichever is chosen, the new algorithm has an exponentially higher complexity than the previous one.

4 Conclusion

Before we started our study, positive learnability results in Gold's model for Lambek Grammars (LG) were still rare and only concerned rigid LG [6,4]. We present here a result of learnability for larger classes of LG, provided that adapted data are available. The advantages of our strategy are very similar to the ones we already argued for Classical Categorial Grammars (CG) [10,11]: types are lexicalized information, easier to justify than structural information. Furthermore the learnability from Typed Examples is even more relevant for LG than for CG. As a matter of fact, the types exemplified in this paper are those of the classical logical formulas associated with words in Montague's tradition. The logical translation of the determiner "a" is classically $\lambda P \lambda Q \exists x[P(x) \wedge Q(x)]$, the one of the quantifier "every" is $\lambda P \lambda Q \forall x[P(x) \implies Q(x)]$, both of type $((e, t), ((e, t), t))$.

With this typing, no CG is compatible with the Typed Example corresponding with "Every man loves a woman", whereas some LG are.

But the problem remains difficult and leads to non tractable strategies, particularly for the most general case of grammars in $\mathcal{LG}_{type}^m$. Nevertheless, despite bad theoretical complexity, the algorithm for $\mathcal{LG}_{type}$ has been programmed and successfully applied on small sets of natural language sentences [9] (built for this purpose and not extracted from a real corpus). The *specialisation strategy* it implements is recognized by psycholinguits as more cognitively relevant than *generalisation strategies*.

Acknowledgements

This paper is an extended version of another one written for the conference "Categorial Grammar" in 2004. The implementation of the algorithm was due to Frederic Dupont. We also thank referees for their useful comments.

References

1. Angluin, D.: Inductive inference of formal languages from positive data. Information and Control 45, 117–135 (1980)
2. Bar Hillel, Y., Gaifman, C., Shamir, E.: On Categorial and Phrase Structure Grammars. Bulletin of the Research Council of Israel 9F (1960)
3. Béchet, D., Bonato, R., Dikovsky, A., Foret, A., Le Nir, Y., Moreau, E., Retoré, C., Tellier, I.: Modéles algorithmiques de l'acquisition de la syntaxe; concepts et méthodes, résultats et problemes, Revue Linguistique de Vincennes, pp. 123–152 (2007)
4. Béchet, D., Foret, A.: Apprentissage des grammaires de Lambek rigides et d'arité bornée pour le traitement automatique des langues. In: CAP 2003, pp. 155–168 (2003)
5. Béchet, D., Foret, A., Tellier, I.: Learnability of Pregroup Grammars. Studia Logica 87, 225–252 (2007)
6. Bonato, R., Retoré, C.: Learning rigid Lambek grammars and minimalist grammars from structured sentences. In: Proceedings of Learning Language in Logic Workshop (LLL), pp. 23–34 (2001)
7. Buszkowski, W., Penn, G.: Categorial grammars determined from linguistic data by unification. Studia Logica, 431–454 (1990)
8. Dudau-Sofronie, D.: Apprentissage de grammaires catégorielles pour simuler l'acquisition du langage naturel à l'aide d'informations sémantiques, PhD thesis, Université de Lille (2004)
9. Dupont, F.: Apprentissage de grammaires de Lambek à partir de types. In: Mémoire DEA d'informatique de Lille1 (2003)
10. Dudau-Sofronie, D., Tellier, I., Tommasi, M.: From logic to grammars via types. In: Proceedings of Learning Language in Logic Workshop (LLL), pp. 35–46 (2001)
11. Dudau-Sofronie, D., Tellier, I., Tommasi, M.: A learnable class of Classical Categorial Grammars from typed examples. In: Proceedings of the 8th Conference on Formal Grammar, pp. 77–88 (2003)

12. Foret, A., Le Nir, Y.: On Limit Points for Some Variants of Rigid Lambek Grammars. In: Adriaans, P.W., Fernau, H., van Zaanen, M. (eds.) ICGI 2002. LNCS (LNAI), vol. 2484, pp. 106–119. Springer, Heidelberg (2002)
13. Fulop, S.: On the Logic and Learning of Language. Trafford Inc., Canada (2004)
14. Gold, E.M.: Language identification in the limit. Information and Control 10, 447–474 (1967)
15. Houdé, O.: Rationnalité, développement et inhibition. Presses Universitaires de, France (1998)
16. Janssen, T.M.V.: Compositionality. In: Handbook of Logic and Language, pp. 417–473. MIT Press, Cambridge (1997)
17. Kanazawa, M.: Learnable Classes of Categorial Grammars. CSLI Publications, Stanford (1998)
18. Lambek, J.: The mathematics of sentence structure, vol. (65), pp. 154–170 (1958)
19. Montague, R.: Formal Philosophy; Selected papers of Richard Montague (1974)
20. Moortgat, M.: Categorial type logics. In: Handbook of Logic and Language. MIT Press, Cambridge (1997)
21. Oehrle, R.T., Bach, E., Wheeler, D.: Categorial grammars and natural language structures. Reidel, Dordrechtz (1988)
22. Partee, B.: Mathematical methods in Linguistics, vol. (30) (1990)
23. Pentus, M.: Lambek calculus is np-complete, Draft (2003)
24. Pinker, S.: Language Acquisition. In: An Invitation to Cognitive Science, pp. 135–182. MIT Press, Cambridge (2005)
25. Retoré, C.: The logic of categorial grammars. In: ACL 2001 and Rapport Inria 5703 (2003)
26. Tellier, I.: Modéliser l'acquisition de la syntaxe via l'hypothése de la primauté du sens, Habilitation thesis, university of Lille3 (2005)
27. Tellier, I.: How to Split Recursive Automata. In: Clark, A., Coste, F., Miclet, L. (eds.) ICGI 2008. LNCS (LNAI), vol. 5278, pp. 200–212. Springer, Heidelberg (2008)
28. van Benthem, J.: The Lambek Calculus. In: Categorial Grammars and Natural Language Structures, pp. 35–68. Reidel, Dordrecht (1988)

Dialogues in Ludics

Marie-Renée Fleury[1], Myriam Quatrini[1], and Samuel Tronçon[2]

[1] Institut de Mathématiques de Luminy, Aix-Marseille Université
[2] Laboratoire "Structures Formelles du Langage", Université Paris 8
fleury@lumimath.univ-mrs.fr, {quatrini,troncon}@iml.univ-mrs.fr

Abstract. In this paper we expose and defend the following claim: Ludics is a relevant framework to ensure both the formalisation and another way for studying dialogues. First we informally introduce a notion of dialogue and explain the correspondence with some fundamental concepts in Ludics, then we give a light technical presentation of Ludics, focusing on the most relevant points for the study of formal dialogues : objects, actions and interactions. At last, we present the concrete part of the model with some examples of dialogues in Ludics.

Introduction

The very recent advances in mathematical Logic seem pertinent to renew the logical anchorage of language studies, for both the philosophical point of view and the formalisation stakes. Ludics is a new logical theory, due to J.-Y. Girard [6], and arises in Proof Theory through postulating *interaction* as most primitive object, from which the usual logical concepts (formulas, proofs) may be recovered. We think that this reversal may be also fruitful in some another domains than mathematical Logic and Computation Theory. Our aim is to understand the relevance of new concepts in Ludics to studies of linguistics with applications to formalization of concepts in this domain. Ludics can be easily related to pragmatics, and more generally to semantics of natural language. However this link is not established in the usual mode. Most of the known issues in this domain are simply formalizations, a.k.a. embeddings of semantic constructions in some formal language. But Ludics opens the way to a very special kind of representation, presaged by the perspectives of Linear Logic, which takes account of both logical and linguistic *internal specificities*. This preservation of their respective properties is probably the fact of the geometrical nature of logic and the cognitive elaboration of language. By this fact, we can expect from this new paradigm the development of a conceptual correspondence providing a theoretical framework in which both engineering and philosophy of meaning would be improved.

Here we focus on dialogues, and we sketch a pattern of ludical formalisation of dialogues. This approach, which investigates the dynamics of interactive situations, offers riche intuitions and mathematical insights easily linkable to the natural structure of our object. In this way, we can analyze further the interactive layer of dialogues, leaving both the propositional and the constructive

S. Pogodalla, M. Quatrini, and C. Retoré (Eds.): Lecomte Festschrift, LNAI 6700, pp. 138–157, 2011.

ones[1]. We expect that such a new perspective may be useful for filling out the current models of dialogues. Nevertheless, the precise relation of our analatycal approach and previous work on dialogues deserves further examination.

The text is build as follows: in the first section, we introduce our model by presenting a not formal notion of dialogue, and by explaining the correspondence with some core concepts of Ludics. These remarks will be useful to understand the continuity between intuitive dialogue (especially seen from the point of view of meaning construction) and formal dialogues. In the second section we give a light technical presentation of Ludics, focusing on the most relevant points for the study of formal dialogues: objects, actions and interactions. Finally, we present the concrete part of the model with some examples of dialogues in ludics. We begin with an *elementary decomposition* by the *intervention-action* matching. Secondly, we introduce a higher level of formalisation, refined approach of the same object, by viewing interventions as complex actions. Finally, we open the level of inside relations, considering superstructures and recursive dialogues.

1   Preliminary Remarks

Intuitively, we can define the dialogue as a common research done by some speakers which want to establish some knowledge by exploring possibilities opened by some thesis and its counter-thesis. This intuitive notion of dialogue corresponds in some way to the greek concept of *dialegesthai* (*gr.* διαλέγεσθαι), which is a primitive notion in the philosophy of knowledge, as opposed to the more traditional *dialectic*.

We describe dialogues as sequences of polarized actions which constitute the chronology of symbolic exchanges underlying the communication of meanings. Their structure represents both the research itself, seen as a process in progress, and the knowledge itself, seen as a stable object, finite at one step of development.

The dialogue carries out three essential functions: exchange of informations, construction of knowledge, resolution of a cognitive tension.

First, at every stage, a speaker is giving a symbol, and this exchange is informative in three ways: it informs us about the *object* discussed (some thesis), the *subject* who is speaking (his approach about this thesis), and the *connection* between a present intervention and some counter-interventions (upstream or downstream, actuals or virtuals).

Second, running dialogue shows arguments interacting like machines built up to explore relevant opportunities of discussion according to some global strategy: *I argue in this way to reach this point, I open these branches to induce some reactions...* So, dialogue is a sort of unfolding structure which represents some knowledge. Evidently, involving friendly but tenacious interlocutors ensures a good (exhaustive) exploration.

Third, by the interaction, the locutors can extract some new information which is about the shape of the interaction, contained in the result of the dialogue: what is stable, what is explored, what is new, what is in latence.

---

[1] Here "constructive" means the way how the arguments logically articulate.

Interpreting ludics as a paradigmatic level which shows natural dynamics in logic, we can find some correspondences between dialogue functions and properties of the logical world described in ludics.

1.1 Action Dynamics

First, we must observe that abstract identity (the same name refers to the same content) is replaced in Ludics by a concrete identity based, as in a game, on a behavioral criterion requiring concrete observation:

> reactions experienced by a player corresponds likewise
> to the actions of his opponent.

Consequently, a logical entity a is characterized by the set of all its interactions with the rest of the logical world. And a is identified with a' when they interact exactly in the same manner with this world. This idea is very close to the fact that conceptual identity does not exist between two natural terms or two sentences, since it is only in the consideration of the context, and so in a definite situation of interaction, that we can evaluate a semantic item.

This property, well known as *holist evaluation* in semantics of natural language, is produced by the localization constraint. In the old logical style we had different occurrences of a same content. Context-sensitive logics, like linear logic, introduces occurrences linked by an orthogonality relation, permitting a strict ressource management. By the fact of localization, occurrences became locations (*loci*) in a geometrical framework and, necessarily, locations are considered as different ones.

So, we have a **first notion of meaning**, assuming that the set of all the possible interactions with other elements of the logical world is the conceptual meaning of my strategy, by the fact that interactions explain what can be expected from my actions. The reaction of my opponent is the meaning of my own action: it is induced by actions I have done, and it induces reactions by me which open or close possible moves. The first step of our model will give sense to this intuition by setting the following elementary decomposition: one intervention is treated as a ludic action, and actions are mirroring themselves.

1.2 Exploration Dynamics

We can also refer to locations in two ways, depending on the cognitive subject position: consumer vs. producer, emettor vs. receptor, speaker vs. addressee, etc. In linguistics this point corresponds to the fact that duality is not an objective reality but a local opposition between persons who can change their positions. Even if we know (at least conceptually) that strategies interact with all the strategies in the world, there is a very special relationship between a set of strategies, its counter strategies (a sort of optimal opponent which explores all the determinations of the player's intentions) and the counter strategies of these counter strategies, that is to say the initial set.

So we have a **second notion of meaning**. My strategies are the meaning of the strategies of my opponent, since he made choices in all the playable strategies in order to select one which can optimally play against mine. Natural language sentences are not considered by themselves but regarding the interpretation processes they suggest. There is a construction of mine, its deconstruction by my opponent, a re-construction knowing that he knows what I said, and his re-deconstruction knowing that I know that he knows...

The second step of our model will focuse to the explorative part of interventions, which are made in order to explore some thesis, by anticipation on the possible ways which would be choosen by an opponent. This will give a second level of formalisation, considering interventions as more complex structures: an intervention is a whole strategy, made of anticipations (about the opponent) and forecastings (about my own further plays).

1.3   Inside Dynamics

Geometrical logics, whose ludics is a very representative one, are founded on the calculus dynamics. That is the crucial point in our attempt considering the fact that too many theories in this domain neglect to develop a really good dynamic part. Till now, we know very expressive systems, based on a lambda-calculus, but without specific attention on β-reduction and η-expansion processes. On the contrary, here, we consider dynamics as the essential part of our research. According to this principle, we propose a **third notion of meaning**: the meaning of our common search is the form of our interaction itself. If we diverge, it means that no durable connection is possible between our games. But we explore, by means of this divergence, some determinations of the invoked strategies. And we would be able, in future games, to modify our intentions in order to greatly explore offered possibilities. In the case of convergence, a really useful exploration is always possible, which produces a new knowledge, not present explicitly in our past determinations. Useful interactions are interactions which urges us to explore more deeply the determinations of our playing intentions.

Considering dynamics, we must introduce a level of complexity, presented in the third part of the model. Inside the on-going dialogue, we must have the capability of duplicating some modules, invoking strategies used in previous stages and dialogues, inserting dead-ends and closed loops, cheating in the argument arborescence, or disrupting opponent's plans. These are complex processes of *de-* and *re-localization* inside the running dialogue, and with outside parts turned inside out, as a sort of high-level *transfer of training* mechanism.

Lastly, let us precise that there is no logical propositions in this model of dialogue. In a more global approach of communication, we suppose a kind of multilevels structure, each level corresponding to a way of taking in account the object. The more abstract level is concerned by the propositional aspects of communication. And we found at the most primitive level the interactive structure of dialogue itself. The work, in the present text, is clearly based on the latter. Fortunatly, it would be possible to invoke some *principle of compilation* between levels which ensure continuity and restore the connection between abstract and concrete views. But, this is another work.

Here, we do not use propositional analysis as in the syntactic style, and structures we present are not based on conceptual contents as in the semantic styles, because we want to get our model away from the semantic/syntactic duality. We propose a third way, based on the exchange itself, considering the dialogue as a sequence of interactions in *some place* at *some time*. So, a *locus* would be a place and a moment of dialogue, and not a linguistic object considered on its own grammatical structure.

2   Ludics in a Nutshell

Ludics can be sum up as an *interaction theory*. It appears in the work of J.-Y. Girard [6] as the issue of several changes of paradigms in "Proof Theory"[2]: from *provability* to *computation*, then from *computation* to *interaction*. The first change of paradigm arises with the intuitionnistic logic, while the second is due to the development of linear logic. Continuing the new approachs of Linear Logic : a geometrical point of view of proofs ; an internal approach of dynamics, Ludics focalizes on the interaction.

The objects of the Ludics are no more proofs but instead incomplete proofs, attempts of proofs. So a rule called *daimon* is available in order to symbolize the giving up in a proof search or a pending lemma. These objects play the role of a proof architecture. Only what is needed for the interaction is kept. This has been made possible by means of the hypersequentialized linear logic introduced by J-M. Andréoli after he has discovered the polarity of formulas. Moreover, this work within polarized objects world allowed to create a link [3] between Ludics and recent works in Game Semantics which share similar motivations. So the Game Theory is a good metaphor for a first approach[3] of Ludics, and it is the point of view often followed in this text.

2.1   The Objects of Ludics

The central object of Ludics is the **design**. By means of the metaphor of Games, a design can be understood as a *strategy*, i.e. as a set of *plays* (**chronicles**) ending by answers of Player against the moves planned by Opposant. The plays are alternated sequences of *moves* (**actions**). The moves are defined as a 3-uplet constitued by : firstly a polarity (positive polarity for a move of Player or negative polarity for a move of Opposant), secondly a locus (a fixed position) from which

---

[2] A deep presentation of the philosophic and epistemologic point of view of the mathematical logic progress (when computer science is concerned in) can be found in the works of J.-B. Joinet [9] and S. Tronçon [10].

[3] Here you find a presentation of the theory in a very simplified version, but we recommend the source texts [6], [7] to the reader concerned with more details on the mathematical notions and rich concepts of Ludics ; we also recommend the reading of this introduction [2].

the move is anchored, and at last a finite number of *positions reachable in one step* (**ramification**). A unusual positive move is also possible : the **daïmon**.

In Ludics, the positions are addresses, **loci** incoded by means of a finite sequence of integers (often noted ξ, ρ, σ ...).

The starting positions (**forks**) are denoted $\Gamma \vdash \Delta$; where Γ and Δ are finite sets of loci such that Γ is either the empty set or a singleton one. When an element belongs to Γ, every play then starts on this element by means of an Opposant move (and the fork is said negative), else Player starts on an element of its choice taken in Δ (and the fork is said positive).

For the hypersequentialized linear logic point of view, a design can be seen as a figure of a proof in this sequent calculus with some particularities : first we can use the *daïmon* rule, for giving up the proof search ; secondly we do not work with formulas but with addresses; lastly only two rules are sufficient for subsuming the usual logical connective rules[4].

Definition 1. *A design is a tree of forks $\Gamma \vdash \Delta$, built by means of these three rules :*

- **Daïmon**

$$\frac{}{\vdash \Delta} \, \dagger$$

- **Positive rule**

$$\frac{\cdots \quad \xi.i \vdash \Delta_i \quad \cdots}{\vdash \Delta, \xi} \, (\xi, I)$$

where I is an eventually empty ramification such that for every couple of indexes $(i,j) \in I$, Δ_i and Δ_j are disconnected and every Δ_i is included[5] in Δ.
- **Negative rule**

$$\frac{\cdots \quad \xi.I \vdash \Delta_I \quad \cdots}{\xi \vdash \Delta} \, (\xi, \mathcal{N})$$

where $\mathcal{N}$ is a possibly empty or infinite set of ramifications such that for all $I \in \mathcal{N}$, Δ_I is included in Δ.

Example 1 (Faggian-Maurel contract in Ludics). Bob offers the following contract to Alice: give me one euro and you can choose either a book or a surprise. In the latter case, I will give you a CD or a DVD. [6]

---

[4] It is a direct consequence of the focalization property : a proof of a formula in usual linear logic can be replaced with a proof of an equivalent formula written by means of polarized synthetic connectives. So only two rules schemes (positive or negative ones) are needed.

[5] Every rule where the union of the Δ_i is strictly included in Δ correspond to the weakening rule (respectively for negative rule when Δ_I is strictly included in Δ).

[6] This contract can be described by means of this Linear Logic formula :

$$1 \, euro \, \multimap \, (1 \, book \, \& (1 \, CD \oplus 1 \, DVD))$$

We are going to represent by means of designs the Alice and Bob's strategies for the dialogue based on this contract. In the next section we shall study this contract in progress by studying the effect of the interaction between these designs. We arbitrarily start the interaction at locus ξ.

Two Strategies of Bob in Ludics. The two strategies begin in a same manner: first Bob sets out the contract (represesented by a positive action $(\xi, \{0\})$); then he is ready to receive one euro and give a book (represented by a negative action $(-, \xi.0, \{1, 2\})$), and he is also ready to receive one euro and choose a surprise for Alice $((-, \xi.0, \{1, 3\}))$.

In the first strategy, Bob ends the exchange by giving the book in return of one euro ; in ludics, we will say that he plays the *daïmon* ; playing the *daïmon* in a strategy allow us to attest that the exchange correctly ends[7]. In the second strategy, Bob gives a surprise in return of one euro.

Then the two strategies differ according on Bob gives a CD or a DVD. "Bob chooses the CD" will be represented by the positive action $(+, \xi.0.3, \{1\})$, while "Bob chooses the DVD" will be represented by the positive action $(+, \xi.0.3, \{2\})$.

$$
\cfrac{\cfrac{\rule{3cm}{0.4pt}}{\vdash \xi.0.1, \xi.0.2}{\scriptstyle\dagger} \quad \cfrac{\xi.0.3.1 \vdash \xi.0.1}{\vdash \xi.0.1, \xi.0.3}}{\cfrac{\xi.0 \vdash}{\vdash \xi}}
\qquad\qquad
\cfrac{\cfrac{\rule{3cm}{0.4pt}}{\vdash \xi.0.1, \xi.0.2}{\scriptstyle\dagger} \quad \cfrac{\xi.0.3.2 \vdash \xi.0.1}{\vdash \xi.0.1, \xi.0.3}}{\cfrac{\xi.0 \vdash}{\vdash \xi}}
$$

Fig. 1. Two strategies of Bob

Three Alice Strategies in Ludics. The three strategies begin in a same manner : she listens to the contract (she plays a negative action $(-, \xi, \{0\})$.

- in the first strategy, "she gives an euro and chooses a book" is represented by the positive action $(+, \xi.0, \{1, 2\})$; in the second and third strategies "she gives an euro and chooses a surprise" is represented by the positive action $(+, \xi.0, \{1, 3\})$.
- in the second strategy, she chooses a surprise, so she is ready for both eventualities : receive a CD or receive a DVD ; so this is represented by two negative actions $(-, \xi.0.3, \{1\})$ and $(-, \xi.0.3, \{2\})$). In these two cases, she ends up the exchange by the positive action: $\dagger$ (great, thank you).
- in the third strategy, she chooses a surprise, but she only is ready for receiving a CD ; this is represented by the negative action $(-, \xi.0.3, \{1\})$. In this case, she ends up the exchange by the positive action $\dagger$ (fine, thank you).

Remark 1. Let us notice that *to receive one euro* and *to give one euro* are represented by the same action. This illustrates, indirectly, the fact that, in Ludics, negation only consists in exchanging the point of view.

---

[7] Another possibility would be to make Bob playing an action ("Bob gives Alice a book") and then make Alice playing the *daïmon* ("Alice thanks Bob").

$$
\cfrac{
\xi.0.1 \vdash \quad \xi.0.2 \vdash
}{
\cfrac{\vdash \xi.0}{\xi \vdash}
}
\qquad
\cfrac{
\xi.0.1 \vdash \quad
\cfrac{
\cfrac{\quad}{\vdash \xi.0.3.1}^{\dagger} \quad
\cfrac{\quad}{\vdash \xi.0.3.2}^{\dagger}
}{\xi.0.3 \vdash}
}{
\cfrac{\vdash \xi.0}{\xi \vdash}
}
\qquad
\cfrac{
\xi.0.1 \vdash \quad
\cfrac{
\cfrac{\quad}{\vdash \xi.0.3.1}^{\dagger}
}{\xi.0.3 \vdash}
}{
\cfrac{\vdash \xi.0}{\xi \vdash}
}
$$

Fig. 2. Three strategies of Alice

2.2   The Interaction

The designs are built on the model of proofs without cut. The underlying signification of the cut is the composition of morphisms or strategies. In Ludics, it is concretely translated by a coincidence of two loci in dual position in the bases of two designs. We can cut for example a design of base $\sigma \vdash \xi$ and a design of base $\xi \vdash \rho$, so forming a cut-net[8] of base $\sigma \vdash \rho$.

The interaction is obtained by means of the cut ; it creates a dynamics of rewriting of the cut-net ; the process continues as long as we may find an negative action corresponding to the current positive one until a *daïmon* is played. When it is not the case the process fails. Otherwise we obtain a design with the same base as the starting cut-net.

Example 2. The interaction between the second strategy of Alice and the first one of Bob:

$$
\cfrac{
\xi.0.1 \vdash \quad
\cfrac{
\cfrac{\quad}{\vdash \xi.0.3.1}^{\dagger} \quad
\cfrac{\quad}{\vdash \xi.0.3.2}^{\dagger}
}{\xi.0.3 \vdash}
}{
\cfrac{\vdash \xi.0}{\xi \vdash}
}
\qquad
\cfrac{
\cfrac{\quad}{\vdash \xi.0.1, \xi.0.2}^{\dagger} \quad
\cfrac{
\xi.0.3.1 \vdash \xi.0.1
}{\vdash \xi.0.1, \xi.0.3}
}{
\cfrac{\xi.0 \vdash}{\vdash \xi}
}
$$

After the first reduction step we get:

$$
\cfrac{
\xi.0.1 \vdash \quad
\cfrac{
\cfrac{\quad}{\vdash \xi.0.3.1}^{\dagger} \quad
\cfrac{\quad}{\vdash \xi.0.3.2}^{\dagger}
}{\xi.0.3 \vdash}
}{
\vdash \xi.0
}
\qquad
\cfrac{
\cfrac{\quad}{\vdash \xi.0.1, \xi.0.2}^{\dagger} \quad
\cfrac{
\xi.0.3.1 \vdash \xi.0.1
}{\vdash \xi.0.1, \xi.0.3}
}{
\xi.0 \vdash
}
$$

After the second reduction step we get:

$$
\cfrac{
\xi.0.1 \vdash \quad
\cfrac{
\xi.0.3.1 \vdash \xi.0.1
}{\vdash \xi.0.1, \xi.0.3}
}{}
\qquad
\cfrac{
\cfrac{\quad}{\vdash \xi.0.3.1}^{\dagger} \quad
\cfrac{\quad}{\vdash \xi.0.3.2}^{\dagger}
}{\xi.0.3 \vdash}
$$

---

[8] A cut-net is a finite graph of designs the bases of which are pairwise connected by cuts ; the cut-net is connected and without cycle. The base of the cut-net is obtained by erasing the cut loci.

For the next step, we first choose[9] the cut on $\xi.0.3$, then we get:

$$\frac{\qquad}{\vdash \xi.0.3.1}{}^{\dagger} \qquad \xi.0.3.1 \vdash \xi.0.1 \qquad \xi.0.1 \vdash$$

which is reduced in:

$$\frac{\qquad}{\vdash \xi.0.1}{}^{\dagger} \qquad \xi.0.1 \vdash$$

The reduction ends up on $\mathcal{D}ai^+$.

Example 3. The interaction between the third strategy of Alice and the second one of Bob:

$$\frac{\xi.0.1 \vdash \quad \dfrac{\dfrac{\quad}{\vdash \xi.0.3.1}{}^{\dagger}}{\xi.0.3 \vdash}}{\vdash \xi.0} \quad \dfrac{\dfrac{\quad}{\vdash \xi.0.1, \xi.0.2}{}^{\dagger} \quad \dfrac{\xi.0.3.2 \vdash \xi.0.1}{\vdash \xi.0.1, \xi.0.3}}{\xi.0 \vdash}$$
$$\frac{}{\xi \vdash} \qquad \frac{}{\vdash \xi}$$

As previously, after two reduction steps we get:

$$\xi.0.1 \vdash \quad \dfrac{\xi.0.3.2 \vdash \xi.0.1}{\vdash \xi.0.1, \xi.0.3}(\xi.0.3,\{2\}) \qquad \dfrac{\dfrac{\quad}{\vdash \xi.0.3.1}{}^{\dagger}}{\xi.0.3 \vdash}\{\{1\}\}$$

The next step produces a **failure** because $\{2\} \notin \{\{1\}\}$.

Example 4. Crucial normalisation: a design against the $\mathcal{F}ax$.
The $\mathcal{F}ax_{\xi,\xi'}$ is the following design which is recursively defined (where $\mathcal{P}_f(\mathbb{N})$ is the set of finite subsets of $\mathbb{N}$) :

$$\dfrac{\dfrac{\dfrac{\mathcal{F}ax_{\xi'_i,\xi_i}}{\xi'.i \vdash \xi.i}}{\vdash \xi.I, \xi'}(\xi',I) \quad \cdots \quad \dfrac{\dfrac{\mathcal{F}ax_{\xi'_j,\xi_j}}{\xi'.j \vdash \xi.j}}{\vdash \xi.J, \xi'}(\xi',J) \quad \cdots}{\xi \vdash \xi'}(\xi,\mathcal{P}_f(\mathbb{N}))$$

The normalization between this design and a design based on $\xi \vdash$ is the copy of the original design. Except that in the whole design, the locus ξ has been replaced with the locus ξ', what justifies its name: "Fax".

Dispute. In Ludics, the notion of *dispute* allows us to report the sequence of the moves (actions) of the play (interaction between two designs connected by a cut), from the point of view of one of speakers.

---

[9] The order chosen for executing the reduction steps is relevant in some rewriting system but it isn't the case in Ludics due to the separation theorem established in [6]

For example, in the first scenario of the foregoing example (FM-contract between Alice et Bob), the dispute, from the point of view of Alice is :

$$(-, \xi, \{0\}), (+, \xi.0, \{1, 3\})(-, \xi.0.3, \{1\})\dagger$$

3   Dialogues in Ludics

In this attempt to provide the dialogues with a formal frame, we shall be interested only in the elements of the dialogue which are supports of the interaction. We superpose then a deconstruction of the dialogue (articulation and analysis of the successive interventions according to the created opportunities) and a reconstruction of strategies (whose aim is the continuation of the dialogue), on which the dialogical interaction is based. In this context, a dialogue is the result of an interaction between the strategies of two speakers.

The formal decomposition of dialogues will be considered at various levels of granularity.

- For an **elementary decomposition**, a dialogue is seen as an alternation of signed interventions, where *intervention* means: one or several successive sentences uttered by a speaker before the turn of its addressee.
- We can then **refine** this approach and decompose the interventions themselves, with regard to the way they are dynamically built.

3.1   Elementary Decomposition

A dialogue and the interventions of each speakers are observed from the point of view of the interaction: on what previous interventions of the speakers a intervention of one of them is attached and which openings are created for the continuation of the dialogue. As announced in the preliminary remark, we do not retain the propositional contain.

Example 5. Tomorrow the weather will be fine, I will go to work to Luminy by bike.' What could be the answers of addressee? With this utterance, the speaker has opened three potential answers:

1. Are you sure? Did you consult the weather forecast?
2. Are you still working at Luminy?
3. I did not know you are so good at sport!

We only are concerned in studying the geometrical aspect of a dialogue. So this utterance with its three created possibilities is represented by the following design:

$$\frac{\xi.1 \vdash \qquad \xi.2 \vdash \qquad \xi.3 \vdash}{\vdash \xi, \Delta} \; (\xi, \{1, 2, 3\})$$

Let us resume what is taken in account in our modelisation of dialogue: a dialogue is an alternated sequence of interventions; an intervention is anchored at a certain locus among those created by the previous interactions and it creates new ones; some interventions allow to close the dialogue.

Our formalization of dialogues is built by means of the following elements:

- An *intervention* of Speaker or Addressee[10] is an **action** (ϵ, ξ, I), where:
    - ϵ is a polarity : $+$ (from the point of view of the speaker who performs the intervention) or $-$ (from the point of view of the one who records the intervention);
    - ξ (the focus), is the point from where the speaker either ends the conversation or follows up on the opportunities created during the previous exchanges ;
    - I (the ramification) is the set of openings created by this intervention.
- A *dialogue* is a sequence of alternated interventions ; the story told by one of the speakers of this alternation will be represented by a **chronicle** or in a more dynamic way by the trace of an interaction between the strategies of each of speakers (a **dispute**). In a same way, in Ludics an alternated sequence of actions can be view either from a static point of view (to tell about a past play) or from a dynamic point of view (to take part into the play in progress).
- A *strategy* of one of the speakers will be represented by a **design**. In order to build a strategy as the tree of its compulsory or offered possibilities, the following rules are used:
    - to play a positive rule / to perform an intervention;
    - to play a negative rule / to record, to anticipate the interventions of the other one;
    - to play the daïmon / to terminate a dialogue.

Example 6 ("Sales of real estates"). Let us consider the following situation and let us imagine several dialogues about it:
P knows that O have three real estate properties A_1, A_2, A_3 ; he heard that O would like to sell some of its real propertiy. P is interested in the real property A_1, also he starts up a dialogue with O. P wants to know if O intends to sell A_1; if yes, at what price does he sell it; he does not want to show immediatly that he is interested in this purchase.

- First possible dialogue : $\mathfrak{D}ial_1$

    P: I have heart that you would like to sell some of your real estates, which one?
    O: I intend to sell A_1 and A_2.
    P: At what price does you sell A_1?
    O: 100000 euros
    P: OK

    This dialogue $\mathfrak{D}ial_1$ can be represented as the result of the interaction between the two following designs:

---

[10] To indicate the actors of a dialogue we shall either use P for Player and O for Opponent as in Games Theory, or Speaker and Addressee as in Dialogues Theory

$$\dfrac{\dfrac{\dfrac{\overline{\dfrac{\vdash \sigma.0.1.5.100,\, \sigma.0.2}{\sigma.0.1.5 \vdash \sigma.0.2}}^{\dagger}}{\vdash \sigma.0.1,\, \sigma.0.2}}{\sigma.0 \vdash}}{\vdash \sigma} \; P \qquad\qquad \dfrac{\dfrac{\dfrac{\dfrac{\sigma.0.1.5.100 \vdash}{\vdash \sigma.0.1.5}}{\sigma.0.1 \vdash \qquad \sigma.0.2 \vdash}}{\vdash \sigma.0}}{\sigma \vdash} \; O$$

Finally, the dialogue $\mathfrak{Dial}_1$ is represented by the following dispute (from the point of view of P) :

$$(+,\sigma,\{0\}) \quad (-,\sigma.0,\{1,2\}) \quad (+,\sigma.0.1,\{5\}) \quad (-,\sigma.0.1.5,\{100\}) \, (+,\dagger)$$

I have heart... ...A_1 and A_2 ... price of A_1?   100000 euros   OK

COMMENT 1.   • σ is the locus where the dialogue starts.
• $\sigma.0$ is the locus of the question I have heard ...
• $\sigma.0.1$ and $\sigma.0.2$ are the loci of the answers I sell A_1 and I sell A_2.
• $\sigma.0.1.5$ is the locus of the question what is the price of A_1?
• $\sigma.0.1.5.100$ is the locus of the answer 100 000 euros.
• P decides to stop the dialogue by playing $\dagger$. He might continue by questioning about the real estates A_2 (by focalizing on $\sigma.0.2$).

– Second possible dialogue : $\mathfrak{Dial}_2$
P: I have heard that ... .
O: I intend to sell A_2 and A_3.
P: Very well, good luck
This dialogue $\mathfrak{Dial}_2$ is seen as the interaction between the two following designs:

$$\dfrac{\dfrac{\overline{\vdash \sigma.0.2,\, \sigma.0.3}}^{\dagger}}{\dfrac{\sigma.0 \vdash}{\vdash \sigma}} \; P \qquad\qquad \dfrac{\dfrac{\dfrac{\sigma.0.2 \vdash \quad \sigma.0.3 \vdash}{\vdash \sigma.0}}{\sigma \vdash}}{} \; O$$

Finally the dialogue $\mathfrak{Dial}_2$ is represented by the following dispute (from the point of view of P:

$$(+,\sigma,\{0\}) \qquad (-,\sigma.0,\{2,3\}) \qquad (+,\dagger)$$

I have heard ... I sell A_2 and A_3 Well, good luck

COMMENT 2.   • σ is the locus where the dialogue starts.
• $\sigma.0$ is the locus of the question I have heard ...
• $\sigma.0.2$ and $\sigma.0.3$ are the loci of the answers I sell A_2 and I sell A_3.
• P is only interested in A_1, so he decides to stop the dialogue by playing $\dagger$.

It is possible to represent by the following design the project of conversation that P has built to obtain the following information: O sells A_1 and if yes at what price?

$$
\cfrac{
\cfrac{
\cdots \ \dfrac{\overline{\hspace{1.5em}}^{\dagger}}{\vdash \sigma.0.1.5.i} \ \cdots
}{\sigma.0.1.5 \vdash}
}{\vdash \sigma.0.1, 0.2}
\qquad
\cfrac{
\cfrac{
\cdots \ \dfrac{\overline{\hspace{1.5em}}^{\dagger}}{\vdash \sigma.0.1.5.i} \ \cdots
}{\sigma.0.1.5 \vdash}
}{\vdash \sigma.0.1}
\qquad
\cfrac{
\cfrac{
\cdots \ \dfrac{\overline{\hspace{1.5em}}^{\dagger}}{\vdash \sigma.0.1.5.i} \ \cdots
}{\sigma.0.1.5 \vdash}
}{\vdash \sigma.0.1., 0.3}
\qquad
\cfrac{
\cfrac{
\cdots \ \dfrac{\overline{\hspace{1.5em}}^{\dagger}}{\vdash \sigma.0.1.5.i} \ \cdots
}{\sigma.0.1.5 \vdash}
}{\vdash \sigma.0.1, \sigma.0.2, \sigma.0.3} \quad \dfrac{\overline{\hspace{1.5em}}^{\dagger}}{\vdash \sigma.0.3} \cdots
$$

$$
\cfrac{\sigma.0 \vdash}{\vdash \sigma}
$$

It is really a strategy of conversation : P imagines the possible answers of O to his initial question and plans how to pursue the dialogue in each case.

3.2   Refined Approach

Until now, we have represented a dialogue as a chronicle or as a dispute. This modelisation seems well adapted to dialogues as long as we only consider a dialogue as an exchange of information. But some *refinement* are needed as soon as we are concerned in more elaborated dialogues, as controversies.

As first refinement we propose that the interventions of a speaker could be more complex than an action: a whole design, possibly a cut-net, can be played instead of an action. Associating a whole design or a cut-net with the intervention of the speaker is the sign that this exchange could be broken down into more elementary ones. We shall perform this operation in order to take care of the dynamics of these exchanges.

The example of the presupposition will illustrate such an extension. An intervention is no more represented by actions (moves) but by whole designs (plays). This extension again will be used in Sect. 3.3 for the studying interventions using elements of the context in the ongoing dialogue (for example, an intervention will be represented by means of a delocalization of a design created in previous dialogues).

At last, Ludics also supplies us with tools to formalize the "picking up again" in a dialogue: each speaker can correct a past intervention and propose a new one.

Presupposition. It is an implicit assumption about the world or background belief relating to an utterance whose truth is taken for granted in discourse. We propose to associate an intervention containing a presupposition with a whole chronicle instead of a only action.

Let consider this well known example due to Aristote ; a judge asks a young delinquent this question: Do you still beat your father?. The judge asks a question that presupposes something that has not necessarily been accepted by the young delinquent. The judge imposes to the delinquent the following exchange:

Do you beat your father? – Yes – Do you stop beating him?

This exchange between the judge J and the delinquent D must be represented by the following interaction according to the previous elementary formalisation:

$$\frac{\dfrac{\xi.0.1.0 \vdash}{\vdash \xi.0.1 \quad \vdash \xi.0.2}}{\dfrac{\xi.0 \vdash}{\vdash \xi}} \qquad \frac{\dfrac{\vdash \xi.0.1.0}{\xi.0.1 \vdash}}{\dfrac{\vdash \xi.0}{\xi \vdash}}$$

$$\text{J} \underline{\hspace{6cm}} \text{D}$$

But the judge utterance: Do you still beat your father? contains a presupposition. So it can't be represented by a only action, but by a whole chronicle:

$$(+, \xi, \{0\}) \ (-, \xi.0, \{1\}) \ (+, \xi.0.1, \{0\}) \ (-, \xi.0.1.0, \{1\})/(-, \xi.0.1.0, \{0\})$$

Do you still beat your father?	yes/no
Judge's intervention	Delinquent's intervention

So J forbids addressee a branch who was due to him (the possibility to answer No). If D agrees to answer according to this configuration (without diverging) he is trapped: he has to record a whole chronicle and answer from the locus $\xi.0.1.0$; so he implicitly answered the question Do you beat your father? by yes .

Picking up again. We want to mean that in a dialogue a speaker can forget the current direction of the discussion and proposes a new one instead of it ; in terms of games, a player can play a new move instead of a previous one.

In linear logic, the exponential formulae were essentially introduced to give the possibility of identifying various occurrences of the same formula (perform a contraction rule in linear logic). In order to integrate this possibility in Ludics, several propositions were advanced. Michele Basaldella and Claudia Faggian in [1] suggest to handle multi-addresses (indexed addresses). These multi-addresses give the possibility (not authorized until now) of replaying a positive action on an already visited locus (provided that this locus is a multi-address).

We shall not clarify more the technical aspects of this notion; we keep in mind this possibility and we shall illustrate it by means of an example read in the text from Schopenhauer "Dialectica Eristica", illustrating its first stratagem.
I asserted that the Englishmen were supreme in drama. My opponent attempted to give an instance to the contrary, and replied that it was a well-known fact that in opera, they could do nothing at all. I repelled the attack by reminding him that dramatic art covered tragedy and comedy alone ....

This dialogue can be represented by the following interaction between two designs (we use an alternative presentation of interaction, which is more relevant to manipulate designs with multi-adresses):

design of P:	design of O :	Dialogue:
$(+, \xi, \{1\})$	$c_1 = (-, \xi, \{1\})$	Englishmen are supreme ...
	$(+, \xi.1, \{3\})$	... useless in opera
$(-, \xi.1, \{\{1\}, \{2\}\})$		... tragedy and comedy alone

In such a case the interaction diverges: there is no negative action corresponding with the positive one. But we may imagine that the dialogue may nevertheless continue: the speaker P is ready to receive a new attempt of O. An account of such a possibility may be given by replacing the first action of P which is $(+, \xi, \{1\})$ by an action where the focus is a multi-address $(+, \xi.\bar{i}_1, \{1\})$.

In this way, the previous exchange can be extented and, for example, it may become: the Englishmen are supreme in drama − it is a well-known fact that in opera, they can do nothing at all − but by "dramatic art" I means tragedy and comedy alone − So, in this case, I agree ....

Which can be represented by the following interaction:

design of P:	design of O :	Dialogue:
$(+, \xi.\bar{i}_1, \{1\})$	$c_1 = (-, \xi.\bar{i}_1, \{1\})$	Englishmen are supreme ...
	$(+, \xi.\bar{i}_1.1, \{3\})$	... useless in opera
$(-, \xi.\bar{i}_1.1, \{\{1\}, \{2\}\})$		but ..
$(+, \xi.\bar{i}_2, \{1\})$	$c_2 = (-, \xi.\bar{i}_2, \{1\})$	... tragedy and comedy alone
	†	So.... I agree

The last intervention of P is represented by the successive actions

$$(-, \xi.\bar{i}_1.1, \{\{1\}, \{2\}\})(+, \xi.\bar{i}_2, \{1\})$$

which precise that P may not receive the argument that his addressee proposed but nevertheless he is ready to accept another attempt: to use a multi-address indeed enables us to play again on the locus which has been already used.

3.3   Towards More Complex Dialogues

Ludics seems to be a fruitful framework to deal with more complex aspects of dialogues. During a dialogue, the speaker builds its strategy by using various elements: he can use pieces of former dialogues ; he can use some contextual elements... And, of course, he can use stratagems or dialectical tricks. It is possible to describe such dialogical facts in Ludics. We rest on the following remark: in Ludics, the designs themselves can be seen as resulting of interactions. We already saw, in presupposition case, that some interventions have to be associated with some designs already built rather than with some elementary actions. We will go further in associating with some elaborated interventions some cut-nets: several interacting designs. Particularly, this will be used to simulate the fact that the strategies supporting one dialogical interaction can be worked out by means of designs which are coming from outside the dialogue in progress. We then need to set that some designs, in fact a set of designs (a context) is available to the locutors when they build their interventions.

We will illustrate this possibility to deal with more complex aspects of dialogues by studying two examples: first application of Ludics is proposed to deal with one of the stratagems suggested by Schopenhauer in *Art of Always Being Right* ; a second one illustrates the possibility to explore in Ludics the core of fallacious sophisms by dealing with the petition of principle.

Study of the 4th Stratagem of Schopenhauer. We sum up the fourth stratagem below:

If you want to draw a conclusion, you must not let it be foreseen, but you must get the premisses admitted one by one, unobserved, mingling them here and there in your talk: otherwise, your opponent will attempt all sorts of chicanery. Or, if it is doubtful whether your opponent will admit them, you must advance the premisses of these premisses; that is to say, you must draw up pro-syllogisms, and get the premisses of several of them admitted in no definite order. In this way you conceal your game until you have obtained all the admissions that are necessary, and so reach your goal by making a circuit. [...]

Let us suppose the following situation: the speaker (here designed by "player" or P while addressee is designed by "opponent" or O) defends a thesis A ; he wants to justify A by resting on the fact that the propositions B and C imply A.

- Some dialogical exchanges took place. The player affirmed B, which was accepted by O. In the same way, P affirmed C, which was also accepted by O.

  That is represented as follows: the proposition B was played on an arbitrary locus α, O recorded this affirmation and accepted it (he gave up). The same for C on an arbitrary locus β.

  The following interactions took place:

$$
\begin{array}{ccc}
 & \dfrac{\quad\quad}{\vdash \alpha.0}{}^{\dagger} & \\
\alpha.0 \vdash & & \\
\hline
\vdash \alpha & \alpha \vdash & \\
P & \underline{\quad\quad\quad} & O
\end{array}
\qquad
\begin{array}{ccc}
 & \dfrac{\quad\quad}{\vdash \beta.0}{}^{\dagger} & \\
\beta.0 \vdash & & \\
\hline
\vdash \beta & \beta \vdash & \\
P & \underline{\quad\quad\quad} & O
\end{array}
$$

  Let us denote by $\mathcal{D}_\alpha$ and $\mathcal{D}_\beta$ the winning designs of P respectively based on $\vdash \alpha$ and $\vdash \beta$.

  The supports of such exchanges have been recorded and will be still avalaible when the speaker P will play its proposition A.
- Now, we come back to the ongoing dialogue: P is asserting its thesis A, arguing it by means of the premises B and C and disclosing its stratagem. This intervention (initiating the (short) ongoing dialogue) is represented by the following design $\mathcal{D}$, located in ξ:

$$
\begin{array}{ccc}
\mathcal{R}_1 & \mathcal{R}_2 & \\
\vdots & \vdots & \\
\xi.1 \vdash & \xi.2 \vdash & \xi.3 \vdash \\
\hline
& \vdash \xi &
\end{array}
$$

  The first action of this design is $(+, \xi, \{1, 2, 3, \})$ where $\xi.1$ is the locus of the argument B, $\xi.2$ the one of C and $\xi.3$ the locus of the proposition $B \wedge C \Rightarrow A$.
- Let us comment the construction of the subdesigns (normal forms of cut-nets) $\mathcal{R}_1$ and $\mathcal{R}_2$ of $\mathcal{D}$:

- the design $\mathcal{R}_1$ is built from the winning design $\mathcal{D}_\alpha$ by using:
  - * one delocalisation from α into $\xi.1.0$ (the proposition B affirmed "out of context" in α or affirmed in the context of the defense of the thesis A in $\xi.1.0$);
  - * one shift (the proposition B affirmed in $\xi.1.0$ is used as an argument when it is localized in $\xi.1$).

  The design $\mathcal{R}_1$, based on $\xi.1 \vdash$, is the normal form of the cut-net consisting in the interaction[11] between $\mathcal{D}_\alpha$ and $\mathfrak{Fax}_{\alpha,\xi.1.0}$.

  Then $\mathcal{R}_1 = \downarrow [[\mathcal{D}_\alpha, \mathfrak{Fax}_{\alpha,\xi.1.0}]]$;

- In the same way: $\mathcal{R}_2 = \downarrow [[\mathcal{D}_\beta, \mathfrak{Fax}_{\beta,\xi.2.0}]]$ and is based on $\xi.2 \vdash$.

− P is then in a good position to win the controversy. Indeed the reaction of O is strongly constrained ; this can be seen by looking at the interaction. After normalization, the design corresponding to the intervention of P is the following:

$$
\frac{\dfrac{\xi.1.0.0 \vdash}{\vdash \xi.1.0} \quad \dfrac{\xi.2.0.0 \vdash}{\vdash \xi.2.0}}{\dfrac{\xi.1 \vdash \qquad \xi.2 \vdash \qquad \xi.3 \vdash}{\vdash \xi}}
$$

In order to converge with this intervention of P, during the dialogue in progress, O has to develop the following design:

$$
\begin{array}{ccc}
\dfrac{\dfrac{\xi.1.0.0\vdash}{\vdash\xi.1.0}\ \dfrac{\xi.2.0.0\vdash}{\vdash\xi.2.0}}{\dfrac{\xi.1\vdash\quad\xi.2\vdash\quad\xi.3\vdash}{\vdash\xi}} & &
\dfrac{\dfrac{\vdash\xi.1.0.0,\xi.2.0.0,\xi.3}{\dfrac{\xi.2.0\vdash\xi.1.0.0,\xi.3}{\dfrac{\vdash\xi.1.0.0,\xi.2,\xi.3,}{\dfrac{\xi.1.0\vdash\xi.2,\xi.3}{\dfrac{\vdash\xi.1,\xi.2,\xi.3}{\xi\vdash}}}}}}{}
\\
P & & O
\end{array}
$$

That is: O has to recognize that $\mathcal{D}_1$ is the shift of one delocalisation of $\mathcal{D}_\alpha$ (and $\mathcal{D}_2$ of $\mathcal{D}_\beta$), and has to remenber that against this designs he may only play the daïmon (to stay coherent with itself).

Then it is the turn to O to play. He is in the position $\vdash \xi.1.0.0, \xi.2.0.0, \xi.3$. The only opening for O would be to play an action located in $\xi.3$ (since either on $\xi.1$ or on $\xi.2$, he can only play the daïmon.) ; if he has nothing to oppose to the proposition $B \wedge C \Rightarrow A$ then O accepts the thesis of P, and plays the daïmon.

---

[11] Such an interaction enables to delocalize the design $\mathcal{D}_\alpha$ from the locus where it was really played until the current exchange.

$$\frac{\overline{\qquad\qquad\qquad}^{\dagger}}{\dfrac{\vdash \xi.1.0.0, \xi.2.0.0, \xi.3}{\dfrac{\xi.2.0 \vdash \xi.1.0.0, \xi.3}{\dfrac{\vdash \xi.1.0.0, \xi.2, \xi.3,}{\dfrac{\xi.1.0 \vdash \xi.2, \xi.3}{\dfrac{\vdash \xi.1, \xi.2, \xi.3}{\xi \vdash}}}}}}$$

$$\frac{\dfrac{\xi.1.0.0 \vdash}{\vdash \xi.1.0} \qquad \dfrac{\xi.2.0.0 \vdash}{\vdash \xi.2.0}}{\dfrac{\xi.1 \vdash \qquad \xi.2 \vdash \qquad \xi.3 \vdash}{\vdash \xi}}$$

Petitio Principii. Our aim now is to understand in Ludics "petitio principii" (or "begging the question"). Rather than an action, rather than an already built designs, we will represent some intervention using such a logical fallacy by a whole cut-net (several design linked by cuts). The loci to which the addressee could cling should appear after the normalisation of such a cut-net but these loci are in fact not available.

- either because these places are pushed back to the infinite. It is the case when the logical fallacy is due to a circular reasoning (traditional usage of the petition principii).
- or because theses places are pinched. It is the case when "begging the question" consists in imposing the premise of a thesis as it was commonly admitted instead of offer it to the discussion ; in presenting evidence (in support of a conclusion) that is less likely to be accepted than merely asserting the conclusion (contemporary usage of the petition principii).

We illustrate the foregoing affirmations on two examples corresponding with the two mentioned cases of petition principii.

- Let us consider at first the following utterance: The soul is immortal because it never dies. This is a traditional usage of "begging the question": circular reasoning. Indeed an affirmation the soul is immortal is justified by an another one it never dies, which has the same meaning.
  We propose to formalize this utterance The soul is immortal because it never dies , by the following (recursively defined) design:

$$\mathcal{D}_{\xi} = \frac{\dfrac{[[\mathcal{D}_{\xi}, \mathfrak{F}ax_{\xi,\xi 11}]]}{\vdash \xi.1.1}}{\dfrac{\xi.1 \vdash}{\vdash \xi}}$$

Let us comment how such a recursive design may be associated with the utterance The soul is immortal because it never dies:
This utterance contains an affirmation the soul is immortal and explicitly contains its argument the soul never dies; it is then reasonable to set that this intervention, do not reduce to be only one action but is a design already built $\mathcal{D}_{\xi}$. The first action: $(+, \xi, \{1\})$ indicates that there is an affirmation (arbitrary located on ξ). The second one: $(-, \xi.1, \{1\})$ expresses the fact that

the locutor is ready to support its argument the soul never dies. The design $\mathcal{D}_\xi$ have to contain also the defense of the soul never dies (which is nothing but because it is immortal). Therefore, the subdesign above $\vdash \xi.1.1$ has the same content than $\mathcal{D}_\xi$, except that the loci of the two affirmations are exchanged. This is expressed by the delocalization of the design $\mathcal{D}_\xi$ from ξ into $\xi.1.1$. Technically speaking, the design above $\vdash \xi.1.1$ is $\mathcal{D}_{\xi.1.1} = [[\mathcal{D}_\xi, \mathcal{F}ax_{\xi,\xi.1.1}]]$. The resulting design is infinite; the loci to which the addressee could cling are never available:

$$
\mathcal{D}_\xi = \cfrac{\mathcal{D}_{\xi.1.1} = \cfrac{\mathcal{D}_{\xi.1.1.1.1} = \cfrac{\cfrac{\vdots}{\xi.1.1.1.1.1 \vdash}}{\vdash \xi.1.1.1.1}}{\cfrac{\xi.1.1.1 \vdash}{\vdash \xi.1.1}}}{\cfrac{\xi.1 \vdash}{\vdash \xi}}
$$

– Let us consider now an another case of the petition of principle. The one consisting in imposing one of the premises of an affirmation as if it was commonly admitted. An intervention using such a petition of principle may be presented by the following schema: Since A (which must have been justified but which is taken for granted) and since A implies B, you will agree about B.

$$
\cfrac{\cfrac{\overline{\vdash \xi.1.1}^{(\xi.1.1,\emptyset)}}{\xi.1 \vdash} \qquad \xi.2 \vdash}{\vdash \xi}
$$

where ξ is the locus were B is affirmed, $\xi.1$ and $\xi.2$ are the loci of the premises of B (respectively A and $A \Rightarrow B$). The subdesign corresponding to the justification of A is the design:

$$
\overline{\vdash \xi.1.1}^{\emptyset}
$$

That is: A appears here as being a data, not needing to be justified. The affirmation of such a data is then an action $(+, \xi.1.1, \emptyset)$. The set of loci from which some speaker could continue the investigation of A is empty.
Once again the loci to which the addressee could cling are not available.

4   Conclusion

The model we proposed has two essential features. The descriptive one, is done by the fact we retrieve the simple form of communicative exchange in the basic structure of formal dialogues. The prospective one, commits us to observe complex processes inside dialogues.

Evidently, being descriptive is required by a genuine notion of model. But, by the fact of this double feature, we obtain a multi-scale theory, giving possibility of viewing objects at differents levels of granularity, depending on what we want to study in them. If our focus is on strategic remodelling processes upon arguments, we could make use of complex operations inside dialogues plans. If we just want to describe the chronology of actions, taking in account the fact that agents anticipate the plays of their opponents, we do not need more than the elementary decomposition level. So the model ensures continuity between fine, refined and complex levels, without change of formal background, just going deep beyond the surface structure of objects.

We must observe that this work opens the way to many others formalisations or conceptual problems. It takes a very important place in our program which consists in investigating possibilities offered by the geometrical turn in furnishing and deploying mathematical means for human and social sciences[12]. The formalisation of dialogues takes a great position in this project, by the fact the notion is intrinsically connected to epistemic, semiotic, pragmatic and semantic layers.

References

1. Basaldella, M., Faggian, C.: Ludics with repetitions (Exponentials, Interactive types and Completeness). In: LICS 2009 (2009) (to appear)
2. Currien, P.-L.: Introduction à la Ludique (2001), http://www.pps.jussieu.fr/~curien
3. Faggian, C.: Travelling on designs. In: Bradfield, J.C. (ed.) CSL 2002 and EACSL 2002. LNCS, vol. 2471, p. 427. Springer, Heidelberg (2002)
4. Gazdar, G.: Pragmatics: Implicature, Presupposition, and Logical Form. Academic Press, New York (1979)
5. Ginzburg, J., Sag, I.A., Purver, M.: Integrating Conversational Move Types in the Grammar of Conversation. In: Kühnlein, P., Rieser, H., Zeevat, H.(eds) Perspectives on Dialogue in the New Millennium, Pragmatics & Beyond, vol. 114, pp. 25-42. John Benjamins, Amsterdam (2003)
6. Girard, J.-Y.: Locus Solum: from the rules of logic to the logic of rules. Mathematical Structures in Computer Science 11(3), 301–506 (2002)
7. Girard, J.-Y.: From foundation to Ludics. In: Ehrhard, T., Girard, J.-Y., Scott, P. (eds.) Linear Logic in Computer Science. London Mathematical Society, Lectures Notes Series. Cambridge University Press, Cambridge (2004)
8. Hamblin, C.L.: Mathematical Models of Dialogue. Theoria 37, 130–155 (1971)
9. Joinet, J.-B.: Logique et Interaction, Habilitation à diriger des recherches, Université Paris 7 (2007)
10. Tronçon, S.: Dynamique des démonstrations et théorie de l'interaction, Thèse de Doctorat, Université de Provence (Encours de publication) (2006)
11. Wittgenstein, L.: Remarques sur les fondements des mathématiques, Gallimard (1983)

---

[12] Some details in Lecomte, A. *Vers une pragmatique théorique*, Note d'intention à l'origine du projet "Prélude", http://anr-prelude.fr/article16.html.

Author Index